FROM MELOS TO MY LAI

War and survival

Lawrence A. Tritle

London and New York

First published 2000
by Routledge
11 New Fetter Lane, London EC4P 4EE

Simultaneously published in the USA and Canada
by Routledge
29 West 35th Street, New York, NY 10001

Routledge is an imprint of the Taylor & Francis Group

© 2000 Lawrence A. Tritle

The right of Lawrence A. Tritle to be identified as the Author of this Work has
been asserted by him in accordance with the Copyright, Designs and Patents
Act 1988

Typeset in Garamond by Taylor & Francis Books Ltd
Printed and bound in Great Britain by Biddles Ltd, Guildford and King's Lynn

British Library Cataloguing in Publication Data
A catalogue record for this book is available from the British Library

Library of Congress Cataloging in Publication Data
Tritle, Lawrence A., 1946–
From Melos to My Lai: War and Survival / Lawrence A. Tritle.
Includes bibliographical references and index.
1. Violence – Greece – history. 2. Violence – United States – history.
3. Violence – cross-cultural studies. I. Title.
HN650.5.Z9 V58   2000
303.6'09495–dc21   99-055816

ISBN 0–415–17160–1 (hbk)
ISBN 0–415–21757–1 (pbk)

FOR MY PARENTS AND MARGARET,
WHO WAITED

CONTENTS

PLATES

PREFACE AND ACKNOWLEDGMENTS

"War," said the Greek philosopher Heraclitus, "is the father of all things and master of all things." He went on to say that in war some acted as gods (i.e. heroically) and others as men (i.e. unheroically), and that some were made slaves to war, and others set themselves free from war.[1] This striking analysis of the nature of war from the ancient Greek world suggests that the grounds for a comparative study of ancient Greeks and modern Americans at war are hardly superficial. When it comes to matters of violence, and how societies cope with conflict, the parallels are many and range from the literary to the artistic, from the psychological to the personal. It will quickly become clear that the present study is not a traditional one. It does not apply the subjective–objective analysis of nineteenth-century positivism, an idea that has dominated the writing of history for the last 150 years. Alternatively, the approach taken here favors a broader view of what history is and finds antecedents in the work of the Cambridge School of the early twentieth century. Scholars in this group, Jane Harrison, W. Ridgway and A.B. Cook among others, investigated classical themes by applying such ancillary tools as anthropology and archeology to their subjects. Jane Harrison, for example, was keenly interested in religion, particularly its rituals. As modern psychology became more widely known, pushed along by the trauma of World War I, she became excited to learn more about psychology from one of its earliest practitioners in England, Dr. W.H.R. Rivers, who had spent a year treating combat exhausted officers at Craiglockhart Hospital in Scotland. Here Rivers' most famous patient was the poet Siegfried Sassoon.[2]

1 Kirk *et al.* 1983: 193–4. The interpretation of Heraclitus' statement is uncertain, but note Guthrie 1967: 447, who also suggests that Heraclitus is thinking of war generally and the nature of its impact on individuals and society.
2 On Harrison and Rivers see Slobodin 1997: 38–9. After his assignment at Craiglockhart, Rivers became psychologist to the Royal Flying Corps and was posted to the Central Hospital in Hampstead, where he remained through the war. Three highly successful novels by Pat Barker, *Regeneration*, *The Ghost Road*, and *The Eye in the Door* discuss these figures and the nature of combat trauma.

This broad cultural approach favors Jacob Burckhardt's notion of history as expressed in his aphoristic definition, "the record of what one age finds worthy of note in another."[3] It might also be thought that the present study with its admixture of "past and present" is some sort of a "new age" history, but in reality it is as old as the writing of history in the Western tradition. Herodotus, Thucydides, and Xenophon, the three great historians of the classical Greek world, contributed their own experiences to their accounts, anticipating what historians today refer to as the "personal voice." Herodotus' travels to Egypt, Thucydides' and Xenophon's experiences and observations of the conflicts through which they lived, illustrate this autobiographical role of the historian. As historian Jeremy D. Popkin has lately concluded, historians "have a right to insist that [their discipline], too, has insights to offer from which others can benefit."[4] Prime among these is the nature of survival, particularly that involving violence resulting from war in all its forms. Thucydides' account of the Peloponnesian War, for example, suggests that his very survival influenced his composition, just as the playwright Aeschylus, a survivor of the Persian Wars, reflected his experiences in his dramas *The Persians* and *Seven Against Thebes*. The human experience with violence, culture, and survival is one that transcends time.

The ancient Greek world, especially in the fifth and fourth centuries BC, was one perpetually at war – peace was an exceptional situation, certainly welcomed but regarded as at best temporary. Modern American society, on the other hand, has not fought a major sustained conflict since the end of the Vietnam War in 1975. The Gulf War of 1990–91 and lesser campaigns such as Panama and Grenada, however, have given the public a taste of what a major conflict might be like. Yet the impact of wars upon the United States in the twentieth century remains substantial – nearly 650,000 dead minimally, amounting to something like 6,500 per year – not to mention the wounded and other survivors, who along with their families share the burdens of conflict and survival.[5] The ancient Greeks did not know numbers such as these, but as will be seen in the pages to come, numbers have little to do with the trauma of violence and its rippling effects through families and generations.

This work owes its inspiration in part to Jonathan Shay, whose *Achilles in*

---

3 Burckhardt was a frequent target of positivist criticism by his contemporaries Ulrich von Wilamowitz-Moellendorff and Julius Beloch, both major figures in classical philology in the late nineteenth century and early twentieth. Yet while these scholars today languish in near obscurity, known mostly only to their modern descendants, Burckhardt's lectures on Greek history and civilization have been newly translated and published. See Burckhardt 1998, with P. Green, "The Oracle of Basel," *Los Angeles Times* (book review), January 24, 1999.

4 Popkin 1999: 748.

5 Figures (compiled by the Public Affairs Office of the Veterans of Foreign Wars) are for "hostile" and "non-hostile" deaths only and do not include the thousands who died "accidentally," i.e. in non-combat-related circumstances such as training exercises. For example, between October 1, 1979 and September 30, 1991, 1,415 soldiers were killed in Germany alone.

Vietnam: Combat Trauma and the Undoing of Character elaborates the trauma of violence on combat soldiers. Shay has been treating a group of Vietnam War veterans in the Boston area for over ten years, and it was during these sessions that he recognized that the experiences of these men reflected those of Homer's heroes. My reading of that book in 1995 led to a review article then a course that I first taught in 1996. For some time though, my friend John Belohlavek, Professor of History at the University of South Florida, had been urging me to investigate the experiences of ancient Greek and modern American societies at war, but it was something I hesitated to do. My own experiences in Vietnam had not yet been confronted, and I was comfortable in the cloistered world of academia. Shay's work gave me the first opportunity to reflect on Vietnam, which in turn led to meeting Shad Meshad, President and founder of the National Veterans' Foundation (NVF), an organization dedicated to assisting veterans and their families. My association with the NVF enabled me to meet and discuss with other veterans the issues of violence and trauma, recovery and survival.

Several of the veterans whom I met through the NVF, and others encountered on my own, have participated in the three "Achilles in Vietnam" classes that I have taught over the last three years at Loyola Marymount University. In teaching this course, as outlined in my essay "Teaching the Vietnam War With the Greeks," I expanded Shay's initial investigation by including a much wider body of Greek sources that also reflect on the experience of violence, culture, and survival.[6] I am grateful to Lou Albert, Ed Cole, Dan Cano, Bill Fitzgerald, Ben Hayes, Vincent Imondi, and Michael Mathis among the vets, whose combat experiences span World War II to Vietnam and who allowed their stories to be told here. A few veterans who have not made public their experiences are represented anonymously. Both Judith Herman and Jonathan Shay agree that recovery from trauma must begin with the individual and that, unless they wish otherwise, their desire to remain private must be respected, and so it is here.[7] The willingness of all the veterans who have met with my students and recounted their experiences has proved invaluable in writing this work. So too have been the reactions and comments of my students. My wife Margaret, who spent an anxious year as a "waiting wife," Linda Clougherty (Army Nurse Corps, Vietnam 1969–71), Terri Hayes, Linda Mathis, and Edith Zimmerman contributed to the discussion of the impact of violence upon women. Additionally, my parents Dorothy and Robert Tritle provided the perspective of the family's role in experiencing the stresses induced by violence. From them too I also learned of the impact of World War II, both on American society broadly and on the individual. Loyola Marymount University provided summer research grants in 1997 and 1998, which

6   Tritle 1998: 1, 36–40.
7   Herman 1997: 3.

enabled me to work on this project; Dr. Kenyon Chan, Dean of the College of Liberal Arts, and Dr. Joseph Jabbra, Academic Vice-President, generously provided additional support that helped fund the production of the manuscript.

I am happy to thank here several friends who helped with this book. Professor John Belohlavek and Dr. Marc Frey[8] (University of Cologne) read most of this book and made numerous suggestions and criticisms. My students Michael Camba, Melissa Naimark, and Michael Young did the same, and their suggestions and criticisms were also useful in improving the sense and clarifying the background. From Chaim Shatan, Bill Mahedy, and Shad Meshad, psychiatrist and trauma counselors, and all co-architects of the Vet Center program organized by the Veterans Administration in the early 1970s, as was also Jonathan Shay, I learned much about the nature of combat trauma and its impact on the individual. I am also happy to thank Richard Stoneman at Routledge for his interest and support in taking on a project and investigation that takes a rather unfamiliar look at the ancient world.

The staffs of the American School of Classical Studies, Athens, especially Ms. Jan Jordan, Art Resource (New York), the Boston Museum of Fine Arts, Corbis Images, the J. Paul Getty Museum (Los Angeles), the Lyndon Baines Johnson Presidential Library (Austin, Texas), the Metropolitan Museum of Art (New York), and the National Archives, were all helpful in providing the photographs used to illustrate the book. The staff of Universal Press Syndicate provided the comic strip from G.B. Trudeau's "Doonesbury" reproduced here. John Buckler, Professor of History at the University of Illinois, generously lent me his sketch of the Monument of Chabrias that once stood in the Agora of ancient Athens. I am especially grateful to Vietnam vet Larry Powell, who allowed me to use several photographs from his award-winning collection, *Hunger of the Heart: Communion at the Wall* (Dubuque, 1995).

None of what follows has been previously published. The discussion in Chapter 4 of the Spartan commander Clearchus was presented as a paper at the Center for Hellenic Studies, Washington D.C. (April 1998) and at the University of Liverpool (July 1999). I am particularly grateful to K. Raaflaub, S. Ruzicka, and C.J. Tuplin for their comments on both this paper and other points discussed here. At a conference in honor of Mortimer Chambers at UCLA in May 1999, I previewed material from Chapter 7 dealing with Thucydides and the idea of survival, and the questions raised by E. Badian, M. Chambers, and S. Lattimore helped clarify several issues.

In general the classical works I have quoted from represent translations well known to the reading public and readily available. In this I have followed the suggestion of Simon Goldhill in making use of such transla-

---

8 M. Frey's *Geschichte des Vietnamkriegs: Die Tragödie in Asien und das Ende des amerikanischen Traums* (Munich: Beck, 1998, reprinted four times) shows the international interest in the Vietnam War.

tions rather than finding the best single translation of each text.[9] In some instances I have adapted a translation when it seemed to clarify the sense or to aid in making my point. Such passages have only been noted occasionally.

Finally, I would also like to thank four classes of students, altogether more than a hundred in number, who have attended my "Achilles in Vietnam" and "Americans in Vietnam" classes since 1996. The interest of these students in learning of the intersection of classical Greek and modern American culture in war and violence – in attempting to understand the impact of such events on a society and culture – gives hope that the experiences that inform this work will in future be matters of intellectual discussion and not painful experience.

9   Goldhill 1986: x.

1

INTRODUCTION

A twentieth-century American odyssey

For Sergeant Harold Brown and Corporal Clarence Brown

When I was a boy growing up in 1950s America, one of the figures who came in and out of my life was an older brother of my mother. Uncle Harold would appear every three or four months, frequently with some new toy for me, so that his visits were always happy occasions. As I grew older, however, I heard more, usually in overheard remarks of my mother and my grandmother – remarks filled with sadness that spoke of Uncle Harold's drinking, his inability to keep a job, the emptiness of a life without a woman's love. I also learned that my uncle had spent two years in the Pacific as an army sergeant in New Guinea and that the experience had changed him radically: from an eager youth who had finished high school, who had a car, job, and girl before going off to war, to a shell of a man who seemed unable to get back on track after confronting the violence, the killing of war in the South Pacific. His troubles were shared by his brother Clarence, who had served in the merchant marine (because he was too tall and skinny for the Marines) and was torpedoed several times. He was later drafted into the army and served in Korea (1951–52), where he was wounded and contracted tuberculosis. This experience transformed him too and left him a recluse and alcohol dependent. These were my earliest contacts with the legacy of war and violence, but they would not be my last. My own turn in the line, so to speak, would come, and while I would try to shut the experience out of my mind for a quarter of a century, when I returned to it, I found it as vivid as ever.

My uncles were not the only veterans I grew up with as a child. My father had flown with the Eighth Air Force in England for three months in 1944 before being shot down over Germany; his father had served as an artillery officer in the European theater and had seen action in Normandy and the Battle of the Bulge. My uncles never talked about their experiences, but from my father and grandfather I did hear accounts of where they had been and something of what they had seen and done. I understand now that what I heard represented only a small part of their experiences and that much had

1

been left out, presumably to avoid telling me anything "bad," as well as avoiding a repetition of their own traumas. In many ways, then, my child-hood was much like that recounted by Ron Kovic in *Born on the Fourth of July* and surely hundreds of thousands of others of the "Baby Boom" genera-tion, the beneficiaries of those who had fought, as Studs Terkel would later tell it, *The Good War*.[1] This upbringing without a doubt influenced the generation that would get caught up in the maelstrom that became Vietnam.

Through the 1950s and early 1960s this legacy imprinted an impression-able youth who were also fed a constant film depiction of these heroics. Films like *The Sands of Iwo Jima* and *To Hell and Back*, television program-ming such as *Combat* and the *Rat Patrol*, offered a fare that today may seem romantically naïve but at the time were as influential as the stories told by our fathers. By the time I was finishing high school in 1964, exotic names of faraway places were rekindling the heroics of war and battle: Laos, Vietnam. In August 1964 the Gulf of Tonkin incident occurred – that shadowy, certainly manipulated incident involving North Vietnamese torpedo boats and US navy destroyers *Maddox* and *Turner Joy* – and spawned the Gulf of Tonkin Resolution.[2] This congressional decision gave nearly *carte blanche* to Lyndon Johnson and then US military forces to escalate the growing war in South Vietnam. Within a year, regular US marine and army divisions had been deployed in Vietnam, and the door was opened to a widening conflict. During the next four years while in college, my own position on this issue would change from one of opposition to support and back again. I had numerous debates with my father and friends about what was going on in Vietnam and who was right. I still recall hearing over the radio in the fall of 1965 news of the Battle of the Ia Drang where the 1st Cavalry Division met and "defeated" for the first time opposing regular units of the North Vietnamese army (NVA). Only later would it be learned that the criterion of victory was simply quantitative – i.e. that of "bodycount" – and even later that the performance of the 1st Cavalry had been characterized by poor lead-ership and tactics.[3]

When I graduated from university in June 1968, parts of Vietnam were still smoldering from the Tet Offensive only four months past. In Los Angeles county thousands of men would be drafted into military service

---

1   Kovic 1976, later made into a film (1989) by Oliver Stone (himself a Vietnam veteran whose upbringing was similar to Kovic's), the second of his "Vietnam" trilogy, the first and third being *Platoon* (1986) and *Between Heaven and Earth* (1992). S. Turkel's *The Good War: An Oral History* was published in 1976.
2   See Moïse 1997: 203–7 and the discussion in this book, pp. 19–26.
3   As told clearly by Moore and Galloway 1992: 215–91, who recount how in the second phase of the battle, units of the 1st Cavalry literally walked into an ambush, simply unaware that the enemy was near.

during the course of the year.[4] It was into the war that I would now be pulled, volunteering for the army with an option to attend officer candidate school within a week of graduation. As it worked out, I spent nearly a year in training before completing infantry officer candidate school in May 1969 and then would spend the usual six months stateside duty before being sent overseas. Luck smiled on me again, however, as my orders were not for USARV (United States Army, Republic of Vietnam) but MACV (Military Assistance Command Vietnam), which meant that I would receive an additional four months of training in Vietnamese language and counter-insurgency techniques before shipping out for Vietnam and duty as an adviser. I finally arrived in Vietnam in May 1970 and was sent to the Mekong Delta, IV Corps, then commanded by J. Paul Vann, one of the few Americans who really understood the nature of the conflict in that country.[5] For nearly eleven months that followed I served as an adviser on a (so-called) Mobile Advisory Team in Ba Xuyen Province in the southern part of the delta. During that time I would advise militia type units of the South Vietnamese army, village self-defense forces (who received just enough training to ensure that they would get killed when the Viet Cong arrived – which did happen on several occasions), and a reconnaissance platoon made up of former Viet Cong. On several occasions I was the particular target of some Viet Cong as I heard the tell-tale "crack" of a rifle round overhead. I learned too that the South Vietnamese were not particularly keen on dying for their country. In turn I adopted their *laissez-faire* attitude, thinking that if dying for their country meant little to them, it meant even less to me. I returned home in March 1971, immediately resuming my education, my goal to become a professor, which I did in 1978. I was also determined to forget Vietnam, which I never seemed quite able to do.

From the time that I returned home and resumed my education and until the mid-1990s, I spoke very little of Vietnam. When it did come up, whenever friends asked me about it or the topic came up in other situations, I found myself "going off" on a sort of Dennis Miller rant. This occurred once while attending the annual meeting of the American Historical Association in December 1993. During the meeting, I attended a "conversations" session at which New York University professor Marilyn Young's new book on Vietnam was being discussed. I arrived late but in time to hear several of the professors gathered there ask what to tell students who asked how the US could have won the war in Vietnam. Annoyed by such naïvety and ignorance on the part of those teaching about Vietnam, I interjected, "I'll tell you how

4   The exact number of men from the county drafted in 1968 is no longer available as the Selective Service figures have been lost. During the year, over 20,000 were drafted into military service from the state of California alone. As Los Angeles County was largest in terms of population, its residents constituted a large percentage of the draftees.
5   For his story see Sheehan 1988. Vann was later killed in a helicopter crash in the Central Highlands of Vietnam in 1973.

3

we could have won. First, you take all the Vietnamese and you put them in boats in the South China Sea and you black-top the country. Then you sink the boats!" This bit of GI sarcasm reveals how illusory any grand plan to victory was. My own lack of patience with those then teaching about Vietnam, who could not understand the futility of the effort there, also brought out all the old anger still seething in me at the time. When I first began teaching in 1978, it became known occasionally that I had served in Vietnam. Students then had grown up with the "television war," and to them Vietnam meant something. I recall talking to them about the war, but in such a steely way that I could see some of them were just scared to death. It was only in early 1995, after I had read Jonathan Shay's *Achilles in Vietnam*, that I was able to put the pieces together and figure out how the Vietnam Experience had affected me and, in some ways, changed my life.

Of violence and survival

> Sweet is war to the untried, but anyone who has experienced it dreads its approach exceedingly in his heart.
> (Pindar, Fragment 110, trans. W.H. Race)

The "Achilles in Vietnam" course that I have taught, and on which this study rests, is not concerned ultimately with the "history" of battles and tactics, either in the ancient Greek world or in Vietnam, though these will be mentioned from time to time. Neither am I concerned with the causes of the Vietnam War or the many wars that the Greeks fought from Homer's great tale of Troy to the campaigns of Alexander. The principal concern is rather to show how societies sustain conflict and violence for prolonged periods, and how the experience of surviving that violence ripples through societies and cultures from one generation to the next.

There is little question that survivors of violence understand its impact differently than those not so exposed. There are a number of passages that demonstrate this truism, including examples from the ancient Greek world, but a pointed one comes from Michael Herr's riveting yet surreal account of the Vietnam Experience, *Dispatches*, and the conversation he relates with a veteran soldier in Vietnam: "Patrol went up the mountain. One man came back. He died before he could tell us what happened."

Herr remarks how he waited for the rest of the story, finally asking, "What happened?" The soldier looked at him, "like he felt sorry for me, fucked if he'd waste time telling stories to anyone as dumb as I was."[6]

---

6 Herr 1977: 6. For an ancient Greek counterpart to this, see Chapter 4, and the account of the Spartan survivor from Pylos, taunted by an Athenian ally for having survived the battle.

Herr's account demonstrates the gap between those who might be, in the words of Jimi Hendrix, "experienced" and those who are not, but his story should not be considered unique. Similar reflections on the toll of violence can be found elsewhere, including ancient Greece. Clearly the study of survivors and range of their experiences would contribute significantly to an understanding of how people are able to see the worst things imaginable and either be consumed by them or rise above them (and occasionally both).

Unlike most historians and other writers who might approach this topic, this investigation begins with the experience of one who has participated in ground combat: witnessing battle, hearing the cries of the wounded, listening to the mourning of families. I also understand the anguish of families torn by separation, not knowing if a husband or son will return from war, and then what to do when confronted by the return of the "honored dead" or the living but disturbed, silent warrior. Marita Sturken suggests in *Tangled Memories* that survivors disrupt history, which she claims "operates more efficiently when its agents are dead."[7] Historian Michael Bentley argues similarly, noting the complications for the historian posed by memory, which a number of historians and psychologists consider a social construct, i.e. something shaped by our own identity, what we read and so on. Bentley avoids an extreme position, and is right to caution on the intersection of memory and history.[8] Yet the view that history can be somehow closed or past seems debatable, for as William Faulkner said, "The past is never dead, it's not even past," and while memories may be influenced by external sources, they also represent a tremendous store of information to the historian.

Instead I would argue that survivors can actually enrich our understanding of events by establishing a living link between past and present. To some extent this happens when autobiographies or oral histories are used in order to bring to life a particular period or event.[9] In my "Achilles in Vietnam" classes I have seen how students are able to broaden their understanding of not only the recent past – Vietnam – but also the distant past – the world of ancient Greece. This results from actively engaging in discussion actual survivors of events. From such discussions comes greater comprehension of what happens in the events that students have been able to learn of only through reading. Moreover, my own experience allows me to look at the Greek evidence attesting the nature of violence, culture and survival and to give this an interpretation that is at once "scholarly" yet also informed by an understanding acquired from first-hand experience of

7 Sturken 1997: 5. See also the discussion below pp. 146–8.
8 Bentley 1999: 154–5, who also questions the view that memory is a social construct.
9 The volumes written by Stephen Ambrose on World War II may serve as examples. These works, in many ways oral histories, have brought to life for many readers the nature of the experience of war, experiences so deeply rooted in survival that the degree to which they may be "social constructs" seems minimal.

violence. A similar example can be seen in Robert Graves' account of his post-war studies at Oxford. Graves disagreed with his tutor, who claimed that Anglo-Saxon literature possessed no intrinsic literary value. He writes how he "thought of Beowulf lying wrapped in a blanket among his platoon of drunken thanes in the Gothland billet ... The War still continued for both of us [i.e. Graves and Edmund Blunden] and we translated everything into trench-warfare terms."[10]

My approach then brings together the personal dimension of a survivor with that of a trained classical historian. This experience does give me an advantage over the historian or writer who has no immediate knowledge of violence and its effects on those caught up in it. This is not to claim that others can never understand what happens in the stress of battle unless they have actually experienced it. But as Michael Herr's story makes clear, those who have been exposed to violence are changed, often in ways not always apparent to them, and see things differently. Again Robert Graves illustrates the point. Returned to England on account of his wounds in 1917, he spoke one day with Bertrand Russell, whose pacifistic views Graves shared. As they discussed what action should be taken with striking munitions workers, Russell was stunned by Graves' response that ordering troops to shoot them would be no different to shooting Germans. When Russell replied, "But they [i.e. the troops] realize that the War's wicked nonsense?" Graves responded, "Yes, as well as I do." Graves comments that, "He could not understand my attitude," and probably few reading Graves today could either.[11]

An empathetic understanding of violence and its effects may be obtained by those who have, fortunately in my estimation, not experienced violence themselves. Nevertheless it is my belief that survivors have an obligation to explain to the wider community what happens when violence is unleashed. Sadly not all are able to do so, which makes it that much more critical that those who can reflect on the consequences of violence do. Societies need to be aware that survivors who are seemingly whole may in fact be psychically damaged, that trauma not only occurs on the battlefield, but may surface years, even decades, later. Viewers of the 1998 film *Saving Private Ryan* have plainly experienced this, seeing old veterans in tears after viewing the film and reexperiencing the original trauma of war and violence. Newspaper and magazine accounts from both the US and Europe are full of such reports, and veterans' groups have reported a surge in telephone calls from families asking for help for fathers and grandfathers alike. The ripple effect of

---

10 Graves 1929/1957: 292–3.
11 Ibid.: 249. It might be added that Graves told Russell that men at the front believed munitions workers (and really anyone behind the lines) to be "skrimshankers," or as they were known in Vietnam, REMFs (Rear Echelon Mother Fuckers). These were basically despised, as they did not share the dangers of the front-line soldier.

violence, then, how it can affect generations of families, also needs to be addressed and explained.

Of violence, survival and culture

> The Greeks, acting on their own initiative, mutilated the corpses, so that the sight of them might cause as much fear as possible among the enemy.
>
> (Xenophon, *Anabasis* 3.4.5)[12]

Xenophon's account of Greek mercenaries mutilating the bodies of their Persian opponents after battling them reflects the violence that existed in the ancient Greek world. This appeared not only in the accounts of the historians but also in the works of the dramatic poets. Euripides and Sophocles refer to heads impaled on spears, and what student of Greek literature does not remember Oedipus gouging out his eyes? Thucydides reports the massacre committed by the Athenians at Melos, just one of many atrocities that occurred during the Peloponnesian War (Thucydides 5.116.2–4). At Melos, as elsewhere, the Athenians killed hundreds of men, stoning them to death or simply cutting their throats. The brutality of such deaths must have been incredible and the reports of such acts left a mark upon those who committed them and those who heard of them.[13] Dramatic scenes and historical accounts alike suggest that the average Athenian and Greek would have been no less often confronted with violence and tales of violence than the average American today watching *Cops!* or the usual gamut of television programs, ranging from PBS' (Public Broadcasting Service) *The Great War* to the daily accounts of World War II that appear on the *The History Channel*, *The Learning Channel*, etc.[14]

Violence in Vietnam was equally pandemic and ranged from the infamous

---

12 Xenophon, *Anabasis* 4.1.22–6 provides another example of Greek violence. The passage describes the capture of two natives who are interrogated regarding directions. The first refused to talk and was killed on the spot, at which the second became quite talkative. This interrogation technique is no different than that applied to the VC in Vietnam (or by the VC for that matter).

13 Thucydides does not tell how the Athenians killed the Melians. At 1.106.2 he reports that Athenians destroyed a trapped army of Corinthians c. 458/7 BC by stoning them to death, which surely intensified Corinthian hatred for the Athenians (see Thucydides 1.103.4 and Lattimore 1998: 50 n). Xenophon (*Hellenica* 2.1.32) reports that the Spartans killed Athenian prisoners taken at Aegospotami by cutting their throats.

14 For another view see Herman 1994: 99–117, who argues that the Athenians succeeded in reducing violence to a minimum. The evidence, as Herman notes, is drawn extensively from forensic rhetoric (a limited body of evidence), and he argues against the value of drama. Moreover, he seems too intent on depicting the Athenians as a "civilized" society. For other views see (e.g.) Dover 1974: 182.

My Lai massacre on the one side to that at Hue on the other, but these are only the best-known (and probably the biggest and most horrific) of many such acts committed by Americans and Vietnamese. Mutilation of the enemy, again by both sides, was a regular practice. These incidents of violence and atrocity in both the ancient Greek world and Vietnam argue powerfully that there exist clear grounds for comparison between one situation and the other.

This argument and conclusion may be unsettling to those readers who favor a narrower notion of human nature than that presented here. These will claim that there is no such thing as human nature and that every culture produces its own values, ethics and morals that relate to and follow from its individual development. This claim to uniqueness is not really challenged here; rather it is made secondary to more basic considerations, namely what happens when humans are threatened, when they are exposed to the prospect of bodily harm. This will be treated more fully below, but here certain biochemical and physiological responses to threats of violence may be noted. When humans (actually all primates) are threatened, hormones secreted by the adrenal gland induce a series of predictable responses that vary only a little.[15] This is the so-called "fight or flight" reflex, and it appears that the Greeks recognized this though they surely did not understand fully the mechanism at work. In Euripides' *Bacchae*, the guard who brings the "Stranger"/Dionysus before King Pentheus of Thebes tells the king, in response to a question about his arrest, that when taken, "our prey here was tame: refused to run or hide, held out his hands as willing as you please, completely unafraid. His ruddy cheeks were flushed as though with wine, and he stood there smiling" (*Bacchae* 436–39). Dionysus' refusal to run or hide (he is a god after all, and moreover, to do so would not develop the drama) should not obscure Euripides' realization that in times of stress the body went through certain physiological changes. While the causes of these would have been beyond his knowledge and that of his contemporaries, physical changes in the body would be the sort of thing that many would have noticed. Surely variable cultural values must be considered, but chemical reactions dictate a rather predictable range of emotions and responses to exposure to stress.

These emotions and responses, then, cut across time and culture and not only "Western" but "non-Western" too.[16] Those interested in Native

15 See Chapter 4 for further discussion.
16 At the Battle of Marathon, an Athenian soldier named Epizelus became blind though he was not struck or wounded – an example of what psychiatrists refer to as "conversion disorder" (earlier "hysterical conversion" or "hysterical blindness"). See pp. 63–5 for discussion. On August 18, 1999, filmmaker Tran T. Kim-Trang presented her short film *Ekleipsis*, which related similar stories of Cambodian women now living in Long Beach, California, who responded in the same way to living under Khmer Rouge terror from 1975 to 1979.

American culture might be surprised, in view of old stereotypes, to find in Mari Sandoz's account of the Lakota war-chief Crazy Horse, the reactions of Crazy Horse and Hump (another warrior) finding a dying friend on the field after the Fetterman fight of 1866:

> [Lone Bear] was face down and when Crazy Horse turned him up, they saw that his hands and face were already white-frozen, his bullet-torn breast a great lump of blood ice. As Crazy Horse lifted him, Lone Bear opened his eyes and even now there was a little shamed smile for this bad luck. So he died in the arms of his friend, with Hump standing beside them, *crying* [italics added].[17]

This human reaction to the trauma of battle finds a companion in Bao Ninh's remarkable novel, *The Sorrow of War*, which reflects his own experiences fighting in the North Vietnamese Army from 1969 to 1975, one of ten out of five hundred in his student brigade who survived the war. After the fighting he was assigned to one of several recovery teams that attempted to retrieve the bodies of those killed.

> "Kien, Kien, what the hell makes you cry so loud?"

> The truck driver's beefy hand pushed through the hammock onto Kien's shoulder, shaking him awake.

> "Get up! Get ready! Quick!"

> Kien slowly opened his eyes. The dark rings under them revealed his deep exhaustion. The painful memory of the dream throbbed against his temples ...

> "You had nightmares. Right?"

> "Yes. Unbelievably horrible. I've had nightmares since joining this team, but last night's was the worst."[18]

His novel reveals plainly the torment of Post-Traumatic Stress Disorder (PTSD) and the struggle of the survivor to live with his survival and what is to be done with the life that has been left to him. The subject of PTSD will

---

17 Sandoz 1942/1992: 204–5, an oral history account based on conversations with Crazy Horse's family and friends. Sandoz adds that Crazy Horse did not cry but instead vowed revenge on those who had killed his friend – just like Achilles after the death of Patroclus.

18 Ninh 1993: 40–1. For other examples of PTSD see e.g. pp. 17, 20, 35.

be treated more fully below (especially in Chapter 4), but it may be noted here that those burdened by it are unable to forget what happened to them and relive experiences daily through dreams, flashbacks, intrusive images, as well as sights and sounds. The reason for this is that traumatic memories form after exposure to fear or pain. These memories are stored in multiple systems of the brain, which increases the likelihood of their being remembered. This function is essential to survival, as a record of danger is created that can be called upon to alert one to similar situations and so survive. Someone suffering from PTSD usually displays hypervigilance, or "overreaction" to stimuli similar to those associated with the event. As this intensifies and becomes pathological, victims of PTSD exaggerate the possibility of danger.[19] As will be seen, this works in the same way for the ancient Greek world as it does for the modern.

Jonathan Shay's *Achilles in Vietnam* provides valuable insight into the nature of violence and trauma. His work, with its rich personal dimension provided by veterans, offers a stimulating and innovative approach, but much remains to be done in analyzing the connections between violence and society and the links between these provided by survivors. One example of the widening investigation into the nature of war and violence, of which Shay's work has played a part, is the current debate in Germany over the exhibition *Vernichtungskrieg: Verbrechen der Wehrmacht 1941 bis 1944* ("War of Extermination: Crimes of the Wehrmacht") sponsored by the Hamburger Institut für Sozialforschung.[20] The impact of violence and trauma, and how it has affected modern German society, will also figure in the discussion that follows.

Professional scholars usually pay little attention to the darker dimensions of human conflict.[21] When I first embarked on this project, I was telling a

19 J.D. Feigenbaum, "Haply I May Remember and Haply May Forget," *Times Literary Supplement* August 22, 1997: 9.

20 For the exhibition catalog see Heer and Otte 1996 (English translation in preparation). The exhibit itself has toured Germany since 1995 and has attracted large crowds as well as tremendous controversy and counter-protests. The controversy over the exhibit took a new turn in the fall of 1999. V. Ullrich, "Von Bildern und Legenden," *Die Zeit* 44, October 28, 1999, 4, showed convincingly that a number of the photographs in the exhibit were either fakes or misinterpreted, i.e. the victims shown in the pictures were those of Soviet atrocities rather than German. See e.g. Thiele 1997 for just one example of the historical debate over the exhibit and what its implications are, not only for German history but also for the nature and role of violence in war, and how its effects must be confronted and examined. It is also interesting to reflect on the reactions of contemporary American society to the nature and meaning of the My Lai massacre. Would Americans respond with the same intensity as have Germans to the "Crimes of the Wehrmacht?" For an example of how Shay's work has influenced recent research in Germany see Schmidbauer 1998.

21 Note the problems encountered by Walter Burkert over his 1972 study *Homo Necans* (translated into English in 1983), which in the eyes of some scholars made him "unfit" to edit a classical journal (cited by Parker 1998: 509–10).

long-time friend and colleague of my planned research into the nature of conflict and violence, comparing the Greek experience with that in Vietnam. After I had given several examples of brutal wartime acts that I knew of first-hand, he said that he had heard enough and asked me to stop. The nature of violence is indeed neither easy to comprehend nor does it make for cheerful discussion.

Such events as these have long occurred, but because society suppresses memory of the cycle of violence, its harmful effects continue. Additionally, scholars attempt to maintain a kind of objective detachment about the brutalizing effects of conflict and its impact on societies. This may be seen in Thucydides' *History of the Peloponnesian War*, especially his account of the destruction of Melos. Many classical scholars see this as simply another event of fifth-century BC Greek history but not as an account reflecting the nature of violence. Yet the Athenian massacre at Melos is hardly different than what happened at My Lai in Vietnam, where American soldiers killed some five hundred civilians. The object of this study, then, is to bring into focus the connections between violence, culture and survival.

An example of this intersection of violence, culture and survival that will be discussed at greater length is the Greek playwright and Athenian citizen-soldier Aeschylus. Though Aeschylus wrote some ninety plays and exerted great influence on the development of Greek tragedy, what he was proudest of was that he had fought the Persians. Not only did he participate in the momentous battles of the Persian Wars, he might have witnessed the death of his brother Cynegirus at Marathon. His epitaph clearly reflects pride in his wartime exploits as well as the mentality of the survivor:

> Aeschylus, son of Euphorion, an Athenian, is covered by
> This tomb; he died in wheat-bearing Gela.
> The famous grove of Marathon can tell his valor
> As can the longhaired Persian who knew it.[22]

These words lend support to the argument that "survivors of historical events are often figures of cultural authority and values."[23] Horace after the civil wars in Rome, Cervantes after Lepanto, and Robert Graves and Siegfried Sassoon after the First World War exemplify this view, as does Aeschylus here. It is of more than passing interest to this study that a battle-field survivor became the first great Athenian playwright, whose literary accomplishments proved so influential for future generations.

---

22 Athenaeus 627c reports the epitaph corroborated by Pausanias, the Greek traveler of the second century AD (1.4).
23 Sturken 1997: 5.

2

LISTENING TO THERSITES

Son of Atreus, what thing further do you want, or find fault
with now? Your shelters are filled with bronze, there are
plenty of the choicest women for you within your shelter,
whom we Achaians give to you first of all whenever we
capture some stronghold. Or is it still more gold you will be
wanting, that some son of the Trojans, breakers of horses,
brings as ransom out of Ilion, one that I, or some other
Achaian, capture and bring in? Is it some young women to lie
with in love and keep her all to yourself apart from the others?
It is not right for you, their leader, to lead in sorrow the sons
of the Achaians. My good fools, poor abuses, you women, not
men of Achaia, let us go back home in our ships, and leave
this man here by himself in Troy to mull [over] his prizes of
honour that he may find out whether or not we others are
helping him.

(Homer, *Iliad* 2. 225–38)

The voice here belongs to Thersites, the only "common" Achaean who
speaks in Homer's great story of the Trojan War. His critical speech reveals a
war-weary soldier who has at last realized that his sacrifice means nothing
and only serves to enrich his lord, Agamemnon. Though his fellow
Achaeans, both lords and commoners, will not listen to him – in fact
Odysseus beats him and his peers laugh (*Iliad* 2. 244–70) – his critique
merits our attention. It points to the emerging democratic voice among the
Greeks that would reach its height in classical Athens of the fifth and fourth
centuries BC, where men would themselves choose to fight or not. Thersites'
dissenting voice also represents the rank and file of another war – Vietnam.
Here by far the greater number of soldiers were,

guys nobody really cares about. They come from the end of the line,
most of them, small towns you've never heard of – Pulaski,
Tennessee – Brandon, Mississippi. Two years high school is about it
... they're the poor, the unwanted ... yet they're fighting for our

12

freedom. They're at the bottom of the barrel and they know it. Maybe that's why they call themselves grunts. Because a grunt can take it – they can take anything. They're the best ... they're heart and soul.[1]

Oliver Stone, himself a well-to-do grunt, described the men he served with in Vietnam in this way in *Platoon*, and the working-class, rural background depicted is in no way inaccurate. Like Thersites, these men never had an opportunity to express their views on being sent half-way round the world to fight in a place that was as different culturally from them as it was far geographically. Yet it remains true that both classical Athens and the United States are examples of democratic societies, and a comparison might reveal some interesting nuances that inform us on how the decision to fight is made, who makes it, and the repercussions of these decisions for all.[2]

The Greek way to war

> The Athenians considered that his [i.e. Pericles'] advice was best and voted as he had asked them to vote.
> (Thucydides, *History of the Peloponnesian War* 1.145.1)

In this manner Thucydides relates how it was that the Athenians voted to go to war with Sparta and her Peloponnesian allies, thus initiating the great Peloponnesian War that violently disrupted the Greek world from 431 to 404 BC. Thucydides' choice of words here points to the discussion and debates that took place in the assembly over the question of war and also to the stature that Pericles possessed. Certainly not all of those Athenians eligible to vote would have done so: many of those residing in the country demes or districts would have found it difficult to travel into the city, while other factors – work as well as inclination – would have kept others away. It remains the case, however, that when the Athenians decided on the question of war with Sparta, the men who voted would do so with the knowledge that they were committing themselves, their sons and families, to war – a circumstance with which all were thoroughly familiar. Hidden within Thucydides' narrative and later sources may also be nuances of detail that shed light on how the Athenians went to war. The deliberate method by

---

1 Dialogue from Oliver Stone's *Platoon*.
2 In some circles it is fashionable to critique the Athenian democracy for its slave owner-ship and denial of voting rights to women. Yet in the democratic United States of America, slave ownership was abolished only in 1863 and women had to wait until 1919 to vote. Ancient Athenian democracy cannot be held to a standard other than its own, and to critique it on modern grounds is, in a sense, to judge the past, which is not the nature of history.

which the Athenians in this case, and other Greek communities we know something about, went to war represents the attitudes and ideas of classical Greek civilization. In earlier eras, as in the Homeric period, the decision to fight was one dominated by the elite but suffered by all, though arguably those lowest in status suffered most. This is the background to Thersites' protest against the decision-making of Agamemnon mentioned above.

The *Iliad* begins with the quarrel that erupted between Achilles and Agamemnon over possession of Briseis, a woman whose family and city Achilles had destroyed, who then became his mistress. Agamemnon, forced to surrender his own spear-won concubine, Chryseis, to appease the gods, forced Achilles to yield Briseis to him. In great anger Achilles retired from the fighting, with the result that Hector and his Trojans inflicted defeat upon defeat, leaving the demoralized Achaeans reeling. As this crisis grew, Agamemnon received a divine dream one night, suggesting that he test the spirit of his disheartened men by asking them, in an assembly, if they should yield to the Trojan might and return home. At dawn he convened this assembly and could say no more than the magical word "home" before his men were racing to their boats to do just that. Of course, this was not what he and the other kings or chiefs – Odysseus, Nestor, Menelaus – had in mind! With some difficulty order was restored and the reluctant warriors were herded back into assembly. It was at this point that Thersites spoke, rebuking Agamemnon for his bankrupt leadership.

There is much in this scene that has attracted scholars and with good reason: it reveals the nature of rule in the Homeric era, how it was an age dominated by the elite. The assembly that in Pericles' day will make decisions, and after him essentially rule the Athenian community, seems little more than a sounding board that the elite can hear and heed or turn a deaf ear to and ignore. Such a view, however, oversimplifies. It has been shown recently that the assembly's view "cannot be ignored lightly" and that it "occupies a crucial position in the community."[3] Decision-making, then, is potentially dangerous. For chiefs like Agamemnon and Odysseus, misreading popular opinion could result in not just a loss of face but loss of control.

The assembly that Thersites disrupted by his outburst also reveals the practice of hoplite warfare, the basic style of war that the Greeks would use for the next five hundred years. The many references that Homer makes to greaves, throwing-spears, and to the "bronze armored Achaeans" generally point to the development of a community-based organization of violence, one in which the role of the commoners like Thersites, over time, became vital.[4] The hoplite phalanx has been much studied by scholars, but the sense

---

3   Raaflaub 1997b: 19.
4   The literature on this is extensive, but see Raaflaub 1997a: 634, 647; Raaflaub 1997c: 49–59; and Osborne 1996: 175–6.

of corporate identity that it created has not always been fully appreciated. In his acclaimed study *The Rise of the West*, William McNeill pointed to the "sense of solidarity and equality among the citizen-soldiers of the phalanx." As one who had served in the ranks, McNeill also observed that close-order drill and repeated exercises "act like a powerful hypnotic, fostering a quite subrational sense of well-being and social solidarity."[5] This sense of group institutionalized violence gradually brought the Thersites and Agamemnons of the Greek city-states together and with the same end in mind: the protection of the community's wealth, the guardianship of the way of life and liberties that all cherished.

With little doubt McNeill correctly noted the social as well as military dimensions of drill and its effects on the members of the phalanx. One further point may be made. As the Greek *poleis* were small in their populations, the men drilling together and fighting together were intimately connected – much more so than in a modern army. The citizen-soldiers were fathers and sons, brothers and near relations. The trauma of watching these die beside you is surely greater than losing a close friend or good buddy. We may gain an understanding of how such deaths may have affected these men in a story told by Stephen Ambrose. A GI nicknamed Junior, a "sweet natured 19 year old kid," had two brothers killed in Normandy (and unlike Private Ryan of Spielberg fame, was not sent home). Afterwards Junior "became a fiend where Germans were concerned. He killed every one he could including any prisoner. It had become a court martial offense to send a prisoner back with Junior."[6]

The Homeric world of c. 700 BC, then, is a world in which the social elite control the land and its peoples as well as the means of production and organization. They dictate actions and situations, but in a tentative manner. Homer's reference to an assembly points to a growing reliance and dependency upon "the many" for military service and how these must be persuaded to fight and guaranteed a reward. From the Homeric era on, what emerges with growing certainty is that the fighting man decides his own destiny, whether he is a prince or a commoner.

The development of democracy in Athens is a long and complicated story, one that would fill (and has indeed filled) many scholarly volumes. It is clear, however, that as the Greek world left its Homeric roots behind, the broadening of society occurred most notably in Athens. This is one reason why the study of ancient Greece has become so fixed on events in Athens. What gradually emerged at Athens was a "horizontal" society or democracy in which citizens related to others as equals. This may be compared with the "vertical" structure, or top to bottom nature, of modern, democratically

5   McNeill 1991: 198–9. More recently McNeill 1995 examines the connection between
      dance and drill.
6   Ambrose 1997: 353.

elected governments. Moreover, as the democratic element grew it saw the need and value to publish popular decisions so that all could see and adhere to what had been decided by the community as a whole. Athens, then, stands out among the Greek communities for its self-announced prominence, as well as its cultural achievements.

In the early pre-classical or "archaic period" (c. 700–500 BC), one example of popular decision-making and war stands out. This is the case of the war waged by Athens and Megara for control of the island of Salamis. Two great personalities figured in this event, Solon and Pisistratus. Solon, sometimes known as the "father" of the Athenian democracy (a title better suited to Clisthenes, c. 500 BC), had carried out a series of reforms c. 594/3 BC and then retired from the political scene. Pisistratus, who emerged as a war-hero in the fight over Salamis, is remembered mostly as the founder of the tyrant dynasty that ruled Athens for some thirty-five years (c. 546–511/10 BC).[7] While in the later classical age Athens would overpower Megara, in this earlier epoch the two states were more evenly matched. The struggle was bitter and exhausting. At one point, after losing ground and momentum, the Athenians became so discouraged that they forbade mention of Salamis, let alone discussion of the idea of further war. Yet Salamis occupied a key position between both communities and Solon realized it. One day he appeared in the agora seemingly bedraggled and confused. He began to rant on the subject of Salamis. Were these the ravings of a madman or a prophet? No one was really sure, but the effect was startling: the Athenians were roused to renew their efforts: Pisistratus emerged as a hero and Salamis became Athenian.[8]

This account of Solon's appeal to the Athenians is fairly typical of the Greek way to war in the classical era as well. Here the great events are the Persian and Peloponnesian wars recounted in all their glory and brutality by Herodotus and Thucydides. In the case of the Great War with Persia, Themistocles took the lead in encouraging Athens to resist literally "to the barricades," and provided a successful strategy. In the later fifth century, Pericles emerged as the architect of Athenian imperial expansion, urged the Athenians to resist Spartan aggression, and devised counter-measures to Spartan power. In both cases, learning about Cimon and his opposition to Themistocles and how Thucydides, son of Melesias, challenged Pericles, and others who might have figured in the debates and offered alternative schemes, is complicated by a shortage of evidence that tells only a partial story.

7   For discussion of Solon and Pisistratus, see e.g. Osborne 1996: 217–25, 283–5. On Clisthenes see p. 29 n. 46 in this book.

8   Solon, Fragments 2, 3 record Solon's rambling reminder to the Athenians not to yield Salamis to the Megarians; see also Jeffery 1976: 156 on Pisistratus' victory.

There are some explanations to these shortcomings. First, it must be kept in mind that the great influence on Herodotus and Thucydides was not some proto-historian, but actually a poet – Homer.[9] In the *Iliad* Homer had established the form, the standard for writing and telling the exploits of great men – identify the heroes and fix the events around them. For these reasons the opponents of Themistocles and Pericles, if they appear at all, are seen only as minor characters. The common man, as illustrated in Homer's account of Thersites' challenge to Agamemnon or in Thucydides' account of the Athenian assembly voting as Pericles asked, is described in general terms.[10] This may also be seen in Thucydides' famous assessment of the Athenian democracy, that it was a "democracy in name, but in reality ruled by the first man," – Pericles (Thucydides 2.65.9).

In the fourth century BC, as Athens became a more sophisticated, more literate community, the process by which the community discussed issues of war and peace also became more complex.[11] Here the great example is the struggle between Athens and Macedon. By the 340s BC, these sophisticated states, one a democracy, the latter a monarchy (and for that reason scorned by the former) were by far preeminent in Greece and, seemingly, on a collision course. The debates that occurred in Athens over the issue of war with Philip of Macedon are skewed by the surviving oratory of the great Demosthenes, and to a lesser extent his antagonist Aeschines.[12] As there exists in some ways a broader body of evidence from this period (some of it reliable, some not) than from the era of the great historians Herodotus and Thucydides, we can discern a greater variety of opinion, a wider group of individuals participating in public debates. Thus the positions and speeches of Demosthenes and Aeschines need to be placed in a broader context that included such equally prominent but now poorly known individuals as the general/politician Phocion, the orators Hypereides and Lycurgus, as well as secondary figures such as Chares and Ephialtes among others.[13] It seems unlikely that the debates in Athens could have been as one-sided as suggested in Demosthenes' oratory.

The process by which the Athenian assembly acquired influence and would eventually decide the issue of war appears first in Thersites' challenge to Agamemnon in the assembly at Troy. This development, which of necessity has been abbreviated here, was also facilitated by population loss

---

9 Griffin 1980: 2.
10 The development of Athenian democracy in the fifth century BC is an immense topic and so is the literature. For discussion of some of the issues see Sinclair 1988, Ober 1996.
11 Developments of the fourth-century Athenian democracy are as complex as those of the fifth. For discussion see Hansen 1991 and Eder 1995.
12 For recent studies of these two antagonists see Sealey 1993 and Harris 1995.
13 For treatments of these less well known but important individuals see Mitchel 1970, and Tritle 1988 and 1993.

Plate 1 The *Bema* or speaker's platform in the Pnyx, a meeting place of the
Athenians in the later fourth century BC. Here individual Athenians could
address their fellow citizens on public matters.

Photo: L.A. Tritle.

through endemic violence, not to mention losses suffered during the great
plague of 431–429 BC. Forces similar to these – the impact of war and the
responses to it – would exert change in the other great state of ancient
Greece – Sparta.

In many ways Sparta was unique. It was a "militaristic" state and community that prepared always for war. In one sense, all Greek communities
prepared for war, but the Spartans were especially cognizant and vigilant
since they were outnumbered in their own land. The enemy within, so to
speak, were the helots, a conquered group of earlier inhabitants who were
reduced to serf-like status and dependency. Later the Spartans conquered
their neighbors the Messenians and reduced them too to this status (see
below, p. 39).[14] The helots, both native and Messenian, remained a
continual worry and threat to the Spartans, hence their constant readiness
for war. To secure themselves further, the Spartans established the

14 See further Osborne 1996: 177, 184, 336.

Peloponnesian League, an alliance system that enabled them to dominate the entire Peloponnese, the southern part of mainland Greece.[15]

The Spartans, then, pushed from within and pulled from without, were frequently at war to defend their lands and intimidate their neighbors. A curious mechanism had evolved in Sparta to register (among other matters) the popular will regarding a declaration of war. According to Plutarch in his *Life of Lycurgus* (6.3–4): "the *damos* [i.e. people] is to have power to give a decisive verdict but if the *damos* speaks crookedly, the *Gerousia* [i.e. the powerful council of elders] and kings are to be removers." What this passage seems to mean, and scholars are by no means in agreement, is that the people, much like the Homeric assembly we have seen already, could indicate their opinion, in effect, be overruled by the kings and elders who could interpret any inconvenient vote "a crooked judgment."

When other Greek communities, in both the classical era and the later Hellenistic (i.e. after Alexander the Great) are examined, the same pattern emerges as for Athens and Sparta. In the rich and populous state of Corinth, one dominated by an oligarchic circle, the assembly retained a voice that the elite had to consider when deciding for or against war.[16] Much better evidence exists for the later Hellenistic age which, in Greece, saw the rise of federal states such as the Achaean and Aetolian Leagues (the largest of these political forms but by no means the only ones). These were highly sophisticated states that practiced a working form of representative government and democracy based around a league council, assembly, and executive, representing a large number of communities that in earlier times had been frequently in conflict. These cities and towns now cooperated under the umbrella of a federal state and in unison through the league assembly; here in the assembly, issues of war and peace were decided by an actual mechanism.[17] This example of representative government stands next to that of the Athenian democracy as the most progressive case of the majority of a community's populace making the most crucial of all decisions, that of declaring war and facing the violent consequences such a decision entails.

America goes to Vietnam

> What the hell is Vietnam worth to me, what the hell is Laos
> worth to me? What is it worth to this country?
>
> (Lyndon Johnson, 1964)

---

15 Osborne 1996: 287–91 discusses Sparta's growth in the Peloponnese, in part at least as a response to the conquest of Messenia.

16 The Corinthian oligarchy reminds us that in the Greek *poleis* power and rule were wielded by adult males and the socio-economic elite.

17 For thorough discussion see Larsen 1955 and 1968.

In the spring of 1997 audiotapes of Lyndon Baines Johnson, never previously heard, were released and made available to scholars and the public alike. These reveal on the one hand Johnson's agony in making the decisions to commit US troops to Vietnam and, on the other, his own skepticism that the cause was at all worth the cost. Politics – his desire to win reelection in 1964 – and his ambitious plans for domestic reforms that would yield significant civil rights and welfare reform victories – pushed Johnson to take the path that would lead to escalation in Vietnam.[18]

The series of decisions that took the US into Vietnam in particular, and Indochina as a whole, was the subject of Robert McNamara's deceiving and self-deceiving memoir *In Retrospect*. In this work McNamara seeks to atone for his acts in advancing the Vietnam War during 1961–67. Whatever else might be said, McNamara makes clear that the Vietnam War resulted from the decisions, and the influence wielded, of a small group of men working first with President John Kennedy and then Lyndon Johnson. A much-celebrated facet of this process of involvement is Kennedy's attitude regarding South Vietnam and the probability of his decision to withdraw US forces. McNamara thinks it "highly probable" that, had Kennedy lived, he would have withdrawn US troops (then consisting of advisers and technical/logistical troops), after coming to the conclusion that the South Vietnamese were incapable of defending themselves. McNamara notes that Kennedy had insisted that his cabinet officers read Barbara Tuchman's *The Guns of August*, the prize-winning and popular work that recounted how the European powers stumbled into war in 1914. Kennedy, McNamara recalls, stated emphatically that "I don't ever want to be in that position," later adding, "We are not going to bungle into war."[19] Yet in conversations with Chet Huntley and David Brinkley only weeks before his death, Kennedy told them that the US should stay in Vietnam, and use its "influence in as effective way as we can ... we should not withdraw. That would be a great mistake."[20]

Kennedy's guarded language is difficult to read more than thirty years after the events. In any event, what policies or decisions Kennedy might have made are academic, something more suited to counterfactual, "what-if" theorizing or computer games, than critical inquiry. The same political forces that Kennedy faced, however, drove Lyndon Johnson, seemingly

18 My focus in this investigation is with the violent consequences of the Vietnam War rather than yet another effort to explain how the policies of the Johnson administration resulted in that war. This topic has been dealt with extensively. Among works recommended to the reader especially for the political developments are Van de Mark 1991, McMaster 1997, and Schulzinger 1997; also valuable for an understanding of Robert McNamara is Hendrickson 1996.
19 McNamara 1995: 96.
20 Ibid.: 86–7.

against his better judgment, to commit US troops on a large scale to Vietnam. Today in the post-communist 1990s it is sometimes difficult to recall the reality of the politics and the threat of imminent conflict that hung over the global community in the 1960s. Indeed, today's generation of students has to be reminded if not taught of this post-World War II reality so as to understand the ideas and fears that may have lurked in the minds of Western, and not just American, political leaders in the 1950s and 1960s.[21] During this turbulent time the struggle between the communist bloc and the "free world" occasionally ignited, as in Korea (1950–53), and threatened to do so in Hungary (1956) and Berlin (1948 [the Berlin Blockade] and 1961). For the US it became an even more critical issue and reality after Fidel Castro's victory in Cuba. In quick succession the abortive Bay of Pigs invasion and Cuban Missile Crisis flared up in 1962. By 1965 these events had convinced many Americans, perhaps even a majority, that containing the communist threat, with a military response if necessary, was a reasonable course of action. What is so tragic in the case of Vietnam is that communism was but a means to an end for Ho Chi Minh, whose sympathies were closer to those of a nationalist than a communist.

It would be tedious to recount in detail the decisions made by Lyndon Johnson and his advisers to escalate the war in Vietnam to the point that half a million American troops had been deployed there by 1967. What is revealing about McNamara's book is the process by which the US government and the military entered the conflict, and the spectator, Thersites-like role played by the American public. A select group of "elites," including McNamara, McGeorge Bundy and George Ball, emerged from similar educational associations (Harvard) and experiences in World War II, and analyzed events in Asia after the fall of "republican" China to the communists, the Korean War, and the expulsion of the French from Vietnam. This group flourished in a hot-house environment and looked inwardly for ideas and policies.

In summarizing the "lessons of Vietnam," McNamara complains that there was an "absence of specialists" in Southeast Asian affairs able to assist the policy-makers in their deliberations.[22] This claim, however, cannot be

---

21 This is occasionally overlooked even in such a thoughtful work as Hendrickson: 1996: 38, 123, who skips over the tenor of these times rather nonchalantly. Yet the American responsibility for "losing" China weighed heavy on American foreign policy experts and domestic politics. The Republicans blamed the Democrats for China's fall to Communism, and during the Korean War President Truman pushed above the 38th Parallel to show he was tough on Communism. This explains in part why Kennedy and Johnson could not show less resolve on Vietnam. Castro's success in Cuba only heightened this policy dynamic. Students today occasionally undervalue or simply ignore these realities, but to do so is to miss much that contributes to an understanding of how Vietnam "happened."

22 McNamara 1995: 322; "absence of specialists" is even indexed!

Plate 2   President Johnson and his advisers at work, July 26, 1965.

Photo: Yoichi R. Okamoto, Lyndon Baines Johnson Library, A 913-12.

treated seriously. McNamara omits any discussion of State Department analysts like Louis Sarris who, as early as October 1963, had submitted a report detailing the declining situation in South Vietnam. In Sarris's case both the Pentagon and McNamara were angered by his findings, which they regarded as an usurpation of Defense responsibilities. The Pentagon made a special effort to rebut Sarris' findings and in the process ignored both a CIA report that echoed Sarris' views and the US military attaché in Saigon, who also noted problems in the South Vietnamese military. The furor subsided and Sarris continued his research. Just before the Tet Offensive of January 1968, he published another report noting the potential for a major Viet Cong attack. This report too fell on deaf ears.[23]

Additionally, there were plenty of "old China" hands who might also have been consulted, as well as academic specialists, scholars such as Owen Lattimore at Harvard and Sar Desai at UCLA. I still recall a course taken at UCLA in the spring of 1967 (US Foreign Policy, taught by William Gerberding, now president of the University of Washington) where a

---

23 L.G. Sarris, "McNamara's War, and Mine," *New York Times* (Op-Ed) September 5, 1995: A17.

teaching assistant gave an informed and balanced lecture arguing against a US role in Vietnam. The advice of these experts, as the State Department analysts, was never asked because McNamara and other policy-makers were supremely confident, perhaps even arrogant, in their own abilities to address and solve the problem in South Vietnam. This self-confidence might have been tempered by consideration of Thucydides' observation that "it is impossible to calculate accurately events that are determined by chance."[24]

The arrogance-induced vacuum in which McNamara and his colleagues in Johnson's cabinet worked is revealed clearly in a remark that George Ball made to Dean Acheson in July 1965. At that point, as the political and military situation in South Vietnam continued to deteriorate, President Johnson and his advisers debated options and actions. George Ball, then serving as Under Secretary for State, and already an avowed skeptic of the effect of strategic bombing, reproached Dean Acheson and others who had persuaded Johnson to commit still more troops and planes in a widening conflict.[25] Ball told them, "you goddamned old buzzards, you remind me of nothing so much as a bunch of buzzards sitting on a fence and letting the young men die. You don't know a goddamned thing about what you're talking about ... you just sit there and say these irresponsible things!"[26]

Ball was one of the few in the government who both criticized the process by which decisions were made and challenged the assumption, widely held by McNamara for example, that the bombing campaign in Vietnam was at all effective. McNamara, in looking back on Ball's criticisms, states that they should have been developed further.[27] At the time, however, McNamara regarded his memoranda, particularly that of October 1964 (titled "How Valid are the Assumptions Underlying our Viet-Nam Policies?") as a "poisonous snake." Ball and McNamara differed fundamentally in approach: Ball looked at the history and culture of Vietnam while McNamara looked only to his data. Moreover, McNamara was a "company man" who disapproved of Ball's direct overture to the president. But in the end McNamara prevailed and Ball was left to reflect on his failed Laocoön-like role in the Johnson White House.[28]

Perhaps the single most important decision and document to emerge from this arrogant and cloistered process was that known today as NSAM-328 (National Security Action Memorandum), issued April 6, 1965.[29]

24 Thucydides 1.84.3.
25 For discussion of Ball's role in the White House during the Vietnam War see Bill 1997: 150–75 and DiLeo 1991.
26 Van de Mark 1995: 176.
27 McNamara 1995: 156–8.
28 Laocoön was the Trojan priest who warned the Trojans against bringing into the city the Horse left by the Greeks. To silence his dissent, Apollo sent serpents out of the sea that killed him and his two sons. See Bill 1997: 160–75 for a fuller discussion of Ball's role in these events.
29 Sheehan 1971: 442–3 (text of NSAM-328, issued as part of the Pentagon Papers), with discussion by Van de Mark 1991: 112–13 and Hendrickson 1996: 161–7.

What this document did was to "change the mission" of US Marine battalions in Vietnam from defensive to offensive postures (i.e. to permit their deployment as regular combat units so as to engage Viet Cong forces). Within a matter of days, additional combat formations of the US Army amounting to three infantry divisions (about forty-five thousand men) were ordered to Vietnam and the build-up that would eventually establish a force of more than a half million men was underway. This decision was virtually made in secret, as Johnson had directed (Point 11 of the document) that "premature publicity be avoided by all possible precautions." Only three people knew of it, McNamara and Dean Rusk (respectively secretaries of Defense and State) and John McCone (CIA Director), and these, as McNamara's later testimony before Senator J. William Fulbright made clear, deceived and otherwise misled Congress. Meanwhile Johnson, as various remarks recorded by McGeorge Bundy show, became increasingly comfortable with his decision to commit more troops and to commit them to battle.[30] NSAM-328 and the decision taken several months earlier to launch Operation "Rolling Thunder" and to bomb North Vietnam, firmly committed the US to full combat operations.[31]

The only thing lacking now to make this mushrooming conflict formal was a declaration of war, but this would never come. A partial explanation for this may lie in the Gulf of Tonkin Resolution passed the previous summer (August 1964).[32] Johnson directed Attorney General Nicholas Katzenbach to investigate how to stretch the Tonkin Gulf Resolution's meaning so as to widen the war. Later as Under Secretary of State, Katzenbach made the point clear, telling the Senate Foreign Relations Committee that a "formal" declaration of war in Vietnam was outmoded, especially when a limited war was being fought and within the scope of the 1955 SEATO Treaty. The result was an interpretation of the document as the "functional equivalent" of a declaration of war. A congressional measure, then, was unnecessary.[33] Hubris, arrogant pride, might explain

30 On McNamara's deceptions of Fulbright and Johnson's remarks as recorded by Bundy, see Hendrickson 1996: 162–3.
31 Note also the hawkish role of W.W. Rostow, who succeeded to the post of National Security Adviser in 1966. Rostow had earlier played a part in the development of the bombing campaign against North Vietnam (the so-called "strike and pause" policy) and also assisted in rebuffing congressional inquiries into the war's conduct, particularly that of Senator Mansfield. See further Olson 1995: 128, 176–7, 182–3.
32 Olson 1995: 133–6 discusses the background, noting that several congressional resolutions similar in nature had passed only a short time before (i.e. the Cuba and Berlin Resolutions). As early as February 1964, the Johnson Administration began thinking of a like measure for Vietnam.
33 See McMaster 1997: 294 and Siff 1999: 110; Moïse 1997 investigates extensively the August 1964 attacks and argues that the attack that provoked the Resolution did not in fact occur as claimed. I thank Marc Frey for pointing this out to me.

the rest of the Johnson administration's decision not to ask for an official congressional act.

McNamara's supreme self-confidence, Dean Rusk's strident anti-commu-nism and McGeorge Bundy's international visions and self-assurance were mirrored in some ways by the personalities, beliefs and values of their coun-terparts in the military establishment. In June 1964 Lyndon Johnson named General William Westmoreland as the new commander of American mili-tary forces in Vietnam (COMUSMACV, or Commander of the United States Military Assistance Command Vietnam), replacing General Paul Harkins whose optimistic reports belied the deteriorating situation in Vietnam. Not long after Westmoreland arrived, so too did Maxwell Taylor, former Chairman of the Joint Chiefs of Staff, now ambassador to Vietnam, replacing Henry Cabot Lodge. Both Westmoreland and Taylor were traditional soldiers from the southern US, well educated and experienced in military and administrative affairs. Taylor's own designated successor, General Earle C. Wheeler, took over the Joint Chiefs' of Staff position, while Harold K. Johnson became Army Chief of Staff. Both Westmoreland and Taylor had distinguished combat records in World War II and Korea, whereas Wheeler and Johnson were primarily administrators with only limited combat expe-rience.[34]

These decision-makers, and others such as Air Force General Curtis Le May, whose idea was "to bomb Vietnam back into the Stone Age," became caught up in inter-service rivalries. This competition impeded their coopera-tion, which resulted in policies for Vietnam being formulated by the White House, which then called upon the Chiefs of Staff to implement them.[35] There were, however, other factors that influenced the decisions of the mili-tary in Vietnam. Chief among these was the confident belief that the American way of war was not only a winning way – witness World War II and, in terms of casualties at least, Korea – but also humanitarian as it saved lives, at least American lives. This belief in the power and success of fire-power and technology would backfire in Vietnam. The Chiefs of Staff, and many others in the US military, would learn that the terrain in Vietnam would appreciably reduce the effectiveness of the firepower available to a ground commander. The nature of the war in Vietnam – small unit, guerilla style hit-and-run – made this even more of a reality. In short, what US mili-tary planners did in Vietnam was to attempt the clichéd square peg in a round hole.

Additionally, American military planners did not appreciate or under-stand the nature of Vietnamese culture and society. Actually, few Americans

34 For further discussion see Van de Mark 1991: 16–18, McMaster 1997: 144 (who notes Johnson's experience as a Japanese prisoner of war in World War II and how this affected him), 108–9 (on Wheeler's administrative as opposed to combat experience).
35 See McMaster 1997: 43 (conflict between Taylor and Le May), 113 (inter-service rivalry), and 114–15, 147 (examples of the Chiefs' inability to formulate policies, etc.).

of any position or rank did, but perhaps more importantly they were powerless to influence the warlord mentality of the Vietnamese generals and
officials with whom they worked. This was especially critical early in the
build-up years of 1963–65, but this situation never really changed. When
the US began to commit large numbers of men to Vietnam following
Operation Rolling Thunder and the issue of NSAM-328, the war slipped
into American hands and out of Vietnamese.

Some Vietnamese were only too happy to let the Americans do the
fighting. Others, such as Tran Van Tuyen, whose family's story Paul
Hendrickson tells in *The Living and the Dead*, regarded this development
with apprehension. Vietnamese politicians of like mind were as concerned
with the growing influence of the Americans as they were with the oppres-
sion of the Vietnamese communists.[36] Tran Van Tuyen's worries, however,
have a Mandarin air to them and seem not to recognize that in many cases
South Vietnamese armed forces were not willing to stand up to their Viet
Cong opponents. While some South Vietnamese army units such as Ranger,
Marine, and Airborne units (and I worked with others such as the 69th and
87th Regional Force battalions) performed ably in the field, others preferred
"search and avoid" type operations to actually engaging the enemy.[37] The
principal problem here was one of leadership. Officers commanding divisions and provinces near Saigon preferred to stand ready to intervene in the
capital's political scene, and their subordinates took their cue from them.
Moreover, officers were frequently reluctant to engage in battle, as they
feared that a defeat with corresponding loss of life would ruin their careers.
Losing men from their unit rosters might also mean a reduction in the unit's
pay, which was frequently a matter of rife corruption. In mid-1965, then, as
Tran Van Tuyen worried about the presence of American soldiers in South
Vietnam, it was clear that the ability of South Vietnamese to prosecute the
war was limited. As a result, American boys began dying in ever increasing
numbers – exactly the situation Lyndon Johnson had sought to avoid.[38]

The political ambitions and rivalries of Vietnamese generals affected US
planning in Vietnam throughout the course of the war. Related to this
problem was that of outright deception and fraud. An early example was the
defeat of a South Vietnamese force in the Mekong Delta in 1963 at a place
called Ap Bac. Here an entrenched Viet Cong force mauled attacking South
Vietnamese and managed to shoot down five American helicopters, killing
three crew members. News coverage of this incident began the careers of

36 For an example of such an attitude see Hendrickson 1996: 300–9, 315–18, 339–43.
37 While operating with a Vietnamese reconnaissance platoon in November 1970
    (consisting of *chieu hoi* or former Viet Cong) in a contested part of the province, I came
    across such a unit, simply waiting in a village to go home at the end of the day.
38 It should also be noted that the South Vietnamese casualties also began to increase as the
    war against the Viet Cong and North Vietnamese became wider and more intensive.

David Halberstam and Neil Sheehan, who encountered American efforts to cover up the defeat and even convert it into a victory.[39] This sort of reaction continued to occur right through the war. In March 1971 I was about to leave for home when word arrived in the Ba Xuyen provincial capital of Soc Trang that a militia outpost had been overrun during the night. Nearly every soldier, about thirty-five men altogether, had been killed. I participated in the relief force sent out the next day and learned that this had in fact occurred, that the Viet Cong had mutilated the bodies by burning them before leaving. Within a week I was in Saigon outprocessing and preparing to leave Vietnam. I went to MACV headquarters and found a civilian official with whom I had worked earlier in my tour. I had reason to believe that the provincial officials, both Vietnamese and American, had covered up this incident rather than report it to higher command. They had – but I was told to forget about it and go home, that saying something would only create problems for myself.[40]

In writing his history in the aftermath of thirty years of war that destroyed Athens, Thucydides concluded "war is a violent teacher." It deprives people, he saw, of the ability to satisfy their needs and brings them down to the level of their circumstances (Thucydides 3.82.2). His remarks actually constitute a sort of afterword to his account of the terrible *stasis* or civil war that had virtually destroyed the community of Corcyra in 427 BC.[41] The analysis, however, may have yet a more general application: first to the McNamaras and Westmorelands, the Agamemnons and the Menelauses who decide on the wars, and then the common soldiers and civilians who get caught up in them. All will find themselves in dilemmas, both intellectual and ethical, and others emotional and moral. There will be inequities too that in the end will oppress most those less able to escape them.

39 The South Vietnamese defeat at Ap Bac was told as early as 1964 by Halberstam 1988: 67–81, who also reports on the effort to conceal the defeat. McMaster 1997: 45, notes too the role played in this by General Wheeler, then an assistant to Taylor, still Chief of the JCS.

40 This long-forgotten incident occurred in Nga Nam district of Ba Xuyen Province. I was leaving Vietnam within a matter of days, and my role in the relief force was to operate a nearby tactical center and this enabled me to listen in on the radio traffic of those actually at the site.

41 Thucydides 3.70–84 records the entire event. I refer to it as an "afterword" here, as Thucydides wrote his account at the end of the war and so could reflect on what had happened. On the manner of Thucydides' composition see Hornblower 1987: 137, who cites Thucydides 2.65.12, 5.26, 6.15 (and other passages could be added) as evidence that Thucydides lived through the war.

Draft-dodging and other inequities

War was a constant in the ancient Greek world and wartime service was a role that perhaps all, or nearly all, free adult males performed as well as resident aliens and even slaves in emergencies. In the *poleis*, the Greek city-states of the classical era (and after), the responsibilities of citizenship called for military service; from the late seventh century BC, the basic form of military service was as the *hoplite*, the heavily-armed foot soldier. During the late fifth and fourth centuries BC, lightly armed (and armored) foot soldiers emerged, *peltasts*, who served alongside the heavily-armed infantry and cavalry in most Greek communities. In Athens those who lacked the wealth to serve in the ground forces could and did find service in the fleet, and it seems likely that other communities that also organized fleets, such as Corinth and Corcyra (at least up to the Peloponnesian War), would have provided similar opportunities for their citizens.[42] In short, most free Greeks, citizens of a *polis*, would have been obliged during their lives to put on military dress, say farewell to wife and family, and march or sail off to war. This farewell theme in fact appears numerous times in Greek vase-painting and sepulchral monuments, which reinforces the idea that this was not simply an artistic convention but a familiar occurrence.

Slaves too could frequently find themselves in a war zone. In Athens there were several occasions in which slaves were given the opportunity to escape their bonds by agreeing to serve, usually in the fleet. This happened, for example, in 406 BC during the Peloponnesian War when the Athenians made a major effort against the Spartans that resulted in the Battle of Arginusae. The comic poet Aristophanes, in his play *The Frogs*, refers to the

---

42　See Anderson 1970: 111–40 for discussion of land warfare. For discussions of fleets see e.g. Jordan 1972 (for Athens) and Salmon 1984: 166–9, 254–6.

slave Xanthias wishing he had volunteered on that occasion so that he would not be serving Dionysus (Aristophanes, *The Frogs* 33–4, 190–92, 693–9; also Xenophon, *Hellenica* 1.6.24). The Spartans too made use of their enslaved, serf-like populace, the helots. As Spartan military manpower declined through the late fifth and fourth centuries BC, the Spartans came to recruit more and more helots to bolster the ranks of the free citizens. These men became known as *neodamodeis*, "New Men," and while they did not enjoy equality with the Spartan elite, they were free. Elsewhere in the ancient Greek world, other cities from time to time called on their servile populations for help in emergencies.[43]

While Greeks both free and unfree could find themselves regularly facing military service, it should not be imagined that all lived up to the standard of Achilles. Desertion was a recurring problem, especially if a campaign became protracted on account of a siege or blockade. A good example of this occurred during the Lamian War of 322/1 BC, when an allied Greek army surrounded the Macedonian Antipater in Lamia in central Greece. Though the Greeks held the upper hand, their forces drifted off to return home, with the result that the Macedonians broke the siege and with it Greek hopes of ending Macedonian hegemony over them.[44]

A related problem was lack of discipline. This was less of a concern for the Spartans than the rest of the Greeks, but was a problem all generals faced: how do you discipline free and equal men?[45] Athenian generals in particular commanded by persuasion as much as authority: one unpopular order or decision would ensure that they would never win election again.[46] An Athenian named Aristogeiton, a popular agitator for war, illustrates the discipline-related problems Athenian generals faced. Once on being called out for military service, Aristogeiton came to the assembly point limping and covered in bandages. Phocion, one of the generals, on seeing him approach, cried out for all to hear that Aristogeiton should be listed as lame and worthless for service (Plutarch, *Phocion* 10.3). Clearly the Athenians, and one suspects the other Greeks as well, were not unfamiliar with "draft-dodgers" and shirkers. A call to support the "fatherland" was invoked by the

43 On helots and *neodamodeis* in Spartan service see Thucydides 4.80.3–5, 5.34.1. See also Socrates of Argos, in Jacoby, *Die Fragmente der griechischen Historiker* 310 F6 and Polyaen. 1.43.1, which record the freeing of slaves in Argos and Syracuse respectively.

44 E.g. Diodorus Siculus 18.17.1; see Pritchett 1971–91: 4, 232–45, who discusses the evidence for the laxity of Greek military discipline.

45 It is usually thought that the Spartans were always brave, never cowardly. For discussion of this Spartan mirage see below pp. 75–77.

46 Clisthenes' reforms c. 500 BC had changed the tribal structure of the Athenian community, requiring a new board of ten generals to command the army. These generals were chosen by direct election, unlike most other magistrates, who were selected by lot. For this reason the generals had to be aware of what their men – the electorate – thought. For discussion see Osborne 1996: 305–6 and Tritle 1988: 61–2 (with sources and authorities).

Athenian Lycurgus after the great defeat at Chaeronea by Philip of Macedon (338/7 BC), and this did produce tangible results. In the years after Chaeronea Lycurgus enacted numerous reforms, some of which were directed towards the military, and these greatly strengthened Athens. When the Athenians faced off against the Macedonians again fifteen years later in the Lamian War, the latter prevailed, but only because Alexander's seasoned veterans secured the victory.[47]

During the classical era, the Athenians realized that indiscriminate levying of troops for services, while democratic, was inherently ineffective, as it brought in numbers of men unfit and unwilling to serve. To counter this problem they created an elite corps of picked troops who were apparently organized independently of other military formations, perhaps extending even to separate battlefield organization as well. Other Greek states during the classical era seem to have encountered similar situations, as they too established elite formations.[48] These measures shed some interesting light on the Greeks and the extent to which the virtues of Homer's heroes influenced them. While many men sought to emulate Achilles, there were others like Aristogeiton who preferred to take a less heroic path and would, if necessary, follow the example of the warrior poet Archilochus who was not above throwing away his shield to save his skin. But these less than heroic actions pale before the gross inequities that emerged from the Vietnam War.

Of the inequities associated with the Vietnam War perhaps the most notorious was the draft, which there is little doubt weighed far more heavily on the less privileged, whether they were found in the rural heartland of America or in inner city ghettos and barrios. Early on, the war in Vietnam was fought by men who had responded to the patriotic appeal of John Kennedy during the Berlin and Cuban crises of 1961/62. Many of the men in the first army and marine units sent to Vietnam in 1964 and 1965 actually volunteered for service in Vietnam or extended their enlistment to do so. Marine veteran Lou Albert, who was one such volunteer, has told me how men not only volunteered for duty in Vietnam, but competed for available slots to get there as soon as possible. It was not always youthful enthusiasm and a belief in one's invulnerability that prompted this, but rather a sense of duty and obligation, of defending freedom against communism. Again in the late 1990s such views seem strange if not quixotic, but they were nonetheless true in 1964–6.

As the war intensified, as casualties and missions widened, the number of US troops on the ground grew. The number of marine and army battalions streaming to Vietnam increased and before long there were simply not

47 See discussion in Sealey 1993: 216–17.
48 For discussion see e.g. Tritle 1989: 54–9.

enough volunteers. As the volunteer pool proved inadequate to the military's needs, the Selective Service Boards began calling up more and more men. The system, however, was far from equal. Those in college gained deferment (i.e. the much coveted II-S or student deferment), while those who lacked access or whose economic status denied them education were increasingly designated I-A and called into service. Another inequity in the draft was felt in rural counties. Here draft boards had a small pool to levy draftees from and yet had to supply a quota: this meant that if you were recently out of high school, not attending college, you could expect to be drafted in a matter of months.[49] My own friends who had graduated in 1964 from high school in a lower middle-class/working-class neighborhood in Los Angeles' San Fernando Valley were, by the spring of 1966, mostly drafted or had volunteered because that was a "normal" thing for "boomers" to do. I had moved from this community into the city of Los Angeles several years earlier. Here I had access to a number of colleges and universities that enabled me to gain deferment from military service, as long, that is, as I remained in school.[50]

My situation was typical of the white middle class. There can be little doubt that the draft fell hard upon the working-class and minority population of America. This is tragic enough, but the enactment and execution of "Project 100,000" makes the draft nearly criminal, the avoidance of service by those able to serve morally bankrupt. What was Project 100,000? It was an effort by the government to widen the draft pool because there were simply not enough men either volunteering or passing Selective Service physical and aptitude examinations. Put into place in 1966, the Project inducted men for service whose scores on the Armed Forces Qualification Tests fell in Category IV, the marginal group placing between the tenth and thirtieth percentile, or those men whose physical fitness was marginal. The program had as its announced goal the education and training of these men who, upon completion of their services, would reenter civilian life and assume productive places in it. Reality was somewhat different. Many of those drafted lacked the intellectual or personal skills to learn any occupation other than those of an infantry soldier, and consequently they were quickly on their way to Vietnam. Approximately half of the 400,000 men taken in under the conditions of Project 100,000 were sent to Vietnam where they met death at a rate nearly twice that of the American forces as a whole. Their deaths – deaths which practically go unknown and unrecorded today (just ask any American of any age group) – are perhaps the most tragic

49 See Appy 1993: 11–15, who lists a number of small towns (i.e. under 500 inhabitants) which lost a half dozen dead in Vietnam.
50 Similar conclusions are reached by Appy 1993: 11–85, and before him by Baskir and Strauss 1978: 6–13.

of all. They are silent testimony to the great inequity of how America chose its warriors for Vietnam.[51]

The figure of Aristogeiton appears in the Vietnam era, too, in the guise of the "war wimps." G.B. Trudeau, in his "Doonesbury" cartoon critique illustrated above, and other American comics, have made frequent allusions to famous American "war wimps" of the Vietnam War – Rush Limbaugh, Patrick Buchanan, Newt Gingrich, as well as Bill Clinton. These all took advantage of the system to avoid military service and allowed others – those certainly lacking their opportunities – to be drafted into military service. These later included, as noted above, many from the Project 100,000 lists, who were surely brought into service because of the flight – whether it was to Canada or to England on a Rhodes scholarship – of these elites. More ambiguous were those like Dan Quayle and George W. Bush, who dodged the draft and active military service by finding a safe-haven in the reserve forces of the Army or Air Force, or the National Guard. This avenue was usually unavailable unless one had a "connection," and if you were poor and minority, your chances of finding such a slot were virtually non-existent. Today these neo-conservative icons profess heroic virtues and claim they would have gone to Vietnam had they been called, but their actions speak otherwise.

A related political development during this era was that of the Young Americans for Freedom (YAF). This group, which formed in the early 1960s and would later provide the nucleus for the "Reagan Revolution," issued its first conservative statement at a conference held at Sharon, Connecticut, in September 1960. Its attitude and position toward the war in Vietnam, however, fit in well with both the draft-dodging of Americans at the time and the social attitudes that created Project 100,000. As a recent study of YAF has noted, "YAF found itself in a difficult position. Opposition to the war and to the draft usually went hand-in-hand. But YAF opposed the draft even while it supported the war."[52] It is argued that this policy was based on "traditional YAF beliefs in anti-communism and individual freedom," but what is overlooked is also the elitist and perhaps unconscious class attitudes which, in effect, gave up the poor, the minorities, and the uneducated to the draft. One day while in Vietnam I escorted a group of YAF students around our province, talking with them and listening to them defend Nixon administration policy in Vietnam. Several of the young men in the group had just graduated from college. I asked them what they would now be doing and to a man they answered, "Oh, I'm starting law school in the fall." None of these eager anti-communists was about to join the armed services, let alone the infantry, and take on the nasty commies themselves! Readers can draw

51 For further discussion of "Project 100,000" see Appy 1993: 32–3, Baskir and Strauss 1978: 122–31.
52 Andrew 1997: 215.

their own conclusions about the anti-communist platform of YAF, but clearly in 1970 there was a big difference between theory and practice.

The process by which American soldiers went to war in Vietnam was dramatically different than that of their Greek counterparts, particularly in the classical world. This is most noticeable in a comparison of the democratic Athenian experience in which the Athenians voted to send themselves into battle. In 1960s America the Government made the decisions and the people were persuaded that it was in the "national interest" to accept these, as well as the process by which their sons and daughters would be sent to Vietnam. Thersites' protest against Agamemnon's corrupt leadership might seem to offer a closer connection to the common soldier sent to Vietnam. Intimidated by the likes of Agamemnon, Odysseus, and Achilles, Homeric soldiers yielded to their chiefs much as average Americans accepted the judgment and decisions of their chiefs, Johnson, McNamara and Rusk. And in the end, Thersites' cynical complaint of Agamemnon's unending greed for wealth and power finds its counterpart in the equally cynical GI description of leaderless policies that brought them to Vietnam:

We are the Unwilling,
Led by the Unqualified,
Doing the Unnecessary,
For the Ungrateful.

3

ACHILLES AND THE HEROIC IDEAL

[Achilles] who stands as a great bulwark of battle over the Achaians.

(Homer, *Iliad* 1.283–4)

In Homer's *Iliad*, Achilles, "the best of the Achaeans," (1.244) dominates as both the model heroic warrior and then, in the words of one scholar, "the be[a]st of the Achaians."[1] This paradox is not simply poetic exaggeration but in fact reality for many who have experienced battle, who enter combat with ideas of martial virtue but then find themselves committing frightful acts of killing and worse. The model of Achilles, like so much more in Homer, provided the Greeks with an exemplary form of conduct that constantly reappears in later poetry and in the commemorative monuments erected in the Greek city-states. This idea of heroic virtue, however, is by no means limited to ancient times. The idealized nature of heroic conduct continues into the present, in the form of the expected *Courage Under Fire*, as the recent Hollywood film puts it, and the corresponding shame of not meeting this standard – of playing the part of the coward.

Closely related to this heroic image is the idea of manliness, a word and concept that today in the early twenty-first century seems, as Harvard scholar Harvey Mansfield has written, "quaint and obsolete."[2] Yet from Homer on, Greek authors tie manliness to war, the latter being the calling and domain of men. Mansfield rightly comments on the passing of manliness as an attribute in today's politically correct society. Yet elsewhere in the world today the idea survives as among the Greeks. Among the Dinka of Sudan, for example, *muoc*, or manliness, derives directly from *moc*, man, who alone may be regarded as *keec*, or courageous – an attribute achieved only in war.[3] Manliness and the heroic virtues appear to possess a universal calling,

1 King 1987: 13–28, at 13.
2 H. Mansfield, "The Partial Eclipse of Manliness," *Times Literary Supplement*, July 17 1998, pp. 14–16.
3 I learned of this in discussions with my Sudanese colleague Jok M. Jok, who told me that this attitude became an issue for women who supported the independence movement in

34

and, despite the millennial breach separating us from antiquity, the expectations of the warrior seem little different today than they were for the Homeric heroes or the Greeks of the classical era.

Greek heroes

> I [Eteocles] will take six men, myself to make a seventh ...
> opponents of the enemy in gallant style.
> (Aeschylus, *Seven Against Thebes* 283–5)

The *Iliad* is Achilles' story, as the poet makes clear at the beginning of the poem: "Sing, Goddess, the anger of Peleus' son Achilles and its devastation, which put pains thousandfold upon the Achaians, herded in their multitudes to the house of Hades" (*Iliad* 1.1–3). In the years that the Greeks had besieged Troy and fought the Trojans and their allies, Achilles had distinguished himself as the bravest of the Greeks, the man on whom the Greeks came to rely for victory. In countless fights and raids Achilles had displayed great courage and skill, but also honor in treating his enemies generously. This can be seen in a statement of Andromache, Hector's wife (*Iliad* 6.414–19), where she relates the death in battle of her father, killed by Achilles, who treated his corpse with dignity – an ironic anticipation perhaps of the death and mutilation of her husband. But things begin to go badly for Achilles as the ignoble Agamemnon takes Achilles' woman Briseis to compensate for his own loss of the captive Chryseis, whom he had been obliged to return to her father. It is this insult that leads Achilles to withdraw from battle, with terrible results: for the Greeks, who suffer horrific casualties at the hands of the emboldened Trojans; for Achilles himself, whose best friend Patroclus is killed by Hector, leaving him to live with the consequences of his survival. Achilles then becomes the heroic model of a survivor trying to make sense of his loss.

In this dramatic and tragic scene there are several situations which may be noted. In the confrontation between Achilles and Agamemnon over the women captives, Achilles delivers a stinging taunt to Agamemnon, "You wine sack, with a dog's eyes and with a deer's heart. Never once have you taken courage in your heart to arm with your people for battle, or go into ambuscades with the best of the Achaians" (*Iliad* 1.225–7). Achilles may be, and probably is, exaggerating Agamemnon's cowardice or skulking, as in the *Iliad* Agamemnon is credited for killing more than a dozen Trojans. Perhaps what Achilles has in mind is that Agamemnon has not killed as many men as he, taken as many towns, or distinguished himself in so many fights.

Sudan and were unable to win equality with the men because only the latter could be manly.

What we have here is actually a "pissing contest," the sort of things that soldiers have always, as we can see here, indulged in, attempting to show that the other is less a man, less courageous, or serving in a less dangerous place than him. Paul Fussell mentions such competition while a graduate student at Harvard after World War II, and Sophocles in his play *Ajax* does so too.[4] Here Menelaus taunts Teucer, brother of the dead Ajax, for his less than manly skills as an archer (Sophocles, *Ajax* 1120–24), and I must admit to doing something similar myself. One day while in from the field, resting but mostly drinking, I began taunting several Signal Corps enlisted men, calling them REMFs ("Rear Echelon Mother Fucker") and candy-asses. With their soft jobs listening to radios all day, they were hardly "real" men going out looking for the enemy, getting shot at and worse. These young guys were about ready to shut me up – actually they were going to beat me up and in my condition I could probably have mustered only feeble resistance – when a sergeant said something like, "Sir, that's enough – you should leave these boys alone." A few days later, after I had sobered up, the men told me that they were about to beat me up when they realized their intended victim was an officer.

It seems that Achilles, angered as well as inspired by drink, has also attempted to paint a picture of Agamemnon as a REMF so as to make himself appear the greater, the more important, so as to justify keeping his captive woman and his honor intact. But if Agamemnon's later actions and victories are any guide to his skill as a warrior, then Achilles is not exactly honest in his description of Agamemnon's martial valor.

Achilles' taunt, his reputation as the "best of the Achaeans," undoubtedly shows that he enjoyed the reputation as the most valiant warrior, one who was unafraid of standing up to anyone, friend or foe, who crossed him. Still there emerges also a picture of a valiant warrior, one who does not strike down the helpless or, in doing so, dishonors himself. The death of Patroclus changed all this. Patroclus, Achilles' alter-ego and boyhood companion, cannot abide the destruction of the Greeks as his friend sulks. He borrows Achilles' armor so as to impersonate Achilles and bring heart and hope to the faltering Greeks. Initially he is successful, but then, as fortune and the poet dictate, he encounters Hector, the great Trojan, who mortally wounds him. With his dying breath, Patroclus tells Hector that Achilles will avenge him and bring destruction to him and the house of Priam (*Iliad* 16).

Patroclus' death brings Achilles back to the fight, but he is a changed man. He is – perhaps strangely to the uninitiated – energized by his friend's death and exacts a fearful toll upon the Trojans. So driven is Achilles to avenge Patroclus that he remarks that,

---

4   See Fussell 1996: 190, and Shay 1994: 205–6, who tries to discourage this attitude, noting that "no person's suffering is commensurable with any other."

neither food nor drink shall go down my very throat, since my companion perished and lies inside my shelter ... Food and drink mean nothing to my heart but blood does, and slaughter, and the groaning of men in hard work.[5]

Achilles' reaction to Patroclus' death and his manner in battle has been described by Shay as "going berserk," but it is a reaction to the stress of battle that knows no time or place.[6] This Achillean terror finally culminates in the climatic battle of the *Iliad*, that between Achilles and Hector, the latter of whom must die and suffer ugly mutilation before all.

Achilles exacts a terrible vengeance upon the body of Hector, and other Achaean warriors join in mutilating the dead Hector before Achilles drags him around Troy (*Iliad* 22.369–404). The gods, however, are bothered by this and Apollo acts to protect Hector's body from actual outrage (*Iliad* 24. 18–25). Slowly Achilles' great rage ebbs, though before it is gone completely he performs human sacrifice over his dead friend's tomb.[7] In the end he makes a peace of sorts with Priam, Hector's father, and returns Hector's corpse to his family so that they might honor him too.

Achilles' name and glory would inspire generations of youths to come, as well as poets and writers who sometimes shaped him anew, reconfiguring him to fit a new need.[8] These new Achillean images ranged from the creations of Livius Andronicus in the third-century BC Roman world to such medieval writers as Benoit de Sainte-Maure, whose story (c. twelfth century) would be translated into Italian and German.[9] After Homer, however, new generations of Greek writers wrote of valor and death, and while they echoed the heroic ideal, they did not always see death in battle as a great thing.

Among these poets were Tyrtaeus and Archilochus, who composed so-called "lyric poems." The term "lyric" suggests lyre, and some of this genre of poetry was sung or spoken to such musical accompaniment. Other instruments, however, were used (such as the *aulos*, an oboe-like instrument), and the poetry itself came in various forms: "melic," meaning "for song," elegy from the elegaic couplet, and iambic, from the iambic meter, a monologue or song, often bawdy or rude.[10] What is most interesting about this poetry, and what sets it apart from the epic poetry that preceded it, is its everyday quality. It refers to contemporary life and issues and not the remote past of

---

5 Homer, *Iliad* 19.209–14.
6 Shay 1994: 77–94.
7 Homer, *Iliad* 24.23.175. For a discussion of this human sacrifice see Richardson 1993: 188, who notes that the practice probably existed within the poet's own time.
8 For discussion see King 1987: 110–217.
9 Ibid.: 110, 229–30.
10 West 1993: vii–x, who provides a much fuller discussion that is only summarized here. West also provides translations of the lyric poets with explanatory notes. See also Mulroy 1992, who provides another translation with explanatory notes.

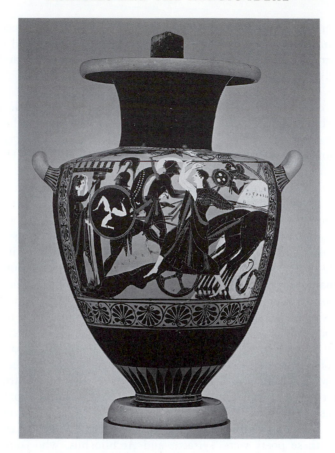

Plate 3 The Wrath of Achilles: having killed Hector, Achilles now drags his body around Troy, mutilating and dishonoring his enemy. Ceramic, black-figure vase painting on a *hydria* (water jar), attributed to the Antiope Group (Athens, Greece; c. 520–510 BC; H. 0.566m; D. 0.33m).

Photo: Museum of Fine Arts, Boston, William Francis Warden Fund.

larger than life heroes. This is personal poetry that is full of remarks about the hopes and fears of real people and how they dealt with these and responded to them. It is also full of value to the present-day ancient historian or classicist. From the poetry of Solon and Theognis, for example, the social and political affairs of Athens and Megara in the seventh century BC come to life. The crises that these two communities faced, the different routes they took to resolve them, leading to very different ends, are vividly, even passionately described.[11] The songs and poems of Tyrtaeus and

Archilochus reveal not only the romances and hardships in the archaic world of the Greeks, but also its heroism.

The poetry of Tyrtaeus is that of desperation amid hardship. Tyrtaeus lived c. 650 BC in Sparta at a time before the feared Spartan military society had emerged. In fact, it was the desperate times of which Tyrtaeus is a witness that would produce the Spartan military machine so well known in the classical era. The cause of this crisis was the conflict between the Spartans and their Messenian neighbors to the west, whom the Spartans had resolved to conquer so as to acquire new lands for a growing population. The Messenians naturally resisted and the result was a conflict that stretched over several generations and is now known to historians as the "Messenian Wars."[12] In the end Sparta prevailed and the Messenians – those who did not flee – were conquered and reduced to helot status.[13] But the conquest of Messenia was neither easy nor quick. The Messenians fought bitterly, and several times the Spartans were repulsed with heavy losses, and the whole community was disheartened and ready to quit. It was at this moment that Tyrtaeus wrote his stirring poetry. Two themes emerge from his writings: the first that it is virtuous to die for your country; the second that the consequences of not doing so lead to hardship and shame.

> For it is fine to die in the front line,
> a brave man fighting for his fatherland,
> and the most painful fate's to leave one's town
> and fertile farmlands for a beggar's life,
> roaming with mother dear and aged father,
> with little children and with wedded wife.[14]

But Tyrtaeus may have been even more concerned to show that the good man is also the brave fighter who does not leave his place in the ranks, who does not abandon the old veterans. The brave fighter is the man who will choose death before dishonor.

> So let us fight with spirit for our land,
> die for our sons, and spare our lives no more.

11 Both Athens and Megara suffered from social-economic ills resulting from the rise of trade and commerce that disrupted the traditional landowning elites. Solon was able to head off unrest and implement compromising policies that, while not agreeable to all, appealed to most. In Megara there was no Solon and the result was political polarization, strife, and political and economic decay – to Athens' benefit. There is no better way to understand Solon's greatness than through comparison with Megara's unresolved conflicts.

12 For discussion see e.g. Jeffery 1976: 114–18 and Osborne 1996: 177–9.

13 As noted above, the Spartans later recruited soldiers from the helots as their own manpower began to decline. But these "new men" never became full-fledged Spartans.

14 Tyrtaeus 10.1–6 (trans. M. West).

You young men, keep together, hold the line,
do not start panic or disgraceful rout.
Keep grand and valiant spirits in your hearts,
be not in love with life – the fight's with men!
Do not desert your elders, men with legs
no longer nimble, by recourse to flight.[15]

The poetry of Tyrtaeus is full of interest as it provides a truer and more realistic picture of hoplite battle than that found in Homer. The *Iliad*, it is true, provides numerous descriptions of combat and death, but these scenes are so grandiose and heroic that they lack a semblance of reality. Tyrtaeus' poetry, on the other hand, allows the reader to sense the fright of what it was like to stand in the battle line and struggle with yourself as to whether to stand and fight or to run. Tyrtaeus' poetry is much more authentic, too, in terms of what really happened amid the terror of battle; witness the old veteran warrior,

with head already white, and grizzled beard,
gasping his valiant breath out in the dust
and clutching at his bloodied genitals,
his nakedness exposed: a shameful sight
and scandalous.[16]

Abandoned by the younger men to face the enemy alone, the old warrior has been killed, as he lies on his back "clutching at [perhaps more accurately "holding"] his bloodied genitals." His posture tells us that he is dead, as a wounded foot soldier will instinctively hug the earth to protect himself from further wounds. That he is holding his genitals reveals that an enemy has added a macabre humiliation, a grotesque joke, to the mutilation of the corpse. In this way Tyrtaeus' poetry depicts the nature of Greek warfare more realistically than anything before.

Tyrtaeus' gritty realism and his call to honor and service surely explain his poetry's survival into the modern era. His value as a guide to noble conduct in war can also be seen in the evaluations of later Greeks. The Spartan king Leonidas, who held the pass at Thermopylae against the Persians in 480 BC – and in doing so died fighting – was once asked his opinion of Tyrtaeus: "A good poet for sharpening the courage of the young" (Plutarch, *On the Cleverness of Animals* 1.1). The imagery of the battlefield is unmistakable and reflects the Spartan ideal clearly. It might be concluded that the values and standard of conduct Tyrtaeus sets forth would speak only to the Spartans. This idea would be mistaken. In the later fourth century BC, the only Greek city-state that could pose a challenge to Philip of Macedon

15 Tyrtaeus 10.13–18 (trans. M. West).
16 Tyrtaeus 10.21–25 (trans. M. West).

was Athens. At the decisive battle of Chaeronea (in 338/7 BC), however, the Athenians suffered a bitter defeat in a hard-fought engagement. In the years after, an Athenian statesman named Lycurgus (though possessing a Spartan sounding name, he was of an ancient Athenian family) would rebuild the economic and moral structures of Athens. In 331 BC he prosecuted for treason a fellow citizen named Leocrates, who had fled Athens in a panic after the Macedonian victory at Chaeronea; some five years later, Leocrates returned, thinking he could resume life as before. Lycurgus thought differently and hauled him into court with deadly seriousness, intent on finding him guilty and securing a capital conviction.[17] In his prosecution speech, Lycurgus cited Tyrtaeus as a poet who taught courage and devotion to the *patria*. Lycurgus' familiarity with Tyrtaeus' poetry, and his endorsement of it for his own program of civic pride and recovery, points once more to the impact of the Spartan poet. Hundreds of years after his death, Greeks outside of Sparta found him a witness to the virtue of patriotism, the virtue of dying for one's country. Tyrtaeus' legacy, combined with Homer's, would remain powerful into the early twentieth century, as evident in the title of Wilfred Owen's great poem "Dulce et Decorum Est," though Owen's take on the theme was rather different.

Similar in vein to Tyrtaeus but yet with a sense of irony and even humor is Archilochus, whose name means literally "Company Commander," who fought and wrote about the same time as Tyrtaeus. Archilochus lived the life of Achilles, fighting during the era of Greek expansionism associated with the foundation of new city-states in the Aegean and elsewhere (a parallel to the Spartans into Messenia), and he may have been an exile, though little about his life is certain. In the fragments of his poems, he shows a flair for humor, as in these lines about his shield: "Some barbarian is waving my shield, since I was obliged to leave it behind under a bush. But I got away, so what does it matter? Let the shield go; I can buy another just as good" (Lattimore 1949: 2 [Epigram 3]). In short, Archilochus shows that fighting to the death does not always make good sense and that preferring discretion to valor may also be heroic. Elsewhere, however, Archilochus reveals the hard life of the soldier, and above all the grim reality of war:

> Shield against shield,
> keep the shield wall tight.
> And the gift of death
> they bring, let no man take.
> In the hospitality of war
> we left them their dead
> as a gift to remember us by.[18]

---

17 See discussion in Tritle 1999: 1227–33
18 Davenport 1964: 8, 64 (Archilochus, Fragments 16, 184).

In one of the longer poems that has survived, however, we find a commonplace oft-repeated among soldiers, "don't cry, get even," when remembering or talking about friends who were killed in battle. In the following poem, Archilochus is telling a friend, surely a fellow warrior and survivor, exactly this:

> Blaming the bitterness of this sorrow, Perikles, no man in all our city
> can take pleasure in festivities:
> such were the men, the surf of the roaring sea washed under, all of us go
> with hearts aching against our ribs
> for misery. Yet against such grief that is past recovery the gods, dear
> friend, have given us strong endurance
> to be our medicine. Such sorrows are variable. They beat now
> against ourselves, and we take the hurt of the bleeding sore.
> Tomorrow it will be others who grieve, not we. From now on act like a
> man, and put away these feminine tears.[19]

This poem is important because it reflects the aftermath of a fight and the grieving over friends lost. Archilochus, however, responds that today it is our turn to mourn but tomorrow it will be the other side that cries. But most important is the final line, "act like a man, and put away the feminine tears." This sentiment is discussed by Shay in his *Achilles in Vietnam*, where he argues that such conduct interrupts the grieving process and makes it difficult for the traumatized warrior or veteran, for example, to find a sort of closure with the death of close friends.[20] Archilochus' statement shows that this reaction, so well known to twentieth-century veterans, is not unique but was also known among veterans/warriors in the ancient world. In Vietnam the term for this was "payback" and it was what motivated many soldiers in seeking vengeance for friends lost. Jonathan Shay refers to one of his veterans who "really loved fucking killing, couldn't get enough. For every one that I killed I felt better. Made some of the hurt went away" [in compensation for friends killed].[21] What this conduct does is to make it more difficult for the veteran to recover from his trauma as he enters a repeating cycle of violence and death.

The study of the poetry of Tyrtaeus and Archilochus, two warrior-poets who experienced battle and wrote of it, reveals differences and similarities with the Homeric poems. In terms of the differences, Tyrtaeus and Archilochus provide a much truer picture of the hoplite fighting that was so typical of the Greeks in the archaic and classical eras. In Tyrtaeus especially we see the emergence of the idea that it is virtuous, even right, to die for

19 Lattimore 1949: 2–3 (Archilochus, Poem 8).
20 Shay 1994: 81–2.
21 Ibid.: 78.

one's *patria* – a powerful idea into the twentieth century, though we might wonder if Archilochus shared this view. There are, however, similarities with these poets, too; chief among these is the virtue of the heroic warrior who takes revenge for the deaths of his friends, for example Achilles for Patroclus, or Archilochus telling Pericles to hold back his tears and get back at the other side. There is also the concept that the good man is the brave man and vice versa. These ideas and others that relate to the study of violence, culture and survival can also be found among the later poets and warriors of the classical age of Greece.

The surviving body of Greek tragedy (written in a poetic idiom, it must be remembered) provides rich resource material with which to investigate the impact of violence on culture. It might appear initially that to make such use of Attic drama is to distort its origins and obscure its place in Athenian society. Yet, as noted above, Aeschylus was prouder of his martial exploits than he was of his dramatic achievements. Next to him stand Sophocles and Euripides. While they did not share the experience of Aeschylus' generation of "Marathon-fighters," they too would have served the community in some sort of military capacity (and in fact Sophocles held the office of *strategos*, or general).[22] Like Aeschylus, then, they can be expected from time to time to reflect on this experience in their dramas, especially as both lived through the Peloponnesian War, which surely gave them much to ponder.[23] Interpretations of Attic drama, then, should not be regarded as final or fixed; nor is there a single simple message to a particular drama. As Simon Goldhill has argued, it is as in the case of Pentheus' body:

> dismembered by the Dionysiac chorus, [it] can only be collected in fragments, but never reconstituted to wholeness, so each person's attempt to comprehend the corpus of tragic texts – through the violence of reading, the selectivity of analysis – can never hope to

22 For Sophocles' generalship see Develin 1989: 89–90. Such service does not necessarily mean that he was also a great commander, only that he possessed sufficient public support to win election to the post. A number of Athenian generals were not particularly "gifted" field commanders but rather prominent citizens seeking to show off. See Xenophon, *Memorabilia* 3.4.1, which records a conversation between Socrates and an unsuccessful candidate for the office of general, Nicomachides, who lost to an inexperienced "political" person, Antisthenes. See Develin 1989: 226, 291.

23 Winkler 1985: 37 argues that "Greek tragedies frequently examine moral issues that become acute under the pressure of warfare." Shay 1995 takes this a step further, arguing that drama was created so as to return combat soldiers to the culture and society of the democratic state. While Shay's position may seem extreme, the combat service of tragedians such as Aeschylus and Sophocles, suggests that this interpretation should be given serious attention. Griffin 1998: 43–4 is skeptical of this view and seems not to place too much value in the battlefield survival of, for example, Aeschylus and Sophocles.

attain the synthesis which can totally efface the signs of *sparagmos* [i.e. dismemberment], the *sparagmos* of signs.[24]

The drama of Aeschylus, it has been suggested above, is that of a revolutionary and innovative poet, one whose experiences in the Persian Wars empowered his art. His plays, as his epitaph suggests, will reflect those formative experiences of youth, and this is certainly the case with his earliest two surviving plays, *The Persians* (472 BC) and *Seven Against Thebes* (465 BC). As with any number of writers whose first works are shaped by their wartime experiences, maturer productions examine other aspects of life and the human experience. In the case of Aeschylus, the "war plays" of *The Persians* and *Seven Against Thebes* will give way to the trilogy of the *Oresteia* and its more complex themes of justice (and the language of justice) and friendship.[25] *The Persians* will be examined in greater detail below, but similar strains of the survivor's mentality and the realism of war can be seen in the less well-known drama, *Seven Against Thebes*.

Seven Against Thebes is a drama rich in the imagery of war and the consequences of violence. The play's plot centers on the curse of Oedipus on his two sons/brothers, Eteocles and Polynices, and how these two bring that curse to life through their own choices.[26] But what stands out in reading this play is, as noted above, the images of war and violence that Aeschylus creates. There are two principal themes. The first is that of the warrior: his equipment and plumage, his fierce reputation and his courage. Related to this idea is the antithesis – cowardice – that Aeschylus notes. These rich descriptions provide the context for the second theme: the civic consequences of failure in war as seen in the destruction of a town, the death, rape, and brutal enslavement of its inhabitants.

The descriptions Aeschylus provides of the seven challengers and their Theban counterparts are alive with images of fierce warriors. Those of the challenger Eteoclus and the Theban Megareus are typical: Eteoclus carries a shield emblazoned with a man in armor mounting a ladder and inscribed with the words "Ares himself shall not cast me from the town" (*Seven Against Thebes* 465–9). Against him stands Megareus, whose own shield shows him capturing enemies as well as their city (477–8). These descriptions reflect Aeschylus' own heroic past and suggest a certain affection for or affinity with his experiences as a warrior. Later Euripides caricatured these descriptions in his *Phoenician Women*, where Eteocles simply selects captains for each gate, without taking time to name them. Peter Burian may be right that Euripides is taking a "cheap shot" at Aeschylus, but the reason for doing so needs clarification.[27] It

24 Goldhill 1986: 285–6. See also Goldhill 1997: 345–6.
25 For discussion of the *Oresteia* see Goldhill 1986: 1–56, 83–4.
26 Argued by Burian 1997: 188.
27 Burian 1997: 195.

may be that Euripides, lacking Aeschylus' military experiences and unable to appreciate them, simply failed to understand the heroic overtones of Aeschylus' rich martial descriptions. It even seems possible that Euripides might have perceived Aeschylus as a sort of "war lover," and was criticizing his descriptions of men and their arms.[28]

Mixed in with these descriptions of warriors and arms are those of cowardice and bravery. In these passages Aeschylus makes plain his views: that bravery is a virtue, cowardice a despicable and unmanly act. These values are conveyed to the audience in various ways. Eteocles, early in the play, rebukes the Thebans for their timidity on hearing of the approach of the Argive host of his brother (*Seven Against Thebes* 181–202). Two warriors, the Argive Tydeus and the Theban Amphiaraus, announce other heroic sentiments: Tydeus rebukes a seer for revealing a cowardly will in the face of battle, thus implying that one should not be afraid, or at least not let it show (383–4). Amphiaraus carries a shield that is blank – no device, no motto. The idea Aeschylus expresses here is that, rather than "seeming to be best" (i.e. by carrying some boastful remark or device), Amphiaraus *is* best by being so (591–3). Finally, in death Eteocles represents the noble warrior dying for his community, the same sort of sentiment revealed earlier in the poetry of Tyrtaeus and so many others (1008–11).

Eteocles' heroic death saved his city from destruction. This is a motif that Aeschylus conveys repeatedly to his reader today, as he did to his audience on staging the drama. This is evident, for example, in the several passages that refer to a city being overrun by the enemy and then being put to the torch (*Seven Against Thebes* 219–22, 432–6). Elsewhere he is much more explicit, revealing clearly the fate of a town that falls to the enemy:

> unlucky indeed the fate of a city captured – murder, fire, and
> rapine, all the city polluted by smoke, and the breath of Ares on it
> maddened, desecrating piety, slaying the people.[29]

In another place Aeschylus notes the fate of the women who survive such an assault, "the girls, new servants, new to misery, must endure a war captive's bed, bed of a man successful. Theirs the expectation of night's consummation but for a triumphant enemy to help their tearful sorrow" (362–7). For Aeschylus, a survivor of war and violence, the past was ever present and was so conveyed in his writing, as shown so clearly and graphically in *Seven Against Thebes*.

Aeschylus' heroic themes find echoes elsewhere in fifth-century BC Greek literature and culture. Herodotus, for instance, is full of such heroisms, particularly in his accounts of the Persian Wars. These include the three

---

28 Suggested by Burian 1997: 195–6.
29 Aeschylus, *Seven Against Thebes* 339–41.

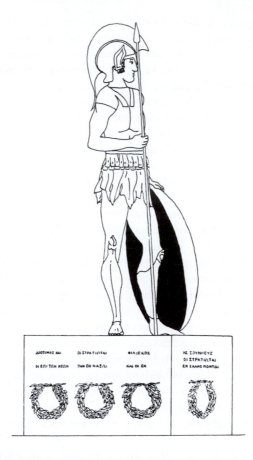

Plate 4   The Monument of Chabrias in the Athenian agora (mid-fourth century BC), erected in honor of the many victories of the general Chabrias. The figure's pose commemorates a challenge to the Spartans to attack his forces *uphill*. They declined.

Sketch courtesy of Professor John Buckler.

Spartans, Posidonius, Philocyon, and Amompharetus, who won great personal distinctions at Plataea in 479 BC, as did the Plataean Callicrates. Mortally wounded before the battle began, Callicrates remarked to a friend before dying, "It is no sorrow to me to die for my country; what grieves me is, that I have not used my arm or done anything worthy of myself, such as I longed to do" (Herodotus 9.72.2). This sentiment evokes the passion for heroic action and death that can be found in Homer, Tyrtaeus, and Archilochus, and shows that these poets' ideals reflected reality.

It is in the account of the struggle at Thermopylae, however, that Herodotus paints a portrait of heroism that lingers into the present. The noble Leonidas, who stayed on in Thermopylae to cover the retreat of the rest of the Greek army after the Persians had found a way round behind him (7. 219–20), is memorialized today at the site with a heroic-size statue. No less valiant were the Thespians who refused to leave the Spartans and died, seven hundred strong, with their Spartan allies (7. 222); and finally the Spartan Dieneces, who gained immortality for his wit and courage. When told that the Persian arrows would block the sun, he replied, "Excellent, we shall have our battle in the shade" (7. 226.1). These remarks could be multiplied easily and have their counterparts in the commemorative monuments that were erected in Athens as well as other Greek cities, and which will be discussed in Chapter 6. Taken together they show that the sentiments of the poets were indeed realized in the attitudes and beliefs of the Greeks of the classical period.

American heroes

> Let it be known that a new generation of Americans has come forth, willing to pay any price, bear any burden, meet any hardship, support any friend, oppose any foe, to assure the survival and success of liberty.
>
> (John F. Kennedy, 1961)

John Kennedy's inaugural speech was a stirring oration, and in the months that followed, many young Americans answered his call to serve the nation.[30] Many joined the newly organized Peace Corps, worked in the civil rights movement in the South, and with the Berlin and Cuban crises, flocked to the armed forces. Kennedy's heroic call to service, to spread the ideas of freedom, democracy, and the American way of life, was widely regarded as a sort of divine mission at the time.[31] This missionary ideal, a legacy of American victory in World War II, would be shattered in the Tet Offensive of 1968.

In the 1950s and early 1960s young Americans growing up in the halcyon days following victory over Germany and Japan were as familiar with images of war and heroism as the ancient Greeks. Sergeant Stryker at Iwo Jima, the exploits of Audie Murphy (who repeated his heroism on screen in *To Hell and Back*), and the comic book hero Sergeant Rock of Easy Company all conveyed influential images of battlefield bravery. Fifty years

---

30 Wills 1992: 212 notes the influence of the Greek rhetorician and sophist Gorgias, particularly the use of antithesis.
31 See the discussion in Turner 1996: 19–22, noting various contemporary sources.

later we can see that it was a strangely one-sided, biased account. It was always the other side, the brutal "kraut" or the little grinning "Jap" (terms used deliberately for effect – I'm fully aware of their connotations) who committed the atrocities, the acts of violence. Only now, and thanks to the heartrending accounts of E.B. Sledge and Paul Fussell, is contemporary America beginning to learn the truths of the American way of war then: the souvenir hunting of Japanese skulls and bones, the mutilation of Japanese dead, and the summary execution of German prisoners of war.[32]

The "all-American" image of the conduct of war influenced the "boomers," namely the generation born in the US following the triumphant return home of American soldiers, sailors, and airmen. Children idealized the exploits of their victorious fathers, and in this they were supported and encouraged by the media. After the war ended there had been several films that raised serious issues concerning the price of victory. One of these was the 1946 film *The Best Years of Our Lives* (which took the Oscar for "Best Picture"), which probed the human toll of war and violence – physical as well as psychological – and the difficulties that servicemen faced in returning to civilian life. In 1950 Marlon Brando made his screen début in *The Men*, a film that explored the psychological dimensions of seriously wounded soldiers, in this case paraplegics.[33] Many civilians, especially those who had not served in combat, were not terribly concerned to learn what happened in the war and treated ex-GIs with studied indifference. The prevailing attitude was, "we won the war; let's get back to the way things were before." Many former servicemen also adopted this view, as many of them wanted to forget the terrors they had experienced and put the war behind them. My own father and other relatives and friends who made the transition from war to peace have also told me this. The problem, however, remains complex, as has been demonstrated by the outpouring of reminiscences of old soldiers upon seeing Steven Spielberg's tribute to the World War II generation *Saving Private Ryan*. Clearly, even in the case of the "Good War," returning home was not a simple matter.

Critically acclaimed work apart, however, it was the "comic book" format films commonly associated with John Wayne and Audie Murphy that soon captured the popular imagination. These stars and their films not only idealized war but also sanitized it. In effect these movies prepared the "boomers" for yet another war. To young people already growing up with the wartime stories of their fathers and uncles, these films delivered messages of sacrifice and heroism, of a sense of duty to succeed their fathers when their own time to serve came. One voice that speaks especially clearly and honestly here is that of Ron Kovic from his own life story, *Born on the Fourth of July*.

32 See E.B. Sledge 1981; Fussell 1988, 1989.
33 Critics rated The Men as one of the best films that year. Another drama that revealed the

Every Saturday afternoon we'd all go down to the movies in the shopping center and watch gigantic prehistoric birds breathe fire and war movies with John Wayne and Audie Murphy ... Castiglia and I saw *The Sands of Iwo Jima* ... The Marine Corps hymn was playing in the background as we sat glued to our seats, humming the hymn together and watching Sergeant Stryker, played by John Wayne, charge up on the hill and get killed just before he reached the top ... every time I heard [the Marine hymn] I would think of John Wayne and the brave men who raised the flag on Iwo Jima that day. I would think of them and cry.[34]

This may sound like so much adolescent hero-worship, and it is, but in Vietnam it became reality. Correspondent Michael Herr describes how "grunts would run around during a fight when they knew that there was a television crew nearby; they were actually making war movies in their heads, doing little guts-and-glory Leatherneck tap dances under fire, getting their

Plate 5   Achilles in Vietnam I. US Marines in Operation Texas, March 1966.
Photo: United States Marine Corps Historical Center, 127-N-A 186820.

complex new social issues of post-war American society was *Home of the Brave* (1949), which examined the war's impact on the changing nature of race relations.
34 Kovic 1976: 54–5.

pimples shot off for the networks. They were insane, but the war hadn't done that to them."[35] What had done this to them was the glorification of war and violence that they had grown up with, as well as the desire to emulate their fathers' victories from an earlier war. What they had not been told, however, was the ugly side of war – how, as Erich Remarque mentioned long before in *All Quiet in the Western Front*, you would do *anything* to stay alive, even if that meant killing your own father.[36] The level of violence that this would lead to was both unknown and unknowable.

Ron Kovic's remarks on his upbringing are typical of the "boomers." Others, such as poet W.D. Ehrhart, another Marine veteran of Vietnam, tell much the same story of growing up in 1950s America.[37] Weaned on the tales of the previous generation and cinematographic images, indoctrinated with lessons of civic virtue and obligation, and imbued with a personal sense of duty, another generation was thus prepared for war. When these influences were reinforced by the "winning is everything" attitude of the star athlete, the result is the prototypical "American hero." Again Ron Kovic speaks for many when he tells how,

> I joined the high-school wrestling team, practicing and working out every day in the basement of Massapequa High School. The coaches made us do sit-ups, push-ups ... "Wanting to win and wanting to be first, that's what's important," the coaches told us. "Play fair, but play to win." ... I won most of my matches that year. When I lost, I cried just like when I lost my Little League games ... not talking to anyone for hours sometimes.[38]

Kovic wanted to make this model of heroism a reality and so, as quickly as possible, he joined the Marines to do his duty as others before him (an attitude expressed also by Oliver Stone in *Platoon*). The experience of the Vietnam War, however, soon made clear the difference between reality and ideal: that the hero's course was not straight and pure. In two tours in Vietnam, Kovic would kill (accidentally) one of his own men, would see women and children killed, and would sacrifice his own body and psyche for the cause. There were other Ron Kovics, however, men like Billy Cizinski who joined the Marines at fifteen and fought his first firefight at sixteen and a half. He was eager to join because

---

35 Herr 1977: 209.
36 Remarque 1929: 113. Sophocles, *Oedipus at Colonus* 1140–6 echoes this in not dissimilar circumstances: i.e. Oedipus' killing of his biological parent Laertes when threatened by him.
37 Ehrhart 1986: 74.
38 Kovic 1976: 62–3.

I grew up in an environment where communism was taboo, better dead than red. Went to a Polish school – same thing – And you can go back to the '50s and see how the country trained kids – the pledge of allegiance to the flag, a lot of militarism.[39]

These same values also impelled Southerners, who were inspired as much by the heroics of their Confederate forebears as those of World War II. One such man was my OCS classmate, Morgan Weed of Decatur, Alabama, who died of wounds during the 1970 invasion of Cambodia. Weed was mortally wounded when, nearly alone, he bravely went to the aid of a group of soldiers pinned down by NVA fire.[40]

It should not be imagined, however, that only young white America was so nurtured. In a series of short stories, Daniel Cano writes of the Chicano experience in Southern California during the 1950s and 1960s. This was virtually identical to Ron Kovic's or Billy Cizinski's experiences. In his semi-autobiogaphical story "Planting the Seeds," Cano relates the boyhood years of David Almas, his alter-ego. David Almas's boyhood activities mirror those of Ron Kovic: he plays Little League baseball on a championship team and listens to the World War II stories of his father and uncles, paratroopers who jumped at Normandy.[41] In the same way Dan Cano and many young Chicanos were reared on the "American ideal" and were prepared to reenact their fathers' wartime exploits. Dan Cano tells basically how he and two friends volunteered for service in 1965:

> David knew some facts, like the 82nd and 101st jumping behind German lines on D-Day, the first American to make contact. He told them about the standoff at Bastogne, the New Year's jump in Belgium, and how many Chicanos from Los Angeles were in the Screaming Eagles, gave their lives for the country ... They talked about war movies, *The Sands of Iwo Jima* and *Guadalcanal Diary*. The three decided to join.[42]

Young black Americans felt the same attractions. Reginald Edwards from Louisiana, while explaining that joining was "the only thing left to do" owing to a lack of any kind of employment opportunities, still thought "the Marines was 'bad.' The Marines Corps built men. Plus just before I went in, they had all these John Wayne movies on every night."[43] But there were

---

39 Cited in Appy 1993: 63 (Appy records Cizinski saying "better red than dead," but this seems erroneous in light of his parents hating communism).

40 Told in Nolan 1990: 263–8, 272–4. On Southerners in Vietnam see generally Wilson 1990.

41 Cano 1995: 22–31, 70.

42 Ibid.: 50–1.

43 Appy 1993: 62.

other young black Americans who believed that the US was their home too, and were motivated by the same sense of patriotic pride and sense of ownership in the American dream. This theme comes out clearly in a number of the stories collected by Wallace Terry in *Bloods: An Oral History of the Vietnam War by Black Veterans*.[44] Lieutenant Archie "Joe" Biggers tells how,

> We are part of America. Even though there have been some injustices made, there is no reason for us not to be a part of the American system. I don't feel that because my grandfather or grandmother was a slave that I should not lift arms up to support those things that are stated in the Constitution of the United States. Before I went to Vietnam, I saw the 'burn, baby, burn' thing because of Martin Luther King. Why should they burn up Washington D.C. for something that happened in Memphis? They didn't hurt the white man that doing business down there on 7th Street. They hurt the black man. They should have let their voices be known that there was injustice. That's the American way.[45]

Others, however, believed themselves exploited yet again and ordered to fight for the cause of freedom, something they did not have at home.

Much the same could be said of Native Americans who served in Vietnam. In his study *Strong Hearts, Wounded Souls*, Tom Holm notes that 44 percent of the veterans he surveyed reported that patriotism, a belief in American values, motivated them to enter military service. This was a percentage point higher than those who joined on account of preserving tribal traditions. One veteran stated that the reason he served was,

> [not out of] any particular loyalty to the United States, but because I have loyalty to my own people, my own tradition. We are pledged by a treaty to provide military assistance to the U.S. in times of war. I know that the U.S. has broken its part of the bargain with us, but we are more honorable than that ... So, it was my obligation to do what I did, even though I didn't really want to.[46]

This explanation is itself essentially heroic, as seen in the value attached to a sense of obligation and duty. These are virtues that any self-respecting hero could identify with and that agree remarkably well with the life stories of other young Americans at the time who believed that they had an obligation to answer the call to duty.

The life story of the Ron Kovics of 1950s/1960s America seems possibly

---

44 Terry 1984: 112, 129, 131, 175, 199.
45 Ibid.: 112.
46 Holm 1996: 118–19.

curious as well as naïve at the beginning of the twenty-first century. His experience, like those of Billy Cizinski and Reginald Edwards and the other young Americans briefly surveyed here, reveals the great impact that winning World War II had upon American society in the 1950s and 1960s.[47] Some readers might think that such attitudes are not to be found among young Americans today. There are in fact, however, young men (and women too) who identify with the values and ideals of Ron Kovic's generation and the ideals of their upbringing. They understand how these men could have joined the Marines at age seventeen or eighteen and could have gone off to Vietnam thinking it was the right thing to do. One student, Sean, wrote in a review discussion of *Born on the Fourth of July* in the spring of 1998 that he too had been raised like Ron Kovic. Born to a newly arrived immigrant family, he had been taught to love God, be a competitor, and believe that the US is the land of freedom and opportunity. There are other young men today who have also grown up learning of the experiences of Vietnam veterans and who have joined the armed services because they too think that such service is the right thing to do. What both cases illustrate is the survival of the dream, the heroic ideal in American society at the dawn of the twenty-first century, much like it was a half century ago.

Yet it may well be true that few young people today would subscribe to views such as those of my student Sean, and just as true that the American dream that nurtured Ron Kovic and W.D. Ehrhart and so many others died violently in Vietnam. Listen to one of the Marine grunts in Gustav Hasford's *The Short-Timers*, Chili Vendor, on defending the American way of life shortly before moving in to take back the Hue Citadel from the NVA during the '68 Tet Offensive:

> You won't come back, Joker. Victor Charlie is gonna shoot you in the heart. [They'll] ship your scrawny little ass home in a three-hundred-dollar aluminum box all dressed up like a lifer in a blouse from a set of dress blues. But no white hat. And no pants. They don't give you any pants. Your friends from school and all of the relatives you never liked anyway will be at your funeral and they'll call you a good little Christian and they'll say you were a hero to get wasted defeating Communism and you'll lie there with a cold ass, dead as a rock.[48]

The cynicism and the inverted values in Chili Vendor's words reflect the destruction of old truths, what in a sense Robert Graves captured in the

---

47 I have omitted from the discussion here those men who either submitted to the draft or volunteered as the result of coercion; also left out are those who went in because of a lack of economic opportunities. All of these are discussed by Appy 1993: 44–55. Even many of these still saw the pull of patriotism and heroic glory.

48 Hasford 1979: 56.

phrase, "Goodbye to all that." Chili Vendor's judgments have been forged by months of brutal combat that have replaced the heroic values of his youth and have changed him and his grunt buddies. The changed personality associated with the violence of battle is now familiar to us as one of the symptoms of PTSD. While this psychological disorder is usually regarded as a creation of the modern age, its first recorded occurrence is in the ancient Greek world.

4

CLEARCHUS' STORY

The heroic ideal transformed

This is the record of a war-lover.
[Clearchus] could have lived in
peace … but he chose to make war.
(Xenophon, *Anabasis* 2.6.6)

In *Achilles in Vietnam* one of Jonathan Shay's principal concerns is to high-light the changes that occur in those who experience combat and, while surviving battle, emerge from the experience transformed. As we have seen, Achilles, though a fierce warrior, was yet honorable before the death of his friend Patrocles. After this death, Achilles turns into a raging fighter who stops at nothing to "get even," "to pay back" the other side for his loss. It should not be imagined that Achilles is the only example of this traumatic character change to be found in the literature or history of the ancient Greek world. Among the other examples that can be noted are the Spartan commander Clearchus, who, we are told, loved war above all else, and even the great Alexander, who in a drunken rage could kill a close friend.

During the course of nearly eleven months in Vietnam, I encountered a number of men, both officers and enlisted men, who were serving their second or third tours, or had been "in country," as the phrase went, continu-ously for two or three years. Such a man was Sergeant X, who had been fighting in different parts of Vietnam for the previous three years and who clearly enjoyed the experience. Once during a firefight with the Viet Cong, he calmly stood upright in the middle of the fight and fired off a long burst of machine gun fire at the enemy. At the time I thought these men were simply crazy or stupid and probably both. Now upon reflection I understand that they had become "hooked" on violence. In a sense they loved war, much like Marrow, the antagonist in John Hersey's 1959 novel *The War Lover*, and, long before that, Clearchus, the veteran Spartan soldier, whom Xenophon in his *Anabasis* described as *philopolemos*, a "lover of war."

What I would argue here is that little separates Clearchus from those soldiers I knew in Vietnam, or others known and recorded elsewhere, who – not in spite of the violence but because of it – loved war. Such ideas have

55

been presented in film, such as the Air Cavalry officer in Francis Ford Coppola's *Apocalypse Now*, who proclaims after assaulting a Vietnamese village, "I love the smell of napalm in the morning." But such responses to violence are not new, as shown in this testimonial from the Western Front in World War I:

> He loved no-man's land and constantly crawled out there at night. On one occasion a star-shell revealed his tall figure, not lying down but standing erect in the open. Whereupon, instead of throwing himself flat, he flung out his arms. "Tell me if I look like a tree," he shouted back to the British trenches.[1]

The question that arises is why men like Clearchus and his counterparts in Vietnam and the Western Front became so entranced with violence. The answer is to be found in the natural "high" that violence induces in those exposed to it, and in the PTSD that follows this exposure. Such a modern interpretation in Clearchus' case might seem forced, but there seems little reason to doubt that Xenophon in fact provides us with the first known historical case of PTSD in the western literary tradition.[2]

Violence and the changing of character

> After a traumatic experience, the human system of self-preservation seems to go onto permanent alert, as if the danger might return at any moment. Physiological arousal continues unabated.
>
> (Judith Herman, *Trauma and Recovery*, 35)

The condition PTSD was diagnosed as such in the early 1970s but had been an object of intense study by the medical community since World War I.[3] During that conflict it was labeled "shell shock," then became known during World War II as "battle fatigue." Only since the 1970s in the aftermath of

---

1 Cited in Jennings and Brewster 1998: 60.
2 Homer's Achilles, as Shay discusses, also suffered from PTSD. But Achilles is a literary figure while Clearchus is historical, hence the distinction made here.
3 PTSD seems to have been recognized previously. During the US Civil War, doctors noted the same reactions but ascribed them to "sunstroke" and "nostalgia." One Union Army doctor, J.M. Da Costa, described such men as suffering from "Soldier's Heart," a condition whose symptoms included rapid heart beat, low blood pressure, and fainting (information from Dr. C. Shatan, noted also by Dean 1997: 131). The discussion by Dean 1997 of Union Army veterans who suffered from PTSD needs to be read carefully, particularly as the author seems intent on disparaging one group of veterans, i.e. those of the Vietnam War, in order to ennoble the sufferings of another. See the review by Shay 1999: 149–55.

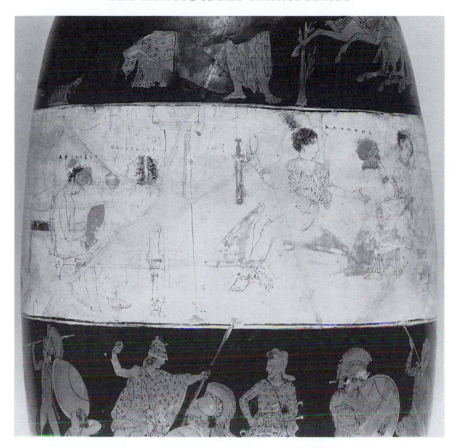

Plate 6   Achilles mourns the death of Patroclus. The death of a friend in battle has
often been the spark igniting the unrelenting desire for vengeance or
"payback." This was true for Achilles at Troy and for many soldiers in
other conflicts since then. Attic red-figure and white ground vase painting
on a *lekythos* (oil bottle), attributed to the Eretria Painter (c. 420 BC).

Photo: Metropolitan Museum of Art, New York, accession number 31.11.13.

the Vietnam War has it been recognized with the label Post-Traumatic Stress
Disorder. Recent studies, including Judith Herman's *Trauma and Recovery*
and Shay's *Achilles in Vietnam*, have examined closely the nature of PTSD and
made the subject much more accessible than ever before.[4] A detailed discussion of PTSD lies beyond the scope of this work, but a brief excursus on the

---

4   In addition note the study of Solomon 1993, which examines PTSD among Israeli army
veterans, particularly from the war in Lebanon, and most recently Schmidbauer 1998,
which focuses on the unresolved trauma of World War II veterans in Germany.

background and symptoms seems essential to understand what happens to individuals confronted by trauma, however incurred. Jonathan Shay provides the following characteristics of PTSD:

1 Loss of authority over mental functions – particularly memory and trustworthy perception
2 Persistent mobilization of the body and the mind for lethal violence, with the potential for explosive danger
3 Persistence and activation of combat survival skills in civilian life
4 Chronic health problems stemming from chronic mobilization of the body for danger
5 Persistent expectation of betrayal and exploitation; destruction of the capacity for social trust
6 Persistent preoccupation with both the enemy and the veteran's own military/governmental authorities
7 Alcohol and drug abuse
8 Suicidality, despair, isolation, and meaninglessness[5]

It should be noted that this list of characteristics differs slightly from those listed in the *Diagnostic and Statistical Manual of Mental Disorders* (fourth edition, usually referred to as *DSM-IV*, the "handbook" of the American Psychiatric Association).[6] I follow Shay here, as his analysis of PTSD includes the ideas of betrayal and destruction of social trust, whereas the *DSM* list omits these and refers to such traits as the avoidance of thoughts, feelings, etc. Shay's emphasis on the devastating personality changes that result from the violence of battle rightly takes into account and gauges the impact of war on character. I also follow Shay because of his extensive work in counseling Vietnam combat veterans.[7] This might seem prejudicial, but in a session of my most recent "Achilles in Vietnam" class, discussion focused on Clearchus and his story.[8] Present for the class were two therapists and Vietnam veterans, William Mahedy and Shad Meshad. Both participated in the creation of the Vet Center Program established in the early 1970s by the US Veterans' Administration to work with troubled Vietnam veterans.

Mahedy and Meshad agree that the above list includes those things that are descriptive of combat veterans rather than just all cases of PTSD. The *DSM* list omits some items because they are not, strictly speaking, clinical

5 These are taken from Shay 1994: xx.
6 C. Shatan informs me that *DSM* I (1950) had a page section on "Gross Stress Reactions," but that this vanished from *DSM* II, published in January 1968, the month of the Tet Offensive.
7 For a more recent contribution to the analysis of PTSD based on additional clinical work, see Shay and Munroe 1999.
8 This was in March 1998.

symptoms, but are reality-based reactions to the violence of battle. Within a week of attending my seminar, Mahedy presented the bulk of the material in this chapter dealing with Clearchus to a group of veterans he counsels at the VA hospital in San Diego. Vietnam veterans saw Clearchus as in some ways reassuring. His story revealed to them that their own bitterness and changed character after combat was not unique, that other warriors from earlier conflicts suffered the same emotional trauma. Some of the World War II veterans were interested in Clearchus as a historical piece. One old Marine veteran of four campaigns in the South Pacific summed it up laconically: "Well, they didn't call it PTSD then, but it's the same thing." These comparisons might seem to be little more than the musings of old soldiers, but clearly the effects of violence on human beings have changed little from the time of Xenophon and Clearchus to the present. A short digression on human physiology will demonstrate this.

Shay and other researchers, such as Stanford University biochemist Robert Sapolsky, have explained the nature of physiological reactions to extreme stress. When humans, as well as other primates, are placed in stressful situations, neurohormones secreted by the adrenal gland, including adrenaline and a group of steroids known as glucocorticoids, induce a predictable range of physical reactions.[9] Neither Achilles nor Hector, Shay observes, "could have remained alive for more than thirty seconds in the absence of cortisol" (i.e. the chemical that enables humans to withstand stress).[10] For present purposes this reaction may be summed up succinctly as the "flight or fight." While no two societies, as well as no two human beings, will display identical reactions, the range of human response will not vary that much from time to time, or place to place. Consequently, there is a strong a priori foundation that validates the basis for the present study and arguments.

Xenophon, Clearchus and PTSD

> [I]n difficult positions the soldiers would give him complete
> confidence ... they said his forbidding look seemed happy.
>   (Xenophon, *Anabasis* 2.6.10)

The *Anabasis*, published in numerous readable editions as *The Persian Expedition* or *The March Up Country*, is possibly Xenophon's best-known work. Perhaps the first war memoir in the Western tradition, the *Anabasis* combines drama, action and a certain amount of suspense in a lively story. Xenophon recounts the courageous and often harrowing march of Greek

---

9 Sapolsky 1997: 120–1.
10 Shay 1994: 92, and p. 8 in this book.

mercenary soldiers over hundreds of miles of uncharted territory. Left leader-less after the treacherous murder of their officers, the Greeks democratically elected replacements and marched on. The *Anabasis*, then, offers much to the historian. It is a commentary on the devastating social fallout of the Peloponnesian War and the thousands of men left traumatized and/or without livelihoods. It provides an account of the "democratic" spirit of the Greeks as they simply elected new officers to replace those who had been killed. It also offers a description of the topography of the Persian Empire and its inhabitants. Additionally, as A. Momigliano noted, the *Anabasis* made a contribution to the development of biography as a literary form.[11] Momigliano emphasized Xenophon's place in biography as one who "must be regarded as a pioneer experimenter in biographical forms."[12] What Momigliano was unable to appreciate, as well as other scholars who have studied the *Anabasis*, was that the snapshot portrait of Clearchus was that of a particularly flawed character. How does Xenophon present the veteran Spartan commander?

1   A man fond of war, who could have lived in peace but chose instead to make war *(Anabasis 2.6.6)*

2   A man who could have lived a life of ease, but preferred a hard one (2.6.6)

3   A man who could have enjoyed riches, but instead spent lovingly what money he had on war and so had even less than he might have had (2.6.6)

4   A man who was fond of adventure, who liked to lead the attack, whose forbidding appearance became happy in times of danger (2.6.7, 10)

5   A tough man, possessing a harsh tone of voice, a brutal disciplinarian, incapable of personal relationships (2.6.11, 13)

6   A man who could not serve under the command of another (2.6.15).

Xenophon's description of Clearchus, summarized here, offers more than just the usual "biographical" label that it has traditionally received. It is rather a diagnosis of what today clinical psychologists would refer to as PTSD. The parallels between the definition and criteria of PTSD outlined above and Xenophon's portrait of Clearchus are striking.[13] As noted at the beginning of this chapter, Xenophon states directly and without qualifica-tion, that Clearchus loved war. To this he adds that Clearchus was incapable

---

11   Momigliano 1971: 51–2.

12   Ibid.

13   See Roisman 1989: 30–52, who argues that Xenophon's sketch of Clearchus is critical and self-serving. Roisman's arguments minimize a good example of Clearchus' character (i.e. the fight with Meno's men discussed on p. 70–1) and discount Clearchus' prominence in the *Anabasis*. Moreover, the impact of more than twenty years' violence on Clearchus, which substantiates Xenophon's assessment of him as a "war-lover," is not addressed.

of personal relationships or friendship – another characteristic of PTSD that relates not just to a betrayal of trust but also to symptoms of psychic numbing. These two pieces of evidence alone validate the argument asserted here that Clearchus was a troubled individual, a warrior who had seen too much war. At this point, however, it would be useful to investigate this intriguing Spartan officer and attempt to reconstruct his early life and career and the events that left him the traumatized warrior he was when Xenophon met him in Asia in 401 BC.

Clearchus and the trauma of combat

> The Lacedaemonians sent a herald and took back their dead. These were the number of men who died on the island and those taken alive: 420 hoplites in all crossed over; 292 of these were brought back alive; and the rest died.
>
> (Thucydides, *History of the Peloponnesian War* 4.41.3)

Clearchus was born c. 450 BC, as Xenophon reports him to have been about fifty years old at the time of his death. His service in the Peloponnesian War after 412 BC is reasonably well known, as Thucydides and other authors tell of his activities in the region of the Hellespont, in the struggle with the Athenians over Byzantium, and other strategic northern sites in the final phase of the Athenian–Spartan conflict. Two things may be briefly said of this. First, Clearchus seems to have been remarkably well connected. Lenschau suggests that he had ties with the Spartan King Agis; his father seems to have been the same Ramphias who traveled to Athens on the eve of the Peloponnesian War and later succeeded Brasidas in the north.[14] Second, and what will be stressed here, is that by the time Clearchus appeared in these northern commands, he had spent nearly twenty years fighting in various campaigns of the Peloponnesian War. Previous accounts of Clearchus, uninformed of the devastating impact of PTSD, have missed a key element in the portrait of the Spartan that Xenophon provides. In the years prior to his appearance in Xenophon, however, he had undoubtedly seen enough fighting to suffer the damaging consequences of PTSD.[15]

Years of hard experience had made Clearchus the veteran commander that Xenophon would meet and record. Xenophon describes him as a vigorous

14 Lenschau 1921: 575–6 collects and discusses the evidence for Clearchus' service in the last phase of the Peloponnesian War. Lazenby 1985: 21 agrees that Ramphias was probably Clearchus' father.
15 K. Raaflaub has suggested to me that the intensity of the Peloponnesian War may have been a sort of catalyst in producing PTSD in Clearchus and others of that generation. On this it should be remembered, as noted by Shatan 1982: 1032, that "a man's life may be changed forever by one flash of combat." Twenty years would more than do it.

man of fifty who marched alongside his men on the road to Cunaxa, leading by example and showing them that if he could do it, then they could too (*Anabasis* 2.3.11). It is of more than passing interest that his career as a soldier began as a youth of nineteen to twenty years old, roughly the same age as most combat soldiers in Vietnam. While the Spartan *agoge* ("training") had surely toughened and prepared Clearchus and his peers for the stress of battle, he still would have been exposed to awful slaughter for which no training is adequate preparation (for discussion of the *agoge*, see e.g. Lazenby 1985: 17, 25, 63). While the places and details of these have not survived, the impact and trauma seems to have been considerable, as Xenophon's portrait shows. In reconstructing Clearchus' early years, it is possible to show convincingly how a youth inexperienced in the horror of war was transformed into the grim, battle-hardened veteran portrayed in Xenophon.

Clearchus would certainly have fought in at least one of the famous battles that occurred in the first twenty years of the Peloponnesian War. One such battle was that of Mantinea (418/7 BC) which Thucydides describes as "the greatest battle that had taken place for a very long time among Hellenic states" (Thucydides 5.74). In the years before this fight, Brasidas, the most energetic and daring of Sparta's warriors at the time, had actively campaigned in northern Greece in an attempt to widen Spartan dominance. In the last phase of the Peloponnesian War, Clearchus served extensively, almost exclusively, in this region. While the evidence permits little more than an inference, Clearchus' service in this region may well have resulted from his attachment either to Brasidas or his father, Ramphias.[16] Clearchus' experiences might then have made him a sort of "northern" expert as far as Spartan authorities were concerned.[17]

The other celebrated military event early in the Peloponnesian War was the Spartan debacle at Sphacteria in 425 BC.[18] While the Spartans who survived this defeat seemed to be distinguished, their return home was probably not pleasant and surely these men would have found themselves poorly regarded by the community. Acceptance and rehabilitation would have been awkward if the treatment accorded the survivors of Thermopylae in 480 BC

---

16 Many of the troops taken by Brasidas on this northern campaign were Peloponnesians including freed helots. But in several places, Thucydides identifies other Spartans with Brasidas (i.e. Ischagoras, Pasitelidas, Clearidas) as well as Brasidas' "own men" (cf. Thucydides 4.70, 4.132.3, 5.2, 5.8, respectively). The second of these passages (i.e. 4.132.3) suggests that Brasidas did take along a small group of Spartiates to provide companionship and, as shown here, to provide him with staff officers etc. This would leave room for Clearchus. Alternatively, he could have accompanied his father Ramphias into the north after Brasidas' death (cf. Thucydides 5.12, 13).

17 Noted also by Mitchell 1997: 82–3.

18 Thucydides 4.26–41. For discussion of the Athenian campaign that ended in the Spartan defeat on Sphacteria (near Pylos) see Wilson 1979.

is any indicator (see pp. 75–7). It is impossible to know if Clearchus fought in this disastrous engagement. On the other hand, the silence in the sources, and his apparent sudden rise after c. 412 BC, could be explained by his service and the time needed to rehabilitate himself and his name. Mounting casualties might also have prompted Spartan leaders to be more forgiving of the Sphacteria survivors. In any event, whether or not Clearchus fought at Sphacteria is not critical to the thesis offered here: that as a young Spartiate, he would have certainly fought in numerous places during these twenty years and undoubtedly saw extensive combat.

Some historians might object that there is no evidence to support the argument for Clearchus' youthful military service and, speaking from a strictly positivist standpoint, they are right. On the other hand, given the nature of Spartan society and the nature of the war going on at the time, it seems logical to ask in return what we might suppose Clearchus was doing during these years. Moreover, as Spartan authorities were recruiting helots for military service and rewarding them as *neodamodeis*, does it stand to reason that an able-bodied Spartiate would not see action? The answer to this is surely no.

We do not know exactly in which battles Clearchus fought as a young man, but fight he certainly did. What would this experience have been like? Much has been written on this subject. Bernard Henderson's study early in the twentieth century depicts heroic warriors in battle, nobly fighting and dying (e.g. his account of the fight at Sphacteria).[19] More recently, Victor Hanson has provided a more authentic account than those of the nineteenth century, but the obscenity of battle – how you will do anything to live – is still depicted in obscure tones.[20] In particular, the psychic toll of battle – how it can turn a survivor like Clearchus into the grim, solitary warrior he became – is not addressed. As Tim O'Brien, Vietnam veteran and novelist puts it, you go into war "clean" and you get dirty, and afterwards you're never the same.[21]

Just how brutal was hoplite fighting? In addition to the shoving of shields and spears, hand-to-hand with sword and knife, the sort of thing we visualize when we read Homer and the historians, there was also the terror and the anger, dimensions which have not received much attention. A rare example of the impact of this is actually seen in Herodotus' account of the Battle of Marathon (490 BC). He tells how,

> Epizelus, the son of Cuphagoras, an Athenian soldier, was fighting bravely when he suddenly lost the sight of both eyes, though nothing had touched him anywhere – neither sword, spear, nor

19 Henderson 1927: 214–15.
20 For additional discussion see Hanson 1989 and 1991.
21 O'Brien 1990: 123.

missile. From that moment he continued blind as long as he lived. I have heard that in speaking about what happened to him he used to say that he thought he was opposed by a man of great stature in heavy armour, whose beard overshadowed his shield; but the phantom passed him by, and killed the man at his side.[22]

Victor Hanson has referred to Epizelus' account of the phantom as a hallucination or creation of fantasy, and seems not to recognize the importance of his own remark on the role here of "battle fatigue" or "battle shock."[23] What happened to Epizelus? Discounting an actual ghost, Epizelus' blindness seems mostly likely to be an example of "conversion disorder," what psychiatrists previously termed "hysterical conversion."[24] David Hackworth, the most highly decorated American soldier now living, provides additional insight as to what happened to Epizelus. In his autobiographical story, *About Face*, Hackworth notes that,

> over time I concluded that a man is like a bottle. On the battlefield, fear is what fills him up and fuels him to perform. But some bottles are smaller than others. When a guy becomes unglued during a firefight, it's just that his bottle has filled up and overflowed; it's time for him to get away and let the fear drain out. But even when it does, there is a catch: from that moment on, the man is like a spent cartridge, and no amount of gunpowder will ever make him a real fighter again.[25]

At Marathon Epizelus watched the man beside him die – clearly a traumatic event. This act, plus the added stress of fighting the Persians, a new enemy, for the first time, pushed Epizelus beyond breaking-point and his mind simply snapped so as to protect the body. Hence the lifelong blindness that Herodotus reports along with the story of the giant warrior – clearly a case of heroic inspired myth-making to explain what to Epizelus and his contemporaries was unexplainable.

Accounts like Epizelus' are critical to understanding how trauma begins: terror at watching your friends go down beside you (why him and not me – he's the better fighter?!), anger at seeing this happen. These thoughts take seconds, but then the realization sinks in that these people are trying to kill

---

22 Herodotus 6.117.2–3. Pritchett 1971–91: 3, 24, refers only to Epizelus' vision and subsequent blindness.
23 Hanson 1989: 192.
24 Weinstein 1995: 383–407. J. Shay also believes Epizelus' injury to be the result of conversion (e-mail message, June 28, 1999). The blindness experienced by Epizelus also occurred in soldiers in both World Wars (see Weinstein) and in the Cambodian women profiled by film-maker Tran T. Kim-Trang (see p.8, n. 16).
25 Hackworth and Sherman 1989: 76.

you! So you fight the harder because you want to live and to win. You go, as Sophocles tells of the Argives in his drama *Eurpylus*, violently trampling over the corpses of the slain – laughing![26] Sounds strange? In 1965 at the Battle of the Ia Drang between the US Army's 1st Cavalry Division and soldiers of the NVA, wounded Americans heard NVA soldiers during the night finishing off other wounded soldiers ("No, No! Please!" – gunfire – NVA soldiers giggling as they went on to the next wounded American).[27] Elsewhere, you find your closest friend whom you had watched fall, and a few steps on you find his killer, whose luck had not been much better. You strip him of his armor, his clothing, and then you mutilate him – you cut off his genitals and place them in his hands as a sort of macabre joke, but also to "pay back" for the death of a friend. This is what Tyrtaeus tells happened during the Messenian Wars of the mid-seventh century BC and Xenophon again reports of the Greeks in the Cyreian army, mutilating the enemy – to scare them, to pay them back for what had happened to their friends.[28] The ancient Greeks, like their modern American and Vietnamese counterparts, knew and practiced mutilation of the dead. In both eras, it was not something done by everyone, or all the time – but surely it happened when some individuals watched their friends and relatives die, and for a moment lost control and exacted the worst possible revenge on their enemy. Mutilation of the enemy is known across both time and culture, and it is not something that only primitives practice. It is in fact a very human thing.[29]

One last point may be made on the traumatic impact of such events as these on survivors like Clearchus. While the Spartan prisoners from Sphacteria were held in Athens, an Athenian ally, one who may not (probably?) have been there at all, began taunting one of the Spartans, asking if the "real" Spartans had died in the battle. The Spartan replied, "It would be some spindle that could pick out the brave man."[30] This laconic statement has attracted much scholarly attention and effort to interpret it. I would agree with both of Thucydides' commentators, A.W. Gomme and S. Hornblower, who place the remark in a context of bravery amid indiscriminate death.[31] Yet the profundity of the Spartan survivor's comment has

---

26 Sophocles, *Eurpylus* 210.47–8, ed. Lloyd-Jones 1992. "Laughing" Argives and mutilations like that recorded by Tyrtaeus cast doubt, in my view, on Lazenby's claim (1991: 102) that the Greeks behaved decently in battle.

27 Recounted by ABC newsman and Ia Drang survivor Jack Smith in the ABC *Day One* program, "They Were Young and Brave," June 29, 1995.

28 Tyrtaeus 10.17–20, Xenophon, *Anabasis* 3.4.5. For discussion of the Tyrtaeus passage see Pritchett 1971–91: 4, 32–3, and Jacoby 1918: 24–5.

29 For further discussion see Tritle 1997a: 124–36.

30 Thucydides 4.40.2. It is not certain where these prisoners would have been held in Athens, but as they were valuable bargaining chips with Spartan authorities they must have been housed in some safe location. Thucydides shows, however, that they were not kept in isolation.

31 Gomme, Andrewes and Dover 1945–81: 3, 480, and Hornblower 1992–96: 2, 196.

remained unappreciated, and Hornblower's description of it as a "joke" simply misses the mark.

The warrior's retort in fact reflects the psychic trauma of a survivor of catastrophe who can relate events only in profound and cryptic fashion. In *Dispatches* Michael Herr tells of an encounter with an apparently psychotic LURP (Long Range Reconnaissance Patrol). In his third tour in Vietnam, when Herr encountered him, he was the sole survivor of his platoon destroyed in the Ia Drang battle of 1965 and of his Special Forces team. Herr relates how he was unable to function at home in "the World," as he passed the time by aiming a rifle out of the window of his parents' home, leading people and cars as they passed by. His parents were, as he himself admitted, "real uptight" about this. But more powerful was the story he told Herr: "Patrol went up the mountain. One man came back. He died before he could tell us what happened." Herr commented that he waited for the rest of the story. When nothing further was said he asked, "What happened?" The LURP "just looked at me like he felt sorry for me, fucked if he'd waste time telling stories to anyone as dumb as I was."[32]

The remarks of both warriors reflect the narration of traumatic events by survivors to bystanders or non-participants for whom in some ways the event they are inquiring about will remain forever a mystery. Only from the perspective of violence-induced trauma can the observer begin to comprehend the magnitude of the effect of that trauma on the participant. Experiences such as these changed Clearchus into that "hard man," that "tough *harmost*," a man with "eine herrschsüchtige und gewalttätige Natur" ("a domineering and violent nature"), that we read of in the literature today.[33] These characterizations are surely true, though only the last, that of German classicist Thomas Lenschau, comes at all close to revealing the extent to which Clearchus' nature, his personality, had been traumatized by these events. It was this experience during the Peloponnesian War that created a commander so aggressive and war-loving that even Spartan authority could not control it; a temperament that led to Clearchus' exile and into Cyrus' employment (Xenophon, *Anabasis* 2.6.1–2). The twenty years of war that preceded Clearchus' first appearance in Thucydides had exposed him to the most violent of situations and, as Xenophon's portrait of him from c. 401 BC shows, left him suffering from the effects of PTSD.

---

32 Herr 1977: 6–7.
33 The assessments respectively of Cartledge 1987: 320, Kagan 1987: 282, and Lenschau 1921: 577.

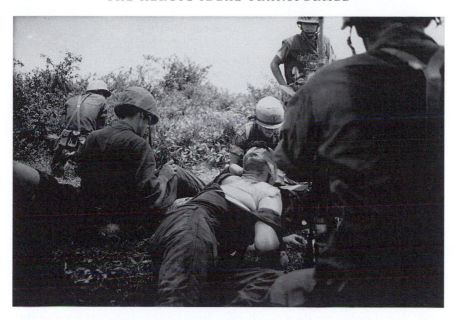

Plate 7   Achilles in Vietnam II. Marine Casualty Clearing Station during Operation
Texas, March 1966. As Clearchus before them, these men were exposed to
a level of violence that would change some of them forever.

Photo: United States Marine Corps Historical Center, 127-N-A186 821.

Xenophon's portrait of Clearchus

> [Clearchus] liked spending money on war just as one might
> spend it on love affairs.
>
> (Xenophon, *Anabasis* 2.6.6)

Even before his service with Cyrus, Xenophon had first-hand experience of
battle and the nature of military life. It seems reasonable, then, that he
would be particularly sensitive and perceptive in detecting human reactions
to stress and violence. Moreover, as noted earlier, Momigliano pointed to
Xenophon's experimentation with the biographical genre, which suggests
that he was interested in what might be broadly called human nature.
Xenophon's literary interests were combined with a keen interest in people,
and the result was the biographical sketches of the Cyreian generals that
have come down to us.

It is reasonable to suppose that Xenophon would have had the opportunity – surely, many times – to observe Clearchus, speak with him, and
listen to him. In some instances Xenophon refers to Clearchus' thoughts,

which suggests that a conversation between the two men is the source of Xenophon's remark (*Anabasis* 2.3.13 and 2.5.24). Such access to Clearchus surely enabled Xenophon to form his appraisal of the Spartan. Yet I suspect that Clearchus was a man of few words, and not simply because he was a Spartan![34] The taciturnity ascribed to him is rather the result of his wartime experiences, experiences which are seldom shared with "outsiders," who are at once mistrusted and perceived as unsympathetic. Mistrusted because they have not shared the experience of the trauma, unsympathetic because they can not understand nor conceive of – as the Joseph Conrad–Francis Ford Coppola symbol Colonel Kurtz in *Apocalypse Now* puts it – "The Horror."

Xenophon suggests that Clearchus, too, was mistrustful of others, a point that would have dire consequences for the Greek army that Clearchus would lead and to which we will return (see pp. 70–1). Such mistrust is reflected in the experiences of Vietnam veterans counseled by Shay and many others, and before them by Revolutionary, World War II and Korean War veterans. Frequently, the returning soldier falls silent because people will not or cannot believe what happens in battle. Moreover, some veterans have been made to feel foolish for their sacrifices or have become alienated because they believe that non-combatants think they should accept the horrors of war as the price of patriotism and resume civilian life as if nothing unusual had happened.[35]

Xenophon seems to have had a pretty clear picture of the kind of man Clearchus was and, as his sketch of the Spartan shows, may have recognized that the man he saw was the product of years of war and violence. Xenophon's description of Clearchus (see p. 60) reflects on my own recollections of soldiers who served multiple tours in Vietnam, or had been there continuously for two or three years. Like Clearchus they too appeared to be war-lovers. What factors could drive these men to face repeatedly such dangers as those found in war?

Several explanations have been offered over the last eighty years. Freud interpreted this phenomenon as an attempt to gain mastery over the traumatic experience by replaying or reliving the initial trauma. Such experience enabled the victim of trauma to absorb and digest the experience. More recently, psychologists and psychiatrists studying Vietnam vets seeking treatment in VA hospitals have offered a more physiological explanation:

---

34 In reading the *Anabasis*, Clearchus' speech seems to assume "Attic-like" qualities when Xenophon gives him a long speech in order to convey the situation facing the Greeks. Elsewhere Clearchus' speech is terse and typically laconic. See e.g. his exchange with Phalinus at *Anabasis* 2.1.18–23 and his speeches to Tissaphernes, the treacherous Persian satrap, at 2.3.21–23, 5.3.3–15.

35 Severo and Milford 1989: 26, 298–314, 327 discuss the dislocation and difficulties of readjustment that returning soldiers encountered.

that reexperiencing traumatic situations stimulates the production of neuro-hormones, particularly endogenous opioids, with psychoactive tranquilizing properties. These block pain, reduce panic, and allow one to respond against attack. These properties explain, for example, why soldiers in battle can sustain numerous wounds and still fight. Nicholas Warr, a Marine lieutenant in the 1968 battle for Hue, tells of a Marine who destroyed two NVA machine gun positions single-handed, not noticing until after it was over that he had been wounded four times.[36] These opioids also seem to impair memory processing. It has been suggested that "freezing/numbing responses may serve the function of allowing organisms not to 'consciously experience' or not to remember situations of overwhelming stress."[37] Researchers have found that stimulating a reexposure to the original trauma caused an endogenous opioid response that had a calming effect on traumatized individuals.[38] What this suggests, then, is that men like Clearchus, the LURP portrayed by Michael Herr, and other men that I knew fought not simply because they "loved" war but because they were attempting, either psychologically or physiologically, to cope with the initial trauma.

This then explains Xenophon's first statement about Clearchus and why he was a war-lover. But evidence of PTSD can be seen elsewhere in his mini-biography. First, when Xenophon says that Clearchus liked to lead the attack, he is actually referring to hypervigilance, the persistent mobilization of body and mind for lethal danger. In his biographical portrait of the Spartan, Xenophon relates how Clearchus clashed with the ephors, the ruling board of magistrates in Sparta, over "his" war with the Thracians (*Anabasis* 2.1.2–3). It was this conflict that seemingly led to his exile; but the matter would seem, on closer examination, a little more complicated. Clearchus' decision to pick a fight with the Thracians suggests an addiction to combat. Many trauma counselors have noted that peace is actually stressful for combat veterans, who find that "too low an arousal level is anxiety-producing." This may point to a psychological or physiological addiction or need for battle, to fight again so as to get that adrenaline "rush" that comes from facing imminent death. Examples of veteran "thrill-seeking" from other wars including Vietnam reflects this need. T.E. Lawrence and his motorcycle has a parallel in Vietnam veterans who went on "Easy Rider" trips through the southern states of the US, hoping that someone would shoot at them. The choice of occupations that many combat veterans make, especially continuing to serve in the military, becoming a

---

36 Warr 1997: 126–8. See also Ambrose 1994: 297–9, who recounts the exploits of airborne Sergeant H. Summers who, on the morning of June 6, 1944, killed or captured over 100 Germans virtually single-handed, and who afterwards could not explain his actions, saying only that he didn't "feel very good."

37 Van der Kolk, McFarlane and Weisaeth 1996: 227.

38 Van der Kolk *et al.* 1989: 108–12. See also Solomon 1993: 75–6, and for more clinical discussions, Friedman *et al.* 1995.

police officer, or fire-fighter, where they will be exposed to dangerous situations, further points to the destruction of social bonds.[39]

In describing Clearchus as a tough, hard man, Xenophon points to the persistent mobilization for danger, keeping combat skills ever-ready. When Xenophon describes Clearchus as incapable of personal friendships, he is reflecting simply on the destruction of social trust, a sense of isolation and the ensuing sense of despair which the destruction of social trust brings about. In the event, these very factors proved Clearchus' undoing in the aftermath, in the negotiations that followed the Battle of Cunaxa and the death of Cyrus. In the negotiations with the Persian satrap Tissaphernes, Clearchus clearly believed himself to be the object of a conspiracy against him. His inability to trust those around him, his willingness to believe that anonymous enemies were plotting against him, enabled Tissaphernes in the end to bait a trap for Clearchus that led to his arrest and death, along with the other commanders in the Greek army.[40] Moreover, the clash that Clearchus had with the ephors points as well to his inability to trust members of his own community. Once the social bond was destroyed, leaving the community and making the decision to live the life of an exile was not really a difficult one: from his perspective he was already cut off from the community, so leaving it was of little consequence.[41] Finally, when Xenophon states that Clearchus could not serve under another man, he is pointing again to what today would be regarded as the absence of social trust as well as a sense of betrayal and exploitation.

These characteristics appear in a passage related by Xenophon to a brawl that was provoked by Clearchus' tough discipline. Xenophon tells how, on the far side of the Euphrates, one of Clearchus' soldiers and one belonging to another general, Meno of Thessaly, got into a dispute. Clearchus decided, perhaps not unsurprisingly, that Meno's man was in the wrong and ordered him beaten. The punishment, we may imagine, was typically Clearchan, i.e. harsh, and nearly got him killed a day or two later, when he chanced to pass through Meno's part of the camp. Meno's men showered him with any sort of missile close to hand and Clearchus became so enraged that he called out his own men and was about to engage his assailants in full battle. Proxenus, another general and Xenophon's friend, attempted to calm Clearchus and quell the dispute, and for his trouble was nearly attacked himself by Clearchus. Only Cyrus, the Persian prince commanding the Greek army, was

---

39 See further (e.g.) Shatan 1997: 212, 221. Shatan also includes pest exterminators, and knows of a Warsaw ghetto survivor and a Korean War veteran, the three times sole survivor of his unit, who took up this line of work. The "Easy Rider" material also comes from Shatan, who heard it in veteran rap groups.

40 Xenophon, *Anabasis* 2.5.24–30. I would like to thank C.J. Tuplin of the University of Liverpool for reminding me of this point.

41 Shatan 1997: 211. Closely connected with this is the idea of "impacted grief," the idea that mourning is emotionally repressed.

able to restore order, and Xenophon remarks that "Clearchus came to himself" upon Cyrus' persuasions (*Anabasis* 1.5ff). This passage could easily be dismissed as an account of soldiers simply behaving like soldiers and little more. Yet Clearchus' rage and the way Xenophon describes him as "coming to himself" or "getting a grip" is typical of combat veterans suffering from PTSD who, to use the usual phrase, "lose it" and "go off." These phrases are routinely used by veterans and their counselors today to describe this kind of explosive behavior and could be documented by any number of case studies and veterans' rap (or discussion) groups. What these incidents demonstrate, however, is what is usually referred to as "pervasive hyperalertness" or the "constant vigilance [that] is the combat survivor's hallmark." Trauma counselor and psychiatrist Chaim Shatan describes "hypervigilance [as] much more enduring and severe in combat survivors than in non-combat veterans or survivors of earthquakes and hurricanes."[42] These terms refer to the persistent mobilization of the body and mind for lethal danger, as seen in Clearchus' fight with Meno's men. It is this persistent mobilization of the body that accounts for such things as the sharp startle response so typical of combat veterans, their inclination to sit with their backs to a wall, to be constantly scanning the surroundings for any possible danger.[43]

The destruction of social skills should not be seen as peculiar to Clearchus because he was a Spartan. In his 1939 novel of World War I, Jules Romains noted this too. He described veterans as being like invalids "who [had] suffered an amputation of all [their] delicate sentiments, like a man who has lost all his fingers and can only feel things with a couple of stumps. And there will be millions ... like that."[44] "Psychic numbing," i.e. the absence of emotion and feeling, perhaps best characterizes Clearchus' character. Many combat soldiers have difficulty achieving sexual intimacy as well as closeness with their children (on the latter point, talk sometime with the son of a combat veteran and it will become clear). Xenophon seems to confirm this diagnosis of Clearchus, noting how he willingly spent money on war just as others did on love affairs (2.6.6).

PTSD in the ancient Greek world

> The violation of human connection, and consequently the risk of a post-traumatic stress disorder, is highest of all when the survivor has not merely been a passive witness but also an active participant in violent death or atrocity.
>
> (Judith Herman, *Trauma and Recovery*, p.142)

42 Shatan 1997: 209.
43 For an example see Fussell 1996: 237.
44 Romains 1939: 430.

Plate 8   At "the Wall," November 10, 1982. Fred Strother of Maine, who lost his leg during the Vietnam War in 1966, views the Vietnam Veterans' Memorial, the first day of its being open to the public. The unforgotten trauma of war.

Photo: UPI/Corbis Bettmann, B & W Print, Number U2098170>2.

Xenophon may not have understood exactly why Clearchus was troubled, but he clearly sensed that he was, and that the reasons for this were to be found in his long years of service as a soldier. This inquiry suggests that Xenophon was rather perceptive, that he was almost the first "psychologist" to recognize the characteristics that today are identified as PTSD. This is evident in another passage of the *Anabasis*, where Xenophon defended his command of the Greek mercenary army at an *euthynai*, or trial, conducted by the army. In this inquest various disgruntled and disappointed soldiers brought forward accusations of various infractions and brutalities. In his defense, Xenophon stated:

> then, too, in cases where a man was *losing his grip on himself and refused to stand up and was giving himself up to the enemy*, I have both struck people and forced them to continue marching [italics added].[45]

This passage with Xenophon's reference to certain "cases" suggests first that the situations where men broke down under the strain of near constant battle occurred more than once. How many times we cannot say, but clearly it was a situation that Xenophon had to deal with on multiple occasions. The condition that Xenophon describes is also one that is identical with cases of battle fatigue known in modern literature from World War I and Remarque's *All Quiet on the Western Front* to Vietnam and O'Brien's *The Things They Carried* and countless other works of poetry and prose.

Xenophon's own battle experiences, his conversations with Socrates and the men he soldiered with, may explain to some degree his ability to recognize the effects of battle on its participants. As a "proto" biographer, Xenophon's sensitivity really comes as no surprise, as the biographic mode of inquiry surely requires a certain intuitive understanding of the peculiarities of the human condition. These sensibilities and perceptions should not be thought of as somehow unique to Xenophon. Other writers, such as the dramatist Sophocles and the historian Herodotus, analyze and discuss figures whose lives seem to be marked by the trauma of PTSD, including the final act of self-destruction – suicide.

Suicide has been the scourge of many Vietnam veterans and their families over the last twenty-five years. It has claimed the lives of anywhere from ten to one hundred thousand Vietnam veterans.[46] The exact number cannot

---

45 Xenophon, *Anabasis* 5.8.14.
46 A reasoned discussion of this often politicized issue may be found in Matsakis 1996: 278–306, who notes *inter alia* that suicides of Vietnam veterans are 23 percent higher than those of other veterans in the same age group (p. 284). Perhaps omitted from these statistical surveys are the deaths, due to suicide and related causes, of the so-called "bush vets," i.e. those men who live cut-off from society in isolation or in camps. In one camp located in Malibu from 1970 to 1976, approximately twenty to twenty-five men took their own lives and are today buried in unmarked graves (information from Shad Meshad, who eventually made contact with this camp and worked with its population).

really be known, as it is sometimes difficult to determine whether a highway accident is an "accident" or instead a means to suicide. This applies equally to drug overdoses and deaths from alcohol abuse – it is simply difficult to know when the wartime trauma ends and the drugs and alcohol begin. In fact, as the symptoms of PTSD would suggest, the two are linked in a causal fashion. Leaving aside the issue of numbers, clearly a significant number of veterans have died from self-inflicted causes, and the number could easily equal that of the battlefield deaths in Vietnam. Such a figure in itself is shocking and points to the depths to which people can be driven by trauma. Suicide, however, as the result of trauma, should not be regarded as a modern, contemporary issue. Both Sophocles and Herodotus relate examples of suicide resulting from the trauma of battle.

In his drama *Ajax* Sophocles tells the story of the great Telamonian Ajax (so-called to distinguish him from the Oelean or "lesser" Ajax), who took his own life when his fellow Greeks denied him the prize of Achilles' armor.[47] His suicide results from his belief that he has been betrayed by those closest to him, his own comrades, and it would seem that he has a point. Ajax's perception of betrayal, as argued above, corresponds well with the diagnosis of PTSD, particularly that aspect of it that focuses on the destruction of the capacity for social trust. So complete is Ajax's capacity for trust that he rebuffs his wife-concubine Tecmessa's plaintive attempt to dissuade him from taking his own life – Ajax cannot even trust her (see further the discussion on pp. 96–8).

The suicide of Ajax could be set beside the real-life suicides of many Vietnam veterans, who finally took their own lives, convinced that everyone had abandoned them, including their wives. While it may be true that Sophocles is exploring aspects of the mind here, it must be seen that the playwright is also describing a warrior, one who had fought many valiant fights, similar to men he had encountered in real life. Like his older contemporary Aeschylus, Sophocles too had seen battle at close quarters and knew what could happen to men locked in battle. The fragment of his play *Eurpylus* already cited, with its reference to Argives "laughing" as they trample over the bodies of the slain, points to a gritty recognition of war's horrors and corresponding trauma. This is known to us from other times. At Tarawa in 1944 Marine private Earle Curtis relates his "uncontrolled laugh" at watching another Marine die, his leg blown off, and then moments later regaining his composure – somewhat.[48] Sophocles' Argives may actually be responding with laughter in much the same way – the trauma of battle. Ajax's suicide, then, need not only be seen in the light of intellectual experi-

---

47 Cartledge 1997: 13 calls attention to the dominance of war in the fifth-century BC Greek world and how this influenced drama, including the *Ajax*. Cf. Winnington with Ingram 1980: 11–56 for an interpretation of Ajax' "mind."
48 Cited in Jennings and Brewster 1998: 249.

ment with ideas of the mind, or of dramatic presentation. It can also be seen as true to life experience.

Ajax as described by Sophocles is a literary creation of the playwright's experiential world. But what of real life Ajaxes, men who were driven to suicide as a result of battle-induced trauma? Two such examples are the Spartans Aristodemus and Pantites, who both survived Leonidas' last stand against the Persians at Thermopylae (480 BC), but not for long as they both took their own lives, albeit in different fashion. With these two warriors we have certain evidence of violence-induced trauma which can only be resolved in self-murder, though again the means used to achieve this are different.

The circumstances by which Aristodemus and Pantites survived Thermopylae are a bit obscure, especially in the case of Aristodemus. Herodotus tells that Aristodemus had been suffering from an eye inflammation and had been sent a safe distance behind the line by Leonidas to recover. Another Spartan, Eurytes, had also gone with him suffering from a similar ailment. When word came of the final fight in the pass against the Persians, the two men responded but rather differently. Eurytes, who could barely see, returned and died. Aristodemus delayed and lived. Herodotus tells how the Spartans were angry with him and virtually cut him off from human contact upon his return home. Much the same treatment befell Pantites. He had been sent to Thessaly by Leonidas on some diplomatic mission and also missed the final battle. Confronted by the same reception as Aristodemus, Pantites hanged himself rather than continue living in disgrace.[49]

Herodotus gives a long explanation about how Aristodemus might not have incurred any resentment had Eurytes also decided to return home rather than fight and die. This explanation, however, is unconvincing in light of what happened to Pantites, who really had a reason for not being at Thermopylae – he was away on official business. Spartan reaction to the survivors of Thermopylae is more complex than Herodotus' account suggests.[50] Moreover, Spartan opinion itself was mixed, which Herodotus' report makes clear was the case.

The story that Herodotus tells represents mostly the perspective of the

---

49 Herodotus 7.230, 232, for Aristodemus and Pantites respectively.
50 Xenophon, *Constitution of the Spartans* 9.3–6 refers to the social disabilities suffered by "cowards" or *tresantes* in Sparta, including the difficulties their sisters faced in marrying. This tells us that the problems Pantites and Aristodemus faced were not isolated incidents but occurred more frequently than may be usually thought. Neither Xenophon nor Herodotus mentions how many times a man had to show cowardice to incur these social sanctions, or if one occasion could be redeemed later by a show of courage, as was the case with Aristodemus. Plutarch, *Agesilaus* 30.6 notes that after the disastrous defeat at Leuctra in 371 BC, the Spartan king Agesilaus decreed that the laws should be allowed to sleep for a day. His intention was to preserve the citizenship of those survivors of the battle who were in danger of slipping into inferior status. See further the discussion in Shipley 1997: 331–4, though he does not note that Aristodemus returned to battle and evidently managed to recover some of his lost honor.

folks at home who were left to live with the trauma of nearly three hundred of their men not returning to them. There must have been much anger as well as pain. Those at home would have found it difficult to understand, much as Michael Herr was unable to understand the story of the lost patrol up the mountain, the plight of the only two survivors. What Herodotus leaves out of his account, and what we today can perhaps appreciate, is the trauma, the guilt that Aristodemus and Pantites felt for having survived the deaths of their friends. As Shay and others have pointed out, the guilt of the survivor creates sometimes an overwhelming burden that leads to self-destruction. Pantites could not bear it, and though he was surely blameless, he took his own life, not because of the disgrace as Herodotus, and perhaps the Spartans too, understood it, but really because of the guilt. So too with Aristodemus. His survival at home until his death in battle at Plataea the next spring makes one wonder just how pervasive the shame, the pointing of fingers, the contemptible looks really were, and how much they were imagined.[51]

At Plataea, a year after Thermopylae, Aristodemus finally got his chance to atone for having lived. What he did there was to go literally "berserk," much in the way described by Shay and which combat soldiers know can really happen. Herodotus tells how Aristodemus rushed "forward with the fury of a madman in his desire to be killed before his comrades' eyes."[52] Yet we need to keep in mind, even if Herodotus does not, that Aristodemus had stood in the line with the rest of the Spartans until the battle began. He waited, that is, under a barrage of arrows until the sacrifices had been made, the paean sung, the orders given. One can imagine him standing there watching and thinking, not on the imminent battle, but rather the haunting memories of his friends killed the previous year. When the battle finally commenced, he then rushed forward, not as Herodotus tells and the Spartans believed, to retrieve his lost honor, but rather out of a sense of guilt at having survived.

It has been suggested that Aristodemus' act would have been "little appreciated by the Spartans who prided themselves on their order and discipline."[53] Yet this claim is contradicted by the discussion after the battle

---

51 Something similar occurred in 391 BC, when a Spartan *mora* or regiment was destroyed by the Athenians in a famous battle at Lechaeum outside Corinth (Xenophon, *Hellenica* 4.5.7–17). Xenophon relates (4.5.10) how the families of those killed, approximately 250 men, went about their business at home as if they were celebrating. This response might as well be like that of Marine Earle Curtis – a response to trauma.

52 Herodotus 9.71.

53 So Marincola 1996: 600. There is also some misunderstanding of the nature of the hoplite phalanx, especially how it tended to lose its integrity once battle began. See Xenophon, *Anabasis* 1.8.18–20, which tells how different parts of the Greek phalanx at the Battle of Cunaxa against the Persians called out to each other to maintain the integrity of their formation.

regarding the prize of valor. Aristodemus' name was indeed considered along with several others; it was only because of the circumstances of Thermopylae that he was not chosen. This discussion shows that, while the Spartans appreciated Aristodemus' courage, they placed a higher premium on the courage of men fighting to live. In other times and cultures, acts much like Aristodemus' can be observed. Note the story of the Bedouin chieftain Tallal told by T.E. Lawrence in *Seven Pillars of Wisdom*. After finding his village destroyed and ravaged by retreating Turkish soldiers, Tallal charged into the retreating Turks only to be killed. Auda Abu Tayi, another Bedouin chief, understood his suicidal charge as he said "God give him mercy; we will take his price." Motivated by "payback," Lawrence and the Arabs attacked and annihilated the Turkish column, taking no prisoners.[54]

Just as suicide is noted in ancient sources, other symptoms of PTSD may be similarly detected. In his *History of Alexander's Anabasis*, Arrian tells a curious story of Alexander's struggle to take the Greek city of Halicarnassus in 334 BC. The Macedonian siege had stalled after various attempts, but success nearly came in an unexpected way. One night two soldiers had been drinking and after more than a few cups, probably taking and making bets, began a two-man assault on the city in the dead of the night. The two drunks were killed almost immediately upon beginning their attack, but the chaotic scene that followed almost brought an unexpected victory for the Macedonians.[55] Within several days Alexander had his city, though he would have to wait another year before gaining possession of the last Persian citadel overlooking the town.

This amusing account reveals one of the usual ways that soldiers pass the time: getting drunk. But alcoholism, especially what could be called chronic alcoholism, is one of the symptoms of PTSD and suggests that there are far deeper troubles hidden underneath the drinking. Such behavior recalls the personality of Alexander the Great. Several years ago J.M. O'Brien's study of Alexander's career made much of his drinking.[56] O'Brien's interpretations of Alexander were not generally well received by scholars. It might be, however, that Alexander's alcoholism, the way he could fly into a rage and kill Cleitus the Black for example, may be considerably illuminated by the realization that Alexander's abuse of alcohol is symptomatic of Post-Traumatic Stress Disorder.

Elsewhere other sources suggest awareness, if not understanding, of the presence of war-induced PTSD in ancient Greek society. The figure of the Athenian general Demosthenes as he appears in Aristophanes' *The Knights* suggests that the playwright also sensed the effects of war on soldiers; he

54 Lawrence 1935: 630–4, at 632.
55 Arrian, 1.21–22.
56 O'Brien 1992: 133–40.

describes Demosthenes in several places as a heavy drinker, which suggests alcoholism. Aristophanes also refers several times to Cleon "stealing" Demosthenes' victory at Pylos, just the sort of thing that could easily create a sense of betrayal in Demosthenes' mind.[57] The Athenian Epizelus and the mute mercenary soldiers who regain their speech, as related in a fragment of the poetry of Poseidippus, all point to PTSD.[58] These overlooked pieces of evidence are reminiscent of director John Huston's controversial post-World War II film *Let There Be Light*, which showed combat veterans undergoing rehabilitative treatment through hypnosis. With such treatments a number of men were able either to recover their lost or impaired speech or to walk again. These are but a few passages which suggest that other writers in the ancient world, and not only Xenophon and before him Homer, recognized that, even in surviving battle, survivors carried with them the burden of guilt, a difficulty in living in peace.

57 Aristophanes, *The Knights* 54–7, 75–6 (Pylos), 85–8 (drink).
58 Herodotus 6.117.2–3; Voutiras 1994: 27–31.

5

PENELOPE AND WAITING WIVES AND LOVERS

> Young men, my suitors now that the great Odysseus has perished, wait, though you are eager to marry me, until I finish this web, so that my weaving will not be useless and wasted.
>
> (Homer, *Odyssey* 19.143–4)

Penelope's weaving of a burial shroud for Odysseus' father Laertes, her own "wily" way of putting off her suitors' demand that she marry one of them, is to some extent obscured by the greater adventures of her husband's return to her. Penelope's story, however, encapsulates the wartime realities of most women throughout history, whose role has been to wait the return of husband or son, father, or brother, from the battlefield. This has only partially changed with the increased military service of women in recent times, something that the ancient world saw only in times of emergency when cities came under direct attack. Assessing the role of women in the ancient Greek world, also as non-Greeks as we shall see in Chapter 5, is made complicated by their "otherness," i.e. to men. The Greeks were fond of polarities and of looking at interrelationships as consisting of opposites – rich and poor, good and bad. Socrates, then (or Thales of Miletus – the attribution varies), could say he was trebly fortunate, "first because I was born a man and not a beast, second a man and not a woman, third Greek and not a barbarian" (Diogenes Laertius 1.33). Other evidence from the classical era shows that such an attitude was not uncommon. In the late twentieth century, however, Socrates' opinion might seem especially odd, not to mention unwelcome in some quarters. But the idea is not really so strange. The recent best seller *Men are from Mars, Women are from Venus* suggests that Socrates' remark is not so chauvinistic or peculiar, at least in terms of suggesting "otherness."

While women do have "other" roles in war, it remains that women both in ancient Greece and in the modern American world share common bonds. First, their duty is mostly to wait for the warriors' return, for, as noted above, the idea of manliness precluded any active participation for them in

Plate 9   Penelope at her loom, with Telemachus her son. This scene depicts the experience historically borne by women, waiting for husband, father, or son, to return from war. Penelope's wait would eventually prove worthwhile – Odysseus returned. Attic red-figure vase painting on a *skyphos* (cup) (c. 450 BC).

Museo Archeologico, Chiusi. *Photo*: Alinari/Art Resource, NY, B & W Print, 50033535, AL 37486.

war. Moreover, women often suffer the most from war's impact, either directly as victims or in dealing with the warriors' survival. Both of these issues occupy a place both in the literature and history of ancient Greece and the modern American experience in Vietnam.

Waiting wives and mothers

> At every window stand lonely girls whose burning eyes are bright with tears ...
>
> (Yvan Goll, *Requiem for a Dead Europe*)

Andromache in the *Iliad* occupies the role of the dutiful waiting wife who simply awaits her man's return from battle and attends to domestic duties. This is revealed clearly in Book 6, which constitutes the principal scene and dialogue between Andromache and Hector. Here it is made clear that, as

Hector puts it, "men must see to the fighting" (*Iliad* 6.492), while Andromache, like Penelope, must attend to her weaving and await the fight's outcome. Later the Athenian poet Aristophanes incorporated the very same sentiment into his own commentary on women and war in his play *Lysistrata*, thus revealing perhaps the standard Greek view on the issue.[1] This division of labor reflects first the apparent subordination of women, whose role it is to remain within the house, with downcast eyes ever deferring to the man. This role, mentioned by Andromache in *The Trojan Women*, omits the truly significant fact that both husband and wife knew when to yield to the other (see Euripides, *Andromache* 645–56). Yet in matters of war Andromache knew that she was powerless to dissuade Hector from the field and that when he said "men must see to the fighting," she knew that this was his place. Until comparatively recent times, the muscle-bound techniques of war placed women at a decided disadvantage and so relegated them to the house.

In telling Andromache that it is for men to see to the fighting, Hector brings to life the age-old silence of men and the toils of war, at least as far as women are concerned. Study of the scene between this devoted couple suggests that what Andromache has learned of the fighting around Hector has resulted from her "peeking" from the walls of Troy. This is most likely a poetic device. It is possible, however, that Andromache's knowledge comes from her own close proximity to the fighting. In other primitive cultures, for example the early Germans, women often placed themselves close to the action so as to provide an inspiration to the men – "if you lose, think of me!" Either way, however, what Andromache reveals regarding the fighting comes from her and not Hector.

What should be stressed here is Hector's silence. He says "men must see to the fighting" and nothing else. This is a sentiment that is timeless and stretches across cultures as well. In numerous cases of traumatized Vietnam veterans, one sees repeated instances of the veterans' silence over the war, what is referred to as the "no talk" rule.[2] Such behavior is a sign of trauma and throws up barriers to any kind of communication between partners. Such silence also extends to letter writing. Many soldiers while serving in combat do not relate their experiences, especially any combat experiences, in letters home to their wives.[3] This was the case for me, and other veterans have told me that they did the same. The underlying rationale for this seems rather simple – so as not to give any cause for worry on the part of the other. Of course, doing this probably has the opposite effect, as in a war zone anything can happen.

The same silence or censorship applies to letters written to the parents

---

1   See e.g. Aristophanes, *Lysistrata* 519–20, 538 and Aeschylus, *Seven Against Thebes* 200.

2   Matsakis 1996: 91, 274, who adds that it is sometimes applied to children as well.

3   This is true in some cases but certainly not all. My friend John Belohlavek, an historian

and families of those killed by their friends, who tell a censured account, as Siegfried Sassoon relates in "Remorse":

> "there's things in war one dare not tell
> Poor father sitting safe at home, who reads
> Of dying heroes and their deathless deeds."

(ll. 12–14)

Because the truth may be more like what Sassoon describes in "The Hero":

> "Jack fell as he'd wished," the Mother said,
> And folded up the letter that she'd read.
> "The Colonel writes so nicely." ...
> He thought how 'Jack', cold-footed, useless swine,
> Had panicked down the trench that night the mine
> Went up at Wicked Corner; how he'd tried
> To get sent home, and how, at last, he died,
> Blown to small bits. And no one seemed to care
> Except that lonely woman with white hair.

(ll. 1–3, 13–18)

Gerald Linderman has written that such silence may be found in letters written home by American and British soldiers in World War II and that not speaking ill of the dead was the soldiers' first principle.[4] Tim O'Brien tells the story of Rat Kiley, who wrote to the sister of his friend Curt Lemon, blown up by a booby-trapped artillery shell. Rat told her what a great guy her brother was: "he would always volunteer for stuff nobody else would," "doing recon or going out on these really badass night patrols. Stainless steel balls," Rat tells her. Rat cried out his heart to Curt's sister and sent the letter: "Jesus Christ, man, I write this beautiful fuckin' letter, I slave over it, and what happens? The dumb cooze never writes back."[5]

Curt Lemon's sister may have been bewildered, horrified, and sickened to hear of her brother's wartime acts and so rejected any association with him. So too the silence of the warrior-husband with the wife is likely to continue

---

of nineteenth-century American history, has pointed out to me that soldiers serving on both sides in the US Civil War did write to their wives telling of their experiences. This also happened in Vietnam. What can be concluded from this is that, in some instances, men did write their wives about what they saw and did in battle, yet I believe that the greater number did not. Moreover, some men will write their parents or a special friend, but will again say nothing to a wife or girlfriend.

4   Linderman 1997: 319.
5   O'Brien 1990: 75–7.

after the war or fighting has ended. The reasons for this are somewhat more complex. The warrior thinks that people generally, as well as his wife, will not want to hear of combat experiences, especially if horrible acts are involved. The veteran is frequently working from a supposition that one who has not shared his experience cannot possibly understand it, which to a certain extent is true. One interesting aspect of this gender conflict over war is that there are cases where a man will speak to a woman about his experiences in war, but one with whom bonds of friendship rather than love are the basis for the relationship. This has been reported to me, for example, among German relations of mine where a veteran feels compelled to bring out past traumatic experiences, but will do it with a friend rather than a spouse.

Yet to dismiss the Andromache–Hector relationship as one-sided and male-dominated risks failing to appreciate the dynamics that this scene and so many others like it represent. John Ruskin, the nineteenth-century critic, artist and essayist, suggests in his lecture "War" that women have a duty of providing moral support for their men: "Wives and maidens, who are the souls of soldiers ... if you fail to do your part they cannot fulfil theirs."[6] Ruskin's notion reflects the nineteenth-century's romantic visions that rested on its perceptions of the classical past. The numerous "departure scenes" on Attic vases that have come down to us suggest that the Greeks also saw women providing moral support to their men. Herbert Hoffmann, in his study of the painter-potter Sotades, argues that these scenes represent the image of feminine virtue exalted by Pericles in the Funeral Oration (see below), and this view is surely right. Additionally he suggests that the giving of the shield and spear by the woman to the warrior conveys "the ideology of the polis, one aspect of which was *thanatos kalos*, 'glorious death,' which was long thought of by most Athenians as the only guarantee of immortality."[7] This view, however, ignores Andromache's fears in the *Iliad* and Penelope's worries in the *Odyssey*. Moreover, if the warrior's farewell in the Munich *stamnos* (see Plate 10) is any guide, the postures and gestures of the women suggest a more complicated and emotional response to the departure than Hoffmann would have us believe.

A similar view has also been argued for the widows and mothers of Athenians who died in battle. Thucydides, in the funeral speech spoken by Pericles, suggests that,

> if I must make mention of womanly virtue, in the case of those who will now be widows, I shall indicate everything in a brief word of advice. Great is your reputation if you do not fall below the nature

6   Ruskin 1903–12: 13, 90.
7   Hoffmann 1997: 74.

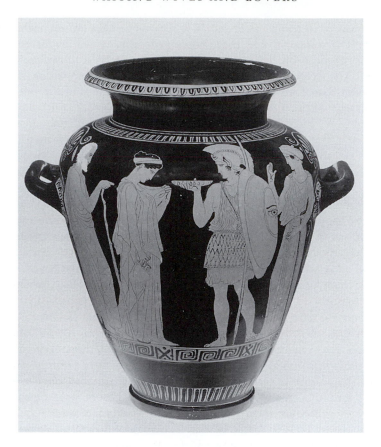

Plate 10   A Greek farewell. In this vase painting on an Attic red-figure *stamnos* (wine jar) of c. 440–430 BC, father, mother, and wife say their goodbyes to the warrior about to depart. The "departure scene" is ubiquitous in Greek art owing to the frequency of war.

Photo: Antiken-Sammlungen, Munich, vas 2415.

that is yours, and great is the reputation of the one who has the least renown among men either concerning her *arete* or her faults.[8]

L. Kallet-Marx has argued that the widows of war heroes were honored by the community in a way that set them apart from other women. The *megale doxa*, the great glory, of the dead was transferred to their widows who, as living representatives, became a reminder of heroic achievement to all. For this reason, then, it would seem unwise to dismiss Andromache's contribu-

8   Thucydides 2.45.2.

tion to Hector's bravery, and that of women through history, of being of little value.[9]

Yet the reality remains that, should Hector fail, the consequences of his defeat and death will be dire for "white-armed" Andromache. Not only will she lose her freedom and be enslaved, but she will work at another's loom and become a beast of burden carrying water, all unwilling actions forced upon her on account of his death (*Iliad* 6.455–9). Hector's and Andromache's dialogue thus brings out not only the narrow margins of life, death, and slavery in the early Greek world, but also the woman's supporting role in sustaining the warrior, which is not to be discounted.

Andromache's poignant appeal to her husband also reveals the great stress that the waiting wife endured. This is evident in the reference to her tears and her clinging to Hector's hand as she implores him to think of her. Should he die there will be nothing left for her but "to sink into the earth" (6.410–13), which can only mean that her own death will follow. Andromache's tears could just as easily be used as a title for a novel or study of the Vietnam wives or lovers as the situations are virtually identical. In a memoir that catches the tenor and tone of the Vietnam War era, Marian Faye Novak's *Lonely Girls With Burning Eyes* conveys simply but effectively the loneliness and anxiety of the waiting woman at home wondering if her soldier husband will return.[10] Many of her remarks ring true in the experience of my wife Margaret during 1970–71. This ranges from the daily wait for the mail to be delivered, which provided a sort of security blanket that said all was safe for another day – even when this could easily have been false – and the courage to endure the nightly news that televised the action. In this waiting the women of Vietnam were more like Andromache than might at first be imagined. All of them could only watch the war's violence and hope that their men would return.[11] Enduring the separation and time apart were daily challenges for Marian and Margaret just as they were for living, rather than literary, Andromaches and Penelopes: Penelope wove her shroud, Andromache and Marian cared for an infant child, and Margaret taught school, all solutions to make time pass as quickly as possible. Andromache, and women like her, may have had the most difficult time, as she had to endure the anxiety of the wait in the absence of any family other than Hector. For, as she says, "I have no father, no honored mother," as all her family had died already at the hands of Achilles. Without Hector she is truly alone, unprotected and vulnerable.

---

9 Kallet-Marx 1993: 140–3.
10 Novak 1991: passim.
11 At least slavery and worse were not fates that awaited American wives, as they did for Greek women. On the other hand, similar fates of prostitution and poverty approaching slavery did happen to Vietnamese women, as portrayed in Le Ly Hayslip's novel *When Heaven and Earth Changed Places*, the source for Oliver Stone's final film in his Vietnam War trilogy, *Between Heaven and Earth*.

This same sentiment of longing after the absent warrior-husband is also expressed by Penelope at the beginning of the *Odyssey*. Here the singer of tales Phemios is asked to tell of the tragic homecoming of the Achaeans from Troy, to which Penelope responds,

> leave off singing this sad song, which always afflicts the dear heart deep inside me, since unforgettable sorrow comes to me, beyond others, so dear a head do I long for whenever I am reminded of my husband.[12]

Here a waiting wife cares not to hear of the sorrowful stories of war no matter how glorious they may be, as they only succeed in reminding her of the lover and husband who is not only absent but who may be dead. Even if Odysseus were sitting next to Penelope she might have said exactly the same thing and Odysseus might just as well agreed. In Book 8 of the *Odyssey* (60–95; cf. 499–534), the singer of tales Demadocus sings the song of Troy's destruction to the court of the Phaeacians, as Odysseus, the unnamed visitor, listens. As he hears and remembers the many friends who died, the violence of the fight under the walls of Troy, he breaks down in tears, pulling his cloak over his head to hide this.[13] Odysseus' reaction has many parallels. In December 1998, NBC news anchor Tom Brokaw was telling about his then new book, *The Greatest Generation*.[14] Asked how he came to write it, he recounted how in 1984 at the fortieth anniversary of the D-Day invasion he met US Representative Sam Gibbons of Florida, who had been a young paratrooper dropping into Normandy the night of June 6th. Surrounded and initially alone, thinking the invasion had failed, Gibbons eventually rallied a small group of men and began fighting the Germans. As he told Brokaw of this, he paused to choke back the tears. His wife said, "You don't have to go on," but he replied, "Yes I do, it's important to tell the story."

Other veterans and their wives have had similar reactions to viewing *Saving Private Ryan* and this has been mentioned in the news and noted by many non-veterans in the audience afterwards. Wives, including my own, find it uncomfortable, even unbearable, to view films and programs that depict the acts of violence in which their husbands participated. As in the case of Penelope in the passage from the *Odyssey* quoted above, this follows in part simply from the identification of the event with the loved one. There is

---

12 Homer, *Odyssey* 1.340–44.
13 Cf. Heubeck *et al*. 1988: 352 for a different view. They argue that "the tears are not unmanly in themselves, but courtesy demanded their concealment unless the grief was shared." They point to Homer, *Odyssey* 4.113ff, 183ff, as examples of this, but neither case involves what could be construed as battlefield trauma, compared with that which Odysseus remembers on hearing Demadocus' song.
14 Broadcast December 23, 1998 on MSNBC, the cable channel of NBC News.

also the fear that if the veteran is exposed to a reenactment of the trauma it will trigger some sort of a flashback or nightmare. Interestingly, the woman's desire to shield her loved one may actually be the wrong thing to do. As Shay argues, the veteran's need to discuss traumatic events, to "communalize" the grief, is an important step toward diminishing the often-terrible consequences of exposure to trauma, be it combat, rape, or natural catastrophe.[15]

In the fifth century BC, during the classical or golden age of Greece, this image of the waiting wife provided the comedian Aristophanes with the material to launch a witty satire of war and its impact on society. In his drama *Lysistrata*, perhaps his most brilliant and probably best-known play, Aristophanes offers up some powerful commentary on the plight of women in war. Lysistrata, the Athenian woman who unites the women of Greece in a sex strike to end the war among the Greeks, makes clear the costs of war to women, a price that Aristophanes would seem to suggest came as a surprise to most men (and probably still does). This is brought out in the dialogue between Lysistrata and the Athenian magistrate who comes to challenge her action and the right of women to bring an end to the war. The magistrate claims that women basically have no reason to think they are entitled to a share in the political process. To this Lysistrata responds, "what of us then, whoever in vain for our children must weep, borne but to perish far away and in vain" (*Lysistrata* 585–90). This remark sends shudders of horror into the magistrate, and surely the Athenian audience as well, who are reminded not only of the yearly toll of war dead, but probably of the recent end of the Sicilian Expedition, where the numbers of Athenian dead far exceeded the annual average. Through Lysistrata, then, Aristophanes suggests that women have a fiduciary claim in the business of war, as it is their sons who are sent off to fight and all too often to die.

In her retort to the magistrate, however, Lysistrata brings up an even more touching reality for the waiting wife and actually all women – the aging process and how this is skewed against them. Men, Lysistrata claims, are able in spite of their gray hair and beards, to find new or younger wives, or mistresses or concubines. Wives, however, prematurely aged on account of worry, are left to tolerate such arrangements (594–7). For the widow, the situation is even worse. She will probably never remarry or if she does it will be to an older relative or an equally unpleasant arrangement and, in either case, will wait out the rest of her life in sorrow and loneliness, as Aristophanes says, clinging to omens and misery.

---

15 Shay 1994: 55.

Plate 11 Modern-day Andromaches mourning? The Vietnam Veterans' Memorial, "The Wall," Washington D.C.

Photo: © Larry Powell, Image number 63 from *Hunger of the Heart: Communion at the Wall.*

Women and the horrors of war

> in a moment look to see
> The blind and bloody soldier with foul hand
> Defile the locks of your shrill-shrieking daughters;
> Your fathers taken by the silver beards,
> And their most reverend heads dashed to the walls;
> Your naked infants spitted upon pikes,
> While the mad mothers with their howls confused
> Do break the clouds, as did the wives of Jewry
> At Herod's bloody-hunting slaughtermen.
>
> (Shakespeare, *Henry V* III. 3.116–24)

Shakespeare's famous speech of Henry V to the citizens of Harfleur in the campaign that led up to Agincourt describes the fate that many a town in the medieval or early modern era would have taken for granted had it been on the wrong end of a successful siege. The speech, however, and the reality it describes also have many counterparts in the literature of ancient Greece. Listen to Aeschylus' similar account from *Seven Against Thebes*:

> Emptied the city walls as the captive spoil, with mingled cries, is led to its doom. This heavy fate is what I fear. It is a woeful thing for maidens unripe, before the marriage rites, to tread this bitter journey from their homes. I would say that the dead are better off than this.[16]

More recently poets and writers of the American experience in Vietnam have also brought out the devastating effect of war on women, particularly Vietnamese women, whose suffering was often no less severe than that of their historic counterparts in Melos, Scione, and other towns of ancient Greece. One poet who related the captive woman's plight was Euripides, who in *Hecuba* tells how the captive woman of Troy, "left the bed of my love and prayed to Artemis. But no answer came. I saw my husband lying dead, and they took me over the sea. Backward I looked at Troy ... and I was dumb with grief" (*Hecuba* 934–41). Yet in the same play, Euripides empowers Hecuba, who leads her servants and the other captive women of Troy in taking revenge, "payback" in the language of Vietnam, on one who had wronged her and thus the Trojans. While women in Vietnam war literature are usually seen as only passive figures or victims, they too have been depicted as architects of violence. Women then emerge not only as the spoil of war, but in some instances practitioners of violence.

The exchange between Andromache and Hector discussed earlier makes it

---

16 Aeschylus, *Seven Against Thebes* 333–8.

clear that the early Greeks certainly were aware of the consequences of defeat and that in fact the living would envy the dead. In the classical drama of the fifth century BC, however, against the backdrop of the Peloponnesian War, this theme received greater attention and discussion. It was, however, not only this intensely brutal conflict that the Greeks waged upon one another for thirty years that provoked discussion of the terrors of war. There was also the simultaneous intellectual experimentation commonly referred to today as the "Greek Enlightenment." This intellectual movement provided dramatists, historians, and philosophers alike with the concepts and tools with which to explore the wide diversity of the human condition.[17] Moreover, it may well also be that the consequences of violence in society received much wider attention than ever before and, quite possibly, an attention and awareness that the world would not see again until the twentieth century.[18]

It might seem that the lessons of Homer provided the Greeks with all that they needed to understand the events of the war around them. Homer was the "teacher" of the Greeks, as any number of authorities from Socrates to Plato confirm, though not always approvingly.[19] Yet while Homer had assumed canonical stature and was admired and quoted, his poems could not provide a forum or a context for examination and discussion of contemporary issues.[20] As William Harris has noted, the minds of Greeks in the classical period were "to a considerable extent remade by contemporary books."[21] Attic drama would take the lead in this process. In the hands of an experimentalist and dramatist like Euripides, the didactic function and role of tragedy would be fully unleashed. Certainly there would have been a variety of views and interpretations of the dramas, but it may be said that the plays of the great dramatists, Aeschylus, Euripides, and Sophocles, and those of their less distinguished contemporaries, provided an unparalleled forum for

17 The bibliography here is extensive, but see especially Guthrie 1971a and b, Solmsen 1975, and de Romilly 1992 for discussion of this development. Note also (e.g.) that the investigations of the Greeks extended into the physical nature of man, as seen in Hippocrates' writings, recently translated by Craik 1998.

18 Note the attention that Thucydides pays to the nature of violence, as e.g. 3.36.6, and his introduction of the Athenian politician Cleon as "most violent" (cf. Hornblower 1992–96: I, 420, who attempts to dilute Thucydides' language). See further Chapter 7 and Thucydides' case study of the *stasis* on Corcyra, and his studied use of different forms of the word for violence *bia* (see Bétant 1843 [1969]: I, 183–4).

19 i.e. the famous criticism of Homer by Plato, see *Republic* 398a, 595a, 603a–604. See also Croally 1994: 17–18.

20 Burian 1997: 193–4 notes several well-known places where the Homeric poems provide setting and background to tragedy, e.g. Hector's dialogue with Andromache in the *Iliad* 6 (see discussion on p. 81) paralleled in Sophocles, *Ajax*, and the homecomings of Agamemnon and Odysseus. Goldhill 1986: Chapter 6, explores this at greater length. There is a difference between these settings and the topics of tragedy.

21 Harris 1989: 84.

debate.[22] In several of Euripides' dramas especially, the place of women and children can be seen as an obvious focus and item for appraisal.

Of the body of Euripidean drama that has survived, three plays, *Andromache* (c. 430–424 BC), *Hecuba* (425/4 BC), and most famously, *The Trojan Women* (c. 416/5 BC) constitute Euripides' "war plays."[23] These dramas take as their subject not only the treatment and fate of women and children in war, but also a wide range of topics involving the relationships of man and gods, man and woman, man and "barbarian." In the years that these dramas were written, Euripides would have had many examples to draw inspiration from: Plataea, taken by the Spartans and Thebans in 427 BC; Mytilene, captured by the Athenians the same year; Scione, recovered by the Athenians in 421 BC; and finally, the unprovoked Athenian attack on Melos in 416 BC, provided innumerable accounts of wartime brutalities in which women clearly would have suffered.[24]

Little evidence survives that gives more than a brief reference to the destruction of these communities. There is one example, however, the Athenian attack on Mycalessus, that provides a brutally lucid picture of what was surely the fate of the others. In 416 BC Thracian mercenaries under Athenian command attacked and destroyed this small insignificant town on their way home to the north, having arrived too late to sail to Sicily with the rest of the Athenian armada. Thucydides relates how the townspeople were caught unawares by the Athenians and Thracians, who "butchered the inhabitants sparing neither the young nor the old, but killing everyone they met, women and children, even the farm animals and every living thing they saw."[25] It is easy to lay this act at the door of the murderous Thracians. Their commander, however, was an Athenian general, Diitrephes, and he was surely not the only Athenian traveling with them. We do not know that he or any other Athenians joined in the slaughter, but there can be little

22 Cartledge 1997: 22–35, at 24, notes "the legitimacy of making tragic drama out of contemporary political experience as opposed to the traditional tales of myth and legend."

23 For a recent study of these dramas see Croally 1994.

24 Croally 1994: 192–4 discusses the imagery of the destroyed city of Troy and how this would have struck the Athenian audience of Euripides. While he is certainly right to note this, it should also be remembered that at this time the Athenians knew from first-hand experience the plight of the destroyed city with which they could easily have identified.

25 Thucydides 7.29–30. Thucydides notes only that they were assigned the task of attacking the enemy as they made their way home, no doubt to cause as much destruction and loss as possible to Athenian enemies (the Athenians may also have wanted to get their money's worth, having bought their services). Thucydides does not explain why the Thracians were so ferocious.

doubt either that the Athenians knew of this incident or that they were in some way responsible.[26]

Intellectually, the wartime dramas of Euripides already mentioned provide a tangible and introspective examination of what happened at such places as Mycalessus and Melos. Additionally, the stage scenery of *Trojan Women* would have conveyed the same type of visceral in-your-face cinematography as Oliver Stone's *Platoon*, where Vietnamese villagers, especially women, are abused, killed, and raped. This scene is inspired by the American destruction of the Vietnamese hamlet of My Lai 4 in March 1968, an event that has numerous parallels of one kind or another (see pp. 122–3). The linkage of Melos and My Lai might be faulted on the grounds that the former was the result of a "state" decision, while the latter spontaneously followed from a combination of "official" and "unofficial" policy regarding the enemy and the suppressed rage of individual soldiers. Yet the results of the two attacks are virtually identical.

A Melian terror permeates Euripides' dramas of *Andromache*, *Hecuba*, and *The Trojan Women*, in which an image of helplessness surrounds the women and children, the real focus of the plays. Hecuba and Andromache, for example, both widowed and thus unprotected, become the property, literally, of another man, to do with as he pleases. Both of them, additionally, must surrender their children to the enemy to be killed. One such example is Polyxena, Hecuba's daughter, who is taken away to be sacrificed at the tomb of Achilles. In *Hecuba* Euripides takes two pages of dialogue to relate the circumstances of her sacrifice and death. While the execution of Polyxena, as well as that of little Astyanax, Hector's son, in *The Trojan Women* is only discussed on stage, its discussion is no less remarkable than the famous execution of a child in Sergio Leone's *Once Upon a Time in the West*. At the beginning of this film, a settler's family is gunned down except for a young boy of seven or eight, the lone witness. When one of the gang calls the leader by name, asking what to do with the kid, the man is compelled to kill the boy so as to leave no witnesses to their crime. In the film's European version, the murder of the boy is shown explicitly. American film editors or censors, perhaps surprisingly today in light of recent action films, cut that scene, which they evidently regarded as too graphic, too upsetting. What should be seen, however, is that both Euripides and Sergio Leone attempt to confront the viewer, the audience, with the realities of violence, including the murder of the young and the helpless.

One dimension to the theme of women and war that Euripides explores in *Hecuba* is that of revenge. After the fall of Troy, Hecuba, witness to the deaths of her husband and most of her sons and daughters, finds a small

---

26 Ibid. See also the discussion below pp. 134–5. While Diitrephes is the only Athenian identified by Thucydides, it seems likely that other Athenians would have been present as staff officers, Diitrephes' friends and entourage (cf. Thucydides 4.132.3).

comfort in the knowledge that her last surviving son, Polydorus, is safe in the care of a friend, Polymestor, king of Thracian Chersonese. Polyxena's body is still warm when servants find that of Polydorus, which is brought before Hecuba. The old ex-queen, now slave, is initially devastated but soon begins planning a wicked revenge: the deaths of Polymestor's sons and the kings' own blinding mutilation. Lured into a tent thinking he will find hidden Trojan treasures, Polymestor and his sons are attacked by Hecuba and her servants: the sons are killed before their father, who is then blinded.[27] By "normal" standards this would be a horrendous act, but after the slaughter at Troy it is one that seems almost trivial. Hecuba's revenge is surely employed by Euripides to demonstrate not only the cycle of violence and how it engenders retribution, but to show too that women as well as men, i.e. mankind itself, can become agents as well as victims in the vengeful cycle.

This vision that women are no less immune to violence, that it is something inherently human, has also been explored in Vietnam war literature. The clearest example is Tim O'Brien's story "The Sweetheart of the Son Tra Bong" in his novel *The Things They Carried*.[28] In this story Mark Fossie, a young soldier who misses his girlfriend, arranges for her to come to Vietnam for a visit. Mary Ann Bell, seventeen and just out of high school, arrives one day, much to the surprise and bewilderment of the other soldiers. Rat Kiley, Mark's buddy, says, in simple amazement, "That fucker."[29] Mary Ann soon settles in, amazed and entranced by the land: wandering the compound, she asks "how [does] a claymore work?," visiting the local ville or village, "like a cheerleader visiting the opposing team's locker room."[30] But then, just as with some grunts, "young and innocent," the "romantic bullshit" yields to reality and Mary Ann gets caught up in the war too. Rat Kiley, O'Brien's teller of the tale, describes how first Mary Ann wanted to learn about the M-16 — how to disassemble it and shoot it. Mark becomes worried and tries to get her to leave, but she resists finally telling him, "To tell the truth, I've never been happier in my whole life. Never."[31] Then she disappears. A frantic search turns up not a trace, but then she reappears just as suddenly in the company of some Green Berets returning from an ambush patrol. The young innocent girl is now a part of the war. The story reaches a climax when Mark goes to Mary Ann to try and get her back. She comes like a shadow before Mark:

> For a long while the girl gazed down at [him], almost blankly, and in candlelight her face had the composure of someone perfectly at

27 Euripides, *Hecuba* 1034–1119.
28 O'Brien 1990.
29 Ibid.: 105.
30 Ibid.: 106–7.
31 Ibid.: 110.

peace with herself. It took a few seconds, Rat said, to appreciate the full change. In part it was her eyes: utterly flat and indifferent. There was no emotion in her stare, no sense of the person behind it. But the grotesque part, he said, was her jewelry. At the girl's throat was a necklace of human tongues. Elongated and narrow, like pieces of blackened leather, the tongues were threaded along a length of copper wire, one overlapping the next, the tips curled upward as if caught in a final shrill syllable.[32]

Mary Ann then disappears, not to be seen again – only to be sensed, as she "had crossed to the other side. She was part of the land. She was dangerous. She was ready for the kill."[33]

Mary Ann, "Sweetheart of the Song Tra Bong", must be seen metaphorically, even surrealistically, like other pieces of Tim O'Brien's writing such as his novel *Going After Cacciato*. Oliver Stone's "Bunny" in *Platoon* talks about how much he "liked it" in Nam – "No one fucks with yah, you get to do what yah want" – and this sentiment is echoed by vet William Broyles and his men.[34] It is expected then that men will "like" war, but to imagine that the same might be possible for women is usually not regarded seriously. To accuse O'Brien, as some critics have, of portraying "women as more masculine than men, hence monstrous and unnatural," particularizes his ideas when in fact they should be universalized.[35] To think that women cannot become caught up in the same cycle of violence fails to comprehend the realities of war and how these can change utterly those who participate in them. O'Brien himself has rejected the antifeminist charge, claiming that in fact he is "utterly feminist." He argues that, if women served in ground combat as did men, then their experiences would duplicate men's, that "they would be going to the same dark side of the human hemisphere, the dark side of the moon, the dark side of their own psyches."[36] O'Brien's account of Mary Ann is not simply antifeminist or a projection of his traumatized wartime experiences, and to interpret the "Sweetheart of the Song Tra Bong" in this context is to misunderstand it.[37] Hecuba's vengeful killing of Polymestor's sons provides not only another example of "payback," but also a reminder that Euripides too could imagine that women as well as men could become not only the recipients of violence but also its agents.

One last dimension of the experience of women in war needs to be raised. This is the role of the nurse, who often witnesses sights far more terrible than many soldiers. Numerous accounts of combat nurses have emerged

2   Ibid.: 120.
33   Ibid.: 125.
34   Broyles 1990: 68–81.
35   Smith 1994: 32.
36   McNerney 1994: 21.
37   Smith 1994: 19.

from the Vietnam War, which demonstrate the trauma that women witnessed and how it left them suffering from PTSD, like the men they so often tended. Women in antiquity, however, would just as often have been in the same situation – treating sons, husbands, and fathers immediately, or nearly so, after battle. Imagine, for example, Athens after the battle of Marathon in 490 BC. There would have been four to five hundred households in which women would have been treating wounded soldiers, some with traumatic amputations, others with ugly belly wounds.[38] One injured Athenian we know of definitely is Epizelus, who was forever blind after the battle, even though he had not been physically wounded (see pp.63–4).[39] Like the Oedipus of drama, his traumatic loss of sight would have left him dependent on others, surely placing greater responsibility for his care on the women of his household. Lynda Van Devanter in her memoir *Home Before Morning* provides a clear idea of what this experience might have been like.[40] Assigned to the US Army's 71st Evacuation Hospital, Lynda Van Devanter saw the worst kind of casualties, those brought in directly from the field. Perhaps her worst memory is that of the young dying soldier she called "the Bleeder," because over the course of a night he slowly bled to death from massive head wounds despite heroic infusions of blood. This experience changed her despite "the deaths of so many others. I had lost an important part of myself. The Lynda I had known before the war was gone forever."[41]

Women, warriors, and survival

> You [Ajax] are my only safety. O my lord, remember even me.
> A man ought to remember if he has experienced any gentle
> thing. Kindness it is that brings forth kindness always.
> (Sophocles, *Ajax* 519–22)

Achilles' death to the "cowardly" Paris' arrow left Ajax, son of Telamon, as the greatest and most formidable warrior among the Greeks at Troy. Once

---

38 Herodotus 6.117.1 numbers the dead at 192. Generally the number of wounded is anywhere from three to four times greater than that of the dead. See Herodotus 6.114 on the amputation of Aeschylus' brother Cynegirus' hand, which probably caused his death.

39 Herodotus 6.117.2–3. How and Wells 1912: 2, 114 attribute Epizelus' blindness to a "vision" and find it strange that the supernatural force that Epizelus identified as the source of his loss of sight was on the Persian side. But in fact the blindness is induced by trauma and the supernatural explanation is itself a heroic myth to account for the loss.

40 Van Devanter 1983.

41 Ibid.: 193–9, at 199. Van Devanter's book was anticipated in her article in the *Los Angeles Times*, May 26, 1980, "In Memory of the Young Bleeder, the Children, the World …"

the funeral games had been celebrated, the moment came to award Achilles' divinely made armor to the most deserving warrior. Ajax believed that he was entitled to this as he ranked just after Achilles as a warrior and fighter. But Ajax was brawnier than he was clever and in the allotting of the armor he was outwitted by the wily Odysseus, who claimed the prize. Ajax did not take this defeat well. He perceived betrayal amid conspiracy and went berserk, slaughtering a herd of animals imagining them to be his enemies, the contemptible Odysseus and his chief allies, the Atreidae, Agamemnon and Menelaus.

In the Sophoclean tragedy of *Ajax*, the hero's madness is attributed to Athena, yet this should be seen as a theatrical device, a way of explaining to the audience what Ajax does. Additionally, "the responsibility for mental states or psychological change is often placed explicitly in the external compulsion or control of the divinities."[42] The Greeks, as other primitive peoples, would have credited the gods with those things they themselves could not understand, and chief among these would have been human psychology, explaining why people do the things they do.

In the case of Ajax we have more than enough reason to think that his emotions are compromised and that he believes himself to have been betrayed. In one passage Tecmessa, his concubine-wife, describes how Ajax has stifled his emotions, he will not cry out and he thinks that those who do are weaklings and cowards (*Ajax* 317–22).

> Then he cried out – long wails of shattering pain,
> Like none I ever heard from him before;
> He always used to say such cries were base,
> Marks of an abject spirit. His own way
> Was not to cry aloud in his distress,
> But low and muffled, like a roaring bull.

Elsewhere Ajax is cool and unresponsive to Tecmessa's overtures that evoke descriptions of other traumatized veterans as "ice men, that is men unable to communicate, who when driven to extremes will take their own lives."[43] Even allowing for cultural differences and formalities, it is clear from Tecmessa's sad remarks that Ajax fits this picture with astounding accuracy. Ajax, then, is to be seen as an ancient Greek equivalent to the traumatized veteran from Vietnam: numbed by extensive combat, then betrayed by his own comrades, who loses control and strikes out at whoever or whatever is nearest to hand. Afterwards nothing is left but suicide. This is Ajax.

After the slaughter of the innocent animals, Ajax came to himself (much like Clearchus following his dispute with Meno's men discussed above), and

---

42 Goldhill 1986: 181. For a similar example see Euripides, *Hippolytus* 26, and Aphrodite arousing Phaedra's passion for Hippolytus.
43 Matsakis 1996: 54–81.

attempted to make sense of his actions and to decide what to do. For a man like Ajax the options were few. He had dishonored himself and death seemed the only avenue open to him. But he also had a wife, Tecmessa, and their son Eurysaces. Tecmessa attempted to ease Ajax's mind, to help him overcome his acts and survive his trauma.

In a long soliloquy, Tecmessa makes an appeal to Ajax in an attempt to help him in his agonized state. She tells him that, abandoned through his death,

> That same day will see me outraged too, forcibly dragged by the Greeks, together with your boy, to lead a slave's life. And then some one of the lord class with a lashing word, will make his hateful comment: "There she is, Ajax's woman; he was the greatest man in the whole army. How enviable her life was then, and now how slavish."[44]

Tecmessa's words echo Hector's to Andromache's (Homer, *Iliad* 6. 455–59) on her fate following his death, and Tecmessa is probably thinking of herself here, should Ajax die. This may be seen in her next appeal, that Ajax should think of his parents and not abandon them to face old age unaided. She reminds him of his son, asking that he show pity, that he not abandon him to a guardian. She then returns to her own fate and, again like Andromache in the *Iliad*, reminds Ajax that he is all she has: "You are my safety" (*Ajax* 519). But as she continues it is clear that there are other issues at play, issues aimed at the wounded warrior and efforts to help him survive.

Tecmessa reminds Ajax that a man needs to remember kindnesses shown to him and that these should encourage reciprocal acts (520–22). Earlier Tecmessa had revealed to the chorus that she recognized the burdens weighing on Ajax's mind, and as she emphasizes the importance of kindnesses, she attempts to show Ajax that there is another way, that he does not have to yield further to the frenzy in his mind. In short, Tecmessa attempts to counsel Ajax much as a modern clinician or Vietnam wife would, trying to help him understand the crisis in which he is embroiled.

The chorus supports Tecmessa, urging Ajax to yield to her words. But Tecmessa is bound to fail as Ajax is already committed to an act – suicide – that will, in his mind at least, wipe away the stain of his dishonor. This is evident in Ajax's long speech to Eurysaces, in which he hopes the boy will have better luck than he did, that Teucer, Ajax's brother, will look after him, and that the boy should take his great shield to his grandfather Telamon (550–77). Finally, Ajax tells Tecmessa not to question further but rather to submit (586–7). He then goes to the death he seeks, one of the few deaths in Greek drama that occurred on stage (814–65).

44 Sophocles, *Ajax* 497–504.

It is poor Tecmessa, the wife who vainly tried to soothe her husband's mind, who finds Ajax dead, fallen on a sword given him by Hector. Tecmessa's response to Ajax's death is both self-centered, as she wonders aloud what her fate will now be, and loving. Her speech over his body is filled with compassion, as she says, "His death was a bitterer thing to me than sweet to them [i.e. Odysseus and others]; but for himself a happiness. For he won his great desire, the death he looked for" (966–8).

Tormented by his repressed emotions and betrayal, Ajax's trauma is beyond repair. Tecmessa attempts to help him find a way out, but the damage and shame are so deep for Ajax that no amount of pleading, reason, or counseling can budge him from his intended end. Tecmessa can neither retrieve Ajax's lost sense of honor nor deter him from the decision he has made. Plainly she is frustrated by her failure, and when she sees Ajax's corpse her reaction is one of peaceful sorrow. The exchange between Tecmessa and Ajax, the woman and the warrior, provides a point of comparison with the literature and reality of Vietnam wives and warriors too. Many of these Vietnam wives would not only recognize Tecmessa's dilemma but could also empathize with her.

One such wife is Kathy Wade, whose husband John served in Vietnam and was present and a participant at the My Lai massacre in March 1968. Their story, told brilliantly in Tim O'Brien's novel *In the Lake of the Woods*, reveals the costs of burying the past as well as imagining that nothing horrific that could occur in a war could change or even destroy relationships.[45] These are the postures that John and Kathy take which, in the end, destroy them both.

Throughout his life, John Wade had survived life's trauma by suppressing, burying deeply his experiences – whether his father's death as a boy or his actions in the massacre at My Lai.[46] At My Lai Wade had mostly watched, horrified, thinking "this is not madness, this is sin."[47] Disoriented and drawn into the slaughter, Wade had killed an old man with a hoe, and then later, startled by another GI, Wade had killed him too.[48] Not only the tragedy of My Lai but the entire Vietnam experience was obscured in his letters home to Kathy, then his girlfriend.[49] As discussed above, this sort of repression is by no means unusual – Hector says nothing to Andromache about the fighting around Troy. His silence can be found in hundreds of other men who will find anything else to discuss with their wives but the

45 O'Brien 1994.
46 Ibid.: 8, 11, 92, 154, 162, 196.
47 Ibid.: 107.
48 Ibid.: 109–10. It should be noted that what O'Brien describes is literary: only one American soldier, Herbert Carter, was wounded in the attack on My Lai (none were killed), and this was possibly self-inflicted so as to escape the carnage. Cf. Hersh 1970: 186, Bilton and Sim 1992: 133, 298–9.
49 Ibid:. 61.

violence and brutalities of war. When Wade returns home he marries Kathy, but the silence regarding the past continues. On one occasion, John tries to tell Kathy about Vietnam but her response is discouraging. She first responds by saying "it doesn't matter," and then, when he tries to push the conversation, she repeatedly changes the subject until he finally breaks off the discussion.[50] It might seem that Kathy is unconcerned with her lover's wartime experiences and oblivious to the trauma that John might have experienced in Vietnam. In fact Kathy Wade acts here as many other wives of combat veterans who, like Penelope, wish not to hear of the violence their lovers have been exposed to and, like Sam Gibbon's wife, would stop the stories if they could. Rather than uncaring, Kathy Wade's apparent rebuff is a loving gesture, one calculated to show that she loves her husband unconditionally.

The story of John and Kathy is fiction but the lives represented are real and could be replaced with the names of actual veterans and their wives. Among the "evidence" O'Brien cites for his novel's storyline is the death of Vietnam vet Robert T'Souvas, a participant in the My Lai massacre, in 1988. After Vietnam, T'Souvas turned to drugs and alcohol to forget what he had done with the rest of the men of Charlie Company. T'Souvas' wife remained with him during these years, and she too was gradually consumed by the violence, possibly killing him finally in a drug induced haze.[51] Numerous other lives and case studies depicted in Aphrodite Matsakis' *Vietnam Wives* illustrate the problems – alcohol and drug abuse, survivor's guilt, and the lingering effects of battlefield trauma – that thousands of women faced since their husbands returned from Vietnam. During the course of this investigation I discussed these life realities with many survivors, the men and women who experienced the sort of trauma related in Sophocles' *Ajax* and Tim O'Brien's *In the Lake of the Woods*. One such case is that of Toni and Bill who experienced the worst year of fighting in Vietnam, 1967–8.

Bill served as a platoon leader, a young lieutenant, in an elite airborne unit of the US Army. Arriving in Vietnam in late December 1967 he experienced the Tet Offensive of January–February 1968, followed by nearly one hundred days of constant action, being hit by the enemy every day. During this time he experienced the deaths of many friends, both within his own platoon as well as fellow officers he had trained with in the US. Typically, as with Hector, little if any of this experience and anguish was ever communicated to Toni, then his fiancée, who spent the year waiting and trying to do something to help by serving with various social organizations. Bill returned home and immediately tried to forget the past year. While in Vietnam he

---

50 Ibid.: 73–4.
51 Ibid.: 261–2. The circumstances of T'Souvas' death were never made clear. For full treatment of his life after Vietnam and his problems in living with the legacy of My Lai, see Bilton and Sim 1992: 358–61.

drank heavily and this continued at an almost suicidal pace and is clearly an effort to erase the past. Nothing was said about Vietnam, and attempts by friends, family, acquaintances to inquire were met by steely eyes and a frozen demeanor that quickly discouraged the attempt. In short, Bill was bent on a self-destructive course and might well have ended up another Vietnam statistic had Toni not persevered and helped him pull through. The nature of her experience is echoed in the words Patience Mason, who speaking from her own experience, describes,

> [finding] yourself crying in corners and vowing that his buddies may have died on him in Vietnam, the brass may have turned its collective back on him, but you will never desert him. He needs you. Whether he can say it or not, whether he can act like it or not, he needs you.[52]

Despite his doubts, Toni and Bill married, raised a family and today enjoy a productive life. The way has not always been easy. Bill was always, as Aphrodite Matsakis describes of other Vietnam veterans, the "ice man," unemotional even when close friends and family died, much to the distress of his children. As his children grew and learned that their father had served in Vietnam and wanted to talk to him about it, he refused to talk. Happily this relationship is changing. As a result of many discussions Bill can talk about Vietnam, remembering things that only a couple of years ago he thought had been forgotten. This remembrance includes his children, who are beginning to learn about their father's Vietnam experience.

Historically, women have borne a terrible burden in war: bearing the sons who will so often fight and die, married to men who will do the same. Frequently they bear the worst of war's horrors as depicted, for example, in Euripides' *The Trojan Women*, and the novels of Larry Heinemann, particularly *Close Quarters*. But as Euripides and Tim O'Brien make clear, women as well as men can respond violently, too, and become agents of violence as well as victims.

52 Mason 1990: 12.

6

WAR, VIOLENCE, AND THE
OTHER

> All who survived ... were stunned and slaughtered, boned
> with broken oars and splintered wrecks: lamentations, cries
> possessed the open sea ...
>
> (Aeschylus, *The Persians* 423–7)

In his drama *The Persians*, Aeschylus provides eyewitness testimony to the
great battles of the Persian Wars, especially the fighting around Salamis
(480 BC), in which he surely participated. His drama is also remarkable for
its portrayal of the very people he and his contemporaries battled against, a
portrayal that is surprising perhaps for the empathy it conveys to the reader.
Additionally, Aeschylus' play reveals that, just as for present-day societies,
the ancient Greeks were confronted by the *Other* and attempted to define and
understand the nature of this relationship. Understandably perhaps, the
perspective taken is Greek.

Socrates' remark on his good fortune in not being born beast, woman, or
barbarian demonstrates the Greek propensity to conceive relationships in
terms of opposites (Diogenes Laertius 1.33). Greek writers of the classical
era, including the historian Herodotus, were interested in the cultures and
societies around them and provided materials that today would be considered as ethnohistory or cultural anthropology. Herodotus also provided some
interesting details on the cultural attitudes of non-Greeks such as the
Egyptians. He tells how the Egyptians used the head of a sacrificial animal
as a scapegoat of sorts, loaded it with curses and then discarded it – unless
there were Greeks present to whom it would be sold![1] Other Greek historians, Xenophon in the early fourth century BC and the historians of
Alexander's campaign in Asia, provide additional information on these
Greek–*Other* relationships.[2] The Greeks knew of the Ethiopians, too, a

---

1   Herodotus 2.39.
2   A number of the so-called "Alexander" historians, i.e. Aristobulus, Ptolemy, Chares of
    Mitylene, were later used by the historian Arrian (second century AD) to write his
    history of Alexander's *Anabasis*, or campaign across the Persian Empire and to the Indus
    River. For a discussion of these see e.g. Bosworth 1988.

people as remote from them geographically as they were different in appearance.

The nature of these attributions or names should be emphasized. The labels used, "Greek," "Persian," "Egyptian," "Ethiopian," are based upon an ethnic concept (*ethnos*, a tribe or people) and not one of race. This shows that the Greeks, and other ancient civilizations, defined people according to their family-kinship descent rather than their exterior or "racial" characteristics, e.g. the texture of their hair, skin color, or the shape of the nose. True, they might describe how people looked. For example the Greeks used the same word, *simos*, pug-nosed, to describe both Scythians and Ethiopians, two peoples who lived far apart. In an era without photographs, the adoption of physical features to identify groups should be accepted at "face value" rather than as an example of ancient racial theory. Martin Bernal asserted such a view in his controversial study *Black Athena*, where he injected, one might say, infected, the ancient world with the disease of twentieth-century racism.[3] Such views and their assertion lack a place in the study of ancient Mediterranean societies.

American classicist Frank Snowden argues that obvious physical and cultural differences between Greek and non-Greek led to a heightened awareness of the *Other*. Some Greeks regarded "barbarians," i.e. non-Greeks, as inferiors, while others admired or took interest in non-Greek peoples. In the classical era, then, there was no unanimity of opinion. The Sophists favored the elimination of common divisions among people and support for a community of all mankind. Plato and Aristotle, however, opposed this view and advocated a distinction between Greeks and "barbarians" that justified war (Plato) and enslavement of non-Greeks (Aristotle). The actions and policies of Aristotle's student Alexander the Great suggest that he did not share his teacher's visions.[4] In the Hellenistic era (323–31 BC), intellectuals such as Eratosthenes and Zeno argued for cultural distinction over ethnic, elaborated by a definition of virtue and vice that could imagine Greeks as bad and barbarians as refined.[5] This debate among the Greeks, presented here in summarized form, is actually of considerable contemporary relevance. Today in the US, for example, there are many intellectuals as well as lay persons who argue that it is culture that matters and not race. If one is open-minded and observant to the ways of the world, more than enough examples of the accuracy of this viewpoint will be found.

The insights of the Greeks become even more striking when compared with present-day societies. Especially in modern America and even in

3   Bernal 1987–91. For criticism of his views see Tritle 1996.
4   On Alexander and his conquest of the East, see Bosworth 1996: 138–42 and Heckel 1997: 213–14. I would argue that the atrocities committed while Alexander was campaigning in the East resulted from the resistance encountered there and not any sort of racial policies or programs.
5   Snowden 1970: 169–71.

Europe, race and racism exert a powerful and profound influence. In the case of the US, the ideology of race has shaped societal attitudes generally. Race has also been directly responsible for the nature of immigration laws in the early twentieth century, the internment of Japanese-Americans during World War II, and the creation of ideas and attitudes of Americans serving in Vietnam. Yet it must be recognized too that race is a state of mind: how else can one explain the marriages between American servicemen of all racial origins and Vietnamese? How can one account for the use of racial epithets by Americans of *all* cultural backgrounds to describe the Vietnamese? Similar attitudes may be found among the Greeks and their views on race and the *Other*. Just as a number of Americans in Vietnam were able to rise above the issue of race, so too among the Greeks there were individuals who rose above their surroundings and treated people as individuals rather than as members of a specified, and stigmatized, group. These issues, as well as questions regarding Vietnamese attitudes toward Americans, will provide various points of comparison with the Greeks.

Greeks and Trojans, Persians and *Others*

> I am your friend and host in the heart of Argos; you are mine
> in Lykia, when I come to your country. Let us avoid each
> other's spears ...
>
> (Homer, *Iliad* 6.224–5)

In the midst of battle at Troy two heroes, Diomedes a Greek and Sarpedon a Trojan ally from Lycia, break away from the fighting to identify themselves and their lineages. This passage, which surely strikes modern readers as a bit odd, reveals actually the nature of heroic warfare, which was remarkably similar to this: formal, ritualistic, and accompanied by a bit of showing off (probably less rather than more). The dialogue also reveals that the Greeks and Trojans in Homer's *Iliad* are virtually the same people culturally and socially. Diomedes and Sarpedon, from homelands far distant from one another, discover their ties of *xenia* or guest-friendship, inherited and binding. Elsewhere it is clear that the Greeks and Trojans recognized the same gods, cults, and rituals. But in the century following the *Iliad*'s composition (c. 750–700 BC) there appears an emerging perception that the Trojans really were different, that they were Asians or Phrygians, that they were the *Other*.[6]

The Asianness of the Trojans and their connection to the Persians is the

---

6　Hall 1988: 15–18 refers to this "barbarization" of the Trojans which had long been ascribed to Aeschylus. On the basis of a reading in the poet Alcaeus (42.15), she argues that this process may have started already in the sixth century BC.

theme that begins the opening chapters of Herodotus' *Histories*, in which he outlines the causes for hostility between the Greeks and the barbarians, i.e. the Persians and Phoenicians. Herodotus attributes the conflict first to the Phoenician kidnapping of Io, daughter of King Inarchus of Argos (*Histories* 1.1), which provoked in turn a Greek response, the kidnapping of the Phoenician king of Tyre's daughter. Finally, though certainly not least, Paris ran off to Troy with Helen, wife of Menelaus of Sparta. A Greek army chased after him and Troy fell (1.2–3).

Herodotus' report is but a preface to his treatment of the Lydian kingdom that exerted such profound influence (e.g. coinage, the political concept of tyranny) upon the Greeks during the archaic era.[7] Interestingly, he credits certain Persian authorities for the origins of the conflict between Greeks and Persians. Herodotus' clear reference to his authorities, however, has been rejected because his account seems such a fundamentally Hellenic attempt to rationalize and otherwise order an event the causes of which were not really known.[8] This view, however, should not be pushed to extreme limits. The ease with which Herodotus could move between Greek and non-Greek societies, converse with people far and wide, suggests that hellenized Persians could have as easily conceived of these explanations as the Greeks. To dismiss outright any Persian contribution seems both unsound and unwarranted. The clash, however, of Greek and Persian had already occurred a quarter of a century earlier in the Persian Wars (490, 480–479 BC). These events Aeschylus related with apparent sympathy and passion, though also with a new recognition for the enemy, the *Other*.

Aeschylus' *The Persians* appeared on stage in 472 BC, only seven years after the final defeat of Xerxes' invasion of Greece and the twin victories of Plataea and Mycale (479 BC). In some ways, however, these battles were anti-climactic in view of the struggle the previous year. During 480 BC had occurred the fall of the pass at Thermopylae and the death of the heroic Spartan king Leonidas, his three hundred Spartans and nearly another thousand men, mostly from the small city of Thespiae. This heroic defeat was avenged later the same year at Salamis, where the combined Greek fleet destroyed Xerxes' great armada.[9] Aeschylus depicts this desperate struggle and aftermath, the Battle of Plataea and the pursuit of the fleeing Persians homeward, in his great drama *The Persians*.

Quite rightly *The Persians* is a story that champions freedom over despotism, the rule of the many over the one. As Simon Goldhill has shown persuasively, *The Persians* both symbolizes the triumph of the Greek forces in a collective victory and represents the "subsumption of the individual into

---

7   Herodotus 1.6–56, 69–94.
8   See Fehling 1971: 50–7.
9   Events portrayed in heroic style by Herodotus 7–9.

the collectivity of the *polis* – a basic factor in fifth-century Athenian political ideology."[10] This political message is brought out forcefully and tersely, as in the chorus of Persian elders' reference to the Athenians as "slaves to none, nor are they subject" (*The Persians* 243). Eighty years later this view still inspired the Greeks, as Xenophon urged the surrounded mercenaries of Cyrus' army to uphold their ancestors' victories and to fight the Persians whom their ancestors had beaten (*Anabasis* 3.2.3–4). Aeschylus contrasts the freedom of the Greeks with the utter dominance of Xerxes, who ruled as "the equal of god" and sovereign ruler even if he failed in battle (*The Persians* 80, 212–14). *The Persians* is also presented as the story of the fate of unbridled arrogance, of how the gods will bring down those who think themselves beyond account (166–8, 345–8). Patriotism aside, however, Aeschylus' drama is also a study in defeat of one's enemy – a study that can only be regarded as one of great sympathy. Simon Goldhill has called attention to this issue, too, and how explanation of Aeschylus' sympathy for his former enemy has remained unexplored. The key here, as noted earlier, lies in Aeschylus' own survival of the trauma of the Persian Wars he so dramatically depicts.

The chorus of Persian elders, it has been argued, "can scarcely be said simply to represent the 'feelings of the spectators.'"[11] The Persian herald, it has also been argued, cannot represent the feelings of the audience either. Yet in most of the passages that display sympathy for the Persians, it is either the chorus or the herald that speaks. It seems possible for the play to have any meaning only if the audience is able to share the experience on stage with something out of their own lives. In the case of the Athenian audience and Aeschylus' *The Persians*, this shared experience can only result from the trauma of war, which Aeschylus and virtually all the men of military age in the audience could understand.

Aeschylus had fought in all the major battles of the Persian Wars and had lost his closest male relative, his brother Cynegirus, in the first battle with the Persians at Marathon (490 BC).[12] This experience Aeschylus related in *The Persians* with its graphic descriptions of what happened on the day of Salamis.

> But when the narrows choked them, and rescue hopeless,
> Smitten by prows, their bronze jaws gaping,
> Shattered entire was our fleet of oars.

10 Goldhill 1988: 190–1.
11 Goldhill 1986: 268.
12 Evidence for Aeschylus' service at Marathon comes from Pausanias 1.21.2 and Athenaeus 627c; the power of the testimony in *The Persians* argues for eyewitness report, and as Aeschylus was still marginally of military age in 480/79 BC (i.e. forty-five or forty-six), there should be little doubt that he fought somewhere in or around Salamis. See further Lefkowitz 1981: 69. On Cynegirus' death, see p. 11.

> The Grecian warships, calculating, dashed
> Round, and encircled us; ships showed their belly:
> No longer could we see the water, charged
> With ships' wrecks and men's blood.
> Corpses glutted beaches and rocks.
> Every warship urged its own anarchic
> Rout; all who survived that expedition,
> Like mackerel or some other catch of fish,
> Were stunned and slaughtered, boned with broken oars
> And splintered wrecks: lamentations, cries
> Possessed the open sea, until the black
> Eye of evening hushed them. The sum
> Of our troubles, even if I should rehearse them
> For ten days, I could not exhaust. Rest
> Content: never in a single day
> So great a number died.[13]

But the action at sea was only one scene of death that day. Aeschylus also relates the Athenian capture of the small island of Psytteleia in the middle of the Saronic Gulf, which the Persians had taken before the battle, possibly to secure a refuge for damaged ships and shipwrecked sailors. The fight here, led by the Athenian commander Aristeides, must have been fierce if Aeschylus' words are any guide.[14]

> For when a god gave Greeks
> The glory, that very day, fenced in bronze
> They leaped ashore, and drew the circle tight
> At every point: mewed up, we could not turn.
> Many rattled to the ground,
> Whom stones had felled, and arrows, shot by bowstring,
> Others killed; and in a final rush,
> The end: they hacked, mangled their wretched limbs
> Until the life of all was gone.[15]

The carnage at Salamis, consisting of hundreds of ships and thousands of men, continued the next year with the great battle at Plataea, "the sacrificial cake of clotted gore made at Plataea by Dorian spear,"[16] where the Persian army was destroyed. The remnants fled north in complete disarray: "some,

---

13 Aeschylus, *The Persians* 413–32.
14 Lattimore 1943: 88 unnecessarily minimizes what happened here. While the struggle might not have made a difference in the battle's outcome, for those who fought here it was a life and death struggle, which is exactly the tone of Aeschylus' words.
15 Aeschylus, *The Persians* 453–63.
16 Aeschylus, *The Persians* 816–17.

in want of precious water, were wracked with thirst ... Thessaly received us, wanting: there most died in hunger and thirst."[17]

The result, as the chorus tells, was "nations wail their native sons, who by Xerxes stuffed up hell" (*The Persians* 921–2). Aeschylus' poetic descriptions should not be regarded as convention or literary flourish, but rather as an attempt to recreate as authentically as he could the terror of these events. Herodotus, who wrote some twenty-five years later, tells the story in much the same way, which suggests that there was little disagreement among the Greeks as to the fate of the Persians.[18]

Absent from the discussions of Aeschylus' play *The Persians* is any consideration of the play from the perspective of the survivor, and how that influences the nature of the historical record and the underlying culture.[19] These points have been noted earlier in the Introduction, but it is useful to review them. Survivors will, on account of their experiences, understand events differently and convey a view of those events at variance with those who have not shared the experience. Survivors then sometimes pose an embarrassment to history or other forms of memory as the nature of their individual experiences may not coincide with the general view of the past or its recollection. At the same time, and perhaps somewhat contradictorily, survivors of violence and violent events are or become figures of cultural authority and values. Aeschylus is himself an excellent example of this conversion from survivor of violence to authority figure whose ideas influence his culture and society.

To see Aeschylus, then, as merely sympathetic or empathetic to his Persian enemies only begins to make sense of the nuances of the relationship. To say that Aeschylus has "mythologized" Salamis, as Paul Cartledge has done, only hints at what Aeschylus is about in this drama.[20] A reexamination of the play from the viewpoint of a survivor of violence, one whose sensibilities have been significantly enlarged and who breaks with accepted norms and expresses himself in truly radical, perhaps even revolutionary fashion, will give a new reading to this drama.

---

17 Aeschylus, *The Persians* 482–91.

18 Cf. Herodotus 8.85–94 (Battle of Salamis), 8.95 (the fight on Psytteleia), 9.69–70 (Battle of Plataea), and 9.89 (the Persian rout through northern Greece). While I would generally agree with Goldhill 1988: 189 that *The Persians* is not a "history" play, its descriptions of the fighting are so powerful and graphic that eyewitness testimony must provide the drama's basis.

19 Hall 1996 is the most recent discussion of *The Persians*. While I would not reject all of the "feminizing 'Other'" arguments that Hall advances, both here and in Hall 1993, I would argue that Aeschylus, the survivor of a traumatic event, should take precedence over Aeschylus' aim to "feminize Asia." For similar criticisms see Sommerstein 1998: 211–12.

20 Cartledge 1997: 25. Pelling 1997:1–2 also attempts to minimize the authenticity of Aeschylus' account of Salamis. Sommerstein 1996: 81–3 appears to take Aeschylus' account at face value.

Other writers and poets who experienced violence turned to writing to express the traumatic shock of the combat experience. The generation of poets forged from the cauldron of World War I – Robert Graves, Wilfred Owen, and Siegfried Sassoon, for example – shattered conventional literary forms with their searing indictment of what befell them on the Western Front.[21] These include Owen's "Dulce et Decorum Est":

> My friend, you would not tell with such high zest
> To children ardent for some desperate glory,
> The old Lie: Dulce et decorum est
> Pro patria mori.[22]

The glamor of war is also stripped away in Siegfried Sassoon's "Died of Wounds":

> I wondered where he'd been; then heard him shout,
> "They snipe like hell! O Dickie, don't go out" …
> I fell asleep … Next morning he was dead;
> And some Slight Wound lay smiling on the bed.[23]

And in much the same way Vietnam War poet W.D. Ehrhart has written in "Fragment: The General's War":

> Paper orders passed down and executed;
> Straggling back in plum-colored rags,
> One legged, in slings, on stretchers,
> In green plastic bags,
> With stubbled faces
> And gaunt eyes hung in sockets;
> Returned to paper
> For some general to read about
> And pin a medal to.[24]

Just as these poems convey the violence and trauma of battle, so too does the poetry of Aeschylus' *The Persians* reveal the reality of Salamis and Plataea. Edith Hall seems reluctant to recognize the degree to which this experience influenced Aeschylus. She refers to Aeschylus as "almost certainly" a war veteran, unnecessarily qualifying his status as if unwilling to accept that such an experience as this could have any impact.[25] She misses

---

21 On the implications of these events for modern poetry see A. Zagajewski, "The Shabby and the Sublime," *The New Republic* April 5, 1999: 32–7.
22 Owen 1973: ll. 25–9. The concluding line of Owen's poem is from Horace, *Odes* 3.2.13, and means "It is sweet and proper to die for your country."
23 Sassoon 1968: ll. 9–12.
24 Ehrhart in Rottmann *et al.* 1972: 25.
25 Hall 1996: 14.

the very real importance of Aeschylus' survival of a traumatic event and all that it entails. It is this experience that informs the reality of scenes that Aeschylus described. Hall refers briefly to Aeschylus' use of *kreokopein* ("to cut meat") in describing the slaughter of the Persians on Psytteleia (*The Persians* 453–63), a phrase that calls to mind James Jones's graphic description in *The Thin Red Line* of the dead and amputated limbs as only "meat."[26] Hall refers to Aeschylus' choice of language as "shockingly bald" – but to whom?[27] To a veteran of infantry fighting this is in fact what happens, and both Aeschylus and his audience of veterans knew it. Similar imagery comes in Aeschylus' description of the Persian and Phoenician sailors stunned and slaughtered, boned with oars (and anything else near at hand) at Salamis. These were memories, and nightmares too I would imagine, lurking still in the minds of his audience. Through Aeschylus' poetry these survivors returned to that day and would have remembered those Persians and *Others* – Egyptians, Phoenicians – with whom they battled and so frequently killed.

Aeschylus' ability to take his fellow warriors back to the very day of Salamis resonates in the discussion surrounding Steven Spielberg's film *Saving Private Ryan* (1998) and before that Oliver Stone's *Platoon* (1987). Both films evoked a tremendous response in the US, where veterans of the Normandy invasion and Vietnam veterans, many for the first time, were able to tell their stories. While neither film is "history," they do succeed in conveying something of the reality of the events they depict, and this is what Aeschylus does in *The Persians*. The experiences of these veterans and those of Aeschylus and the Athenians in *The Persians* coincide remarkably. This is true not only in the telling of the survivors' stories, but also in terms of the ownership of memory. Edith Hall refers to Richmond Lattimore's argument that *The Persians* had distorted the past by omitting the collaborative nature of the pan-Hellenic defense of Greece against the Persians.[28] In the aftermath of the opening of *Saving Private Ryan* in Europe in the fall of 1998, the reactions of many to the film were almost identical to Lattimore's criticism of *The Persians* ... the Americans had cut the Europeans out of history.[29] While both criticisms are understandable, they also misunderstand what the playwright and the director are attempting to unravel: the nature of violence and trauma, the effects of these on the survivor.

Aeschylus knew, as do so many others who have fought, that so long as you are fighting, you have only one idea in your mind – survival. Your survival, and after that your friends' around you, comprise the world that you know. What happens three hundred yards away, not to mention miles

---

26 Jones 1962: 5, 44, 373, 446 (the last reference is to a Japanese soldier cannibalized by other Japanese, the body utilized literally as "meat").
27 Hall 1996: 142.
28 Ibid.: 11, following Lattimore 1943: 90–3.
29 Noted in a CNN European program, October 1998.

away, is essentially unknown and irrelevant. This is the so-called "fog of battle," an idea made well known by military historian John Keegan. As for the enemy, he is to be killed, and it does not really matter how this is done. But after the fighting is over, it becomes possible to look back and see that your enemies were not that much different than you, just other men doing the same thing ... trying to survive.

This explains Aeschylus' sympathy for his old enemies the Persians. This point has troubled numerous critics. Simon Goldhill claims that, "it is difficult to imagine anything similar [i.e. to Aeschylus' *The Persians*] in the years following the First or Second World War."[30] Edith Hall suggests that it was probably not Aeschylus' priority to give the Persians a "sympathetic hearing" and points to his brother's death at Marathon as a rationalization of his disdain for Persian suffering.[31] Both Goldhill and Hall ignore the nature of the survivor's experience. In his own case, when Aeschylus wrote *The Persians* in 472 BC, he would have been about fifty-three years old and eight years removed from Salamis, eighteen from Marathon. At this point in his life he was able to reflect on what he had experienced. In this respect, his reflections on the terrible deaths of the Persians seem remarkably like those of Robert Graves and Siegfried Sassoon.[32] Both had survived years in the trenches, yet even during the war and immediately after could see sympathetically the German soldiers with whom they fought so bitterly. In February 1918 in his poem "Remorse" (ll. 6–14) Sassoon could wonder,

> "Could anything be worse than this?" – he wonders,
> Remembering how he saw those Germans run,
> Screaming for mercy among the stumps of trees:
> Green-faced, they dodged and darted: there was one
> Livid with terror, clutching at his knees ...
> Our chaps were sticking 'em like pigs ... "O hell!"
> He thought ... "there's things in war one dare not tell
> Poor father sitting safe at home, who reads
> Of dying heroes and their deathless deeds."

And nine months later at the end of the war, Sassoon could write in "Reconciliation,"

> When you are standing at your hero's grave,
> Or near some homeless village where he died,
> Remember, through your heart's rekindling pride,
> The German soldiers who were loyal and brave.

---

30 Goldhill 1988: 193.
31 Hall 1996: 3.
32 Graves 1929: 293–4.

Men fought like brutes; and hideous things were done;
And you have nourished hatred harsh and blind.
But in that Golgotha perhaps you'll find
The mothers of the men who killed your son.[33]

Some American writers of the Vietnam Experience have written similarly moving accounts of their enemies, such as Tim O'Brien's story of "The Man I Killed" that will be examined later. Real-life expressions of reconciliation have come from other Vietnam veterans. Some have traveled to Vietnam and met their former enemies and shared memories and meals. The current US ambassador to Vietnam, Pete Peterson, a prisoner of war in Hanoi, married a Vietnamese woman in Hanoi in May 1998 and the occasion was perhaps the most significant event to occur between the two countries since the end of the Vietnam War in 1975. Other US veterans have gone to assist the Vietnamese in locating the mass graves of Vietnamese soldiers killed by Americans and then buried afterwards. Vietnamese leaders and clergy were then able to honor these dead with the appropriate religious rites and observances. In these acts, memory of the *Self* and *Other* clearly intersect and in doing so bring both closer together.

So Aeschylus' sympathetic portrait of the Persians knows many parallels. In the case of the Persians, he can still consider them "slaves" and ruled by a despot, and make a statement about the superiority of the Hellenic political order. He can offer a view on the reasons for the failure of such a massive military undertaking: that the gods deceived Xerxes and doomed him to failure; that it was the Greeks united as one who were greater than the Persian many. At the same time, however, it remains possible to see the humanity of the Persian enemy and to understand him on those terms. It is this, I would argue, that explains the "Asia unmanned" theme that Hall has discussed. When Aeschylus refers to an "emptiness of men" in Asia (*The Persians* 166) and Persian wives "manless" (289), he is referring to the realities of the violence of war and its human toll. These descriptions and pathetic pictures of the battles of the Persian Wars evoke a sympathetic portrayal of the fate of the Persians who invaded Greece.[34] Aeschylus aims at this theme in *The Persians*: an understanding that may actually transcend "sympathy"; it is more like realizing that the differences separating enemies are imaginary, that "friend" and "enemy" are only labels, that the *Other* is really *Self*.

Herodotus, who wrote after Aeschylus and the generation of "Marathon-

33 Sassoon 1983: 136.
34 I would accept many of Hall's observations (e.g. Hall 1993: 118–21) regarding this play, but in some instances, feminist literary theory gets the better of her, as in pp. 126–7 and the argument for feminine seduction. Here Aeschylus would seem to be reflecting on the agony of young widows grieving for their dead husbands. This strikes me as a very human thing, an act of sympathy.

fighters," as Aristophanes called them, provides extensive information regarding the Persians and their empire. He relates details on their origins and culture and provides a history of their expansion from a small tribe to the dominant power in the Near East. His account of the clash with the Greeks is detailed and eloquently told. It is also a history that is very "Hellenic," one that interprets events from a Greek perspective. For example, the famous "Constitutional Debate" that Herodotus attributes to the Persian nobles Darius, Otanes, and Megabyzus following the end of Cyrus the Great's dynasty is surely influenced, despite Herodotus' contrary assertions, by political events in Athens in the years before Herodotus wrote (3.80–83).

The Herodotean account of the Persians and other Western Asiatic peoples seems free of "racism," bias, or prejudice. The Persians are in some contexts referred to as "barbarian," a word that can bear a number of meanings depending on the context, just as, for example, the intonation of the voice can convey a variety of meanings. Herodotus, however, had spent much time in the company of Western Asiatic peoples, and his account offers a sympathetic portrait, one that suggests in the mid-fifth century BC, Persians and 'Others' were not always marked by negative connotations. As evidence of this, Herodotus ascribes acts of cruelty and brutality to both Greeks and Persians. Two incidents from the end of his *Histories* dealing with the aftermath of Xerxes' failed campaign into Greece show this clearly. On the Greek side, Xanthippus (father of Pericles the Athenian statesman) crucified the Persian governor Artaÿctes, who in dying watched his son stoned to death (*Histories* 9.120.3). On the Persian side, Xerxes, his advances refused by a noble's wife, retaliated by ordering her to be horribly mutilated (9.107–13, at 112).

Of even greater interest perhaps is Xenophon's gripping account of the "march up country" of the Greek mercenaries left stranded in the Persian Empire after the death of their employer, the Persian prince Cyrus. As translator Rex Warner observed, the *Anabasis* is valuable, as "unlike most of classical literature [it is] an account of the day-to-day life of ordinary men and soldiers."[35] It is not "ideal," like the work of a philosopher, or "dramatic" like that of a poet. It is in fact about "real" people in a stressful and dangerous position, told by a great writer with a flair for bringing the everyday realities of an army on the march to life.

In the course of his narrative Xenophon refers to the Persians and the other peoples encountered by the Greeks as they marched through the interior of Asia. Xenophon generally refers to the Persians as such, but when referring to the non-Persian peoples he adopts the usual Greek term of *barbaros* to identify them generically.[36] This suggests that Xenophon made a

---

35 Warner 1946: 11–13.

twofold distinction: Greek–Persian, Greek–Barbarian. The latter distinction is not so much a pejorative judgment as it is a qualitative one: barbarians were generally people who lacked the same sort of civilized accomplishments as the Greeks and Persians and were seen as "primitive" peoples. Xenophon's reason for this judgment probably comes from the march during which the Greeks encountered a number of different peoples with some rather exotic customs. There were the Chalybes, who decapitated the corpses of their enemies and then carried the heads around singing to them (*Anabasis* 4.7.16)! The Mossynoici practiced unusual sexual relations by Greek standards, having sexual intercourse in public, and attempted to introduce this custom to the women traveling with the Greek army (5.4.3–4). But perhaps Xenophon's most telling and poignant account comes in his report of the arrival of the Greeks in the land of the Taochi. Here the Greeks were pushing their way homeward to the sea, but the Taochi were in the way. The Taochi, thinking themselves to be the object of a foreign invasion, resisted. The Greeks fought back and, with their determination and skills, prevailed after a hard fight. At this point Xenophon tells of,

> a terrible spectacle. The women threw their children down from the rocks and then threw themselves after them, and the men did the same. While this was going on Aeneas of Stymphalus, a captain, saw one of them, who was wearing a fine garment, running to throw himself down, and he caught hold of him in order to stop him; but the man dragged him with him and they both went hurtling down over the rocks and were killed.
>
> (*Anabasis* 4.7.13–14)

Xenophon emphasizes that this was "a terrible spectacle," and clearly others thought so too. Aeneas, who must have been an able and brave soldier to hold his rank, was similarly moved by the sight of this mass suicide and attempted to stop it. Cynics might think that there is no compassion here and that Aeneas acted out of greed, perhaps to get the "fine garment" that Xenophon describes. In this case, however, inaction would seem the simpler option. If Aeneas really wanted the clothes only, all he had to do was wait, climb down the height and strip the body. Xenophon's unadorned description of "a terrible spectacle" argues that Aeneas' act was spontaneous and impelled by humanitarian considerations. This brief incident about these Greek soldiers marching and fighting their way through the wilds of Asia Minor to return home tells much. While Xenophon, Aeneas, and their fellow Greeks did encounter peoples of certainly non-Greek culture, they did not automatically despise them. Rather as Aeneas' selflessness shows,

36 Cf. Xenophon, *Anabasis* 1.8.29 (Persian) and 2.5.42 (barbarian). For discussion see Hirsch 1985: 3–4.

they responded to them as fellow human beings, perhaps, as in the case of the Mossynoici, people with strange habits, but as people all the same.

At the beginning of this chapter, it was discussed how the Greek perception of the Trojans evolved from the time of the *Iliad*'s and the *Odyssey*'s composition to the mid-fifth century BC when the Trojans came to be regarded as both "Oriental" and *Other*. Fifth-century drama makes clear the ambiguities regarding the *Other* during this era. During the crisis of the Peloponnesian War, however, such brutality would be practiced by the Greeks that the notion of the barbarian's identity became quite confused. The sharpest example of this occurs in the "war plays" of Euripides that were staged ostensibly against the background of the Trojan War. Again, these plays need to be contextualized by the era and the events of the Peloponnesian War, and the steadily escalating level of violence that became commonplace.

In *The Trojan Women*, staged by Euripides with the background of a ruined city, the Greek herald Talthybius comes to tell Hecuba and the other Trojan women that the Greeks have debated the fate of young Astyanax, and that,

> The council has decreed ...
> They will kill your son. It is monstrous ...
> Odysseus. He urged it before the Greeks, and got his way.
> He said a hero's son could not be allowed to live.[37]

These lines, enclosed by shouts of grief from Andromache at the prospect of her son's death, show the "civilized" Greeks gathered together calmly and rationally discussing the murder of a child. Note Odysseus' rationalization that this act is necessary to defend against the prospect of a resurgent Troy seeking "payback" should Astyanax live. Talthybius, the reluctant herald, hates his mission and himself for his role in this affair, saying "I am not the man to do this. Some other without pity, not as I ashamed, should be herald of messages like this" (*The Trojan Women* 786–9). He cautions Andromache not to cry out or curse the Greeks "for fear the army, savage over some reckless word, forbid the child his burial" (*The Trojan Women* 734–6).

Talthybius, however, must submit to his "orders" and bring the decision of Astyanax' death. He may not like carrying out this order, but like so many other soldiers past and present, he has to. Clearly, he strains under the assignment which, as his remarks show, are subjecting him to stress which will surely create in him a certain amount of guilt and trauma for having assisted in the killing of a child. But in this scene Euripides reveals even more awareness of the ugly side to war. His description of the potential evil

37 Euripides, *The Trojan Women* 713, 719, 721, 724.

that lurks within an army coming out of a bitter fight – heartless and fully capable of committing any barbarity – shows that Greeks can commit the foulest of acts like any people, barbarians or *Others*.

Talthybius' role in *Hecuba* is remarkably similar to the role he plays in *The Trojan Women*. The Greeks have again killed a young non-combatant, this time Hecuba's daughter Polyxena (her lone surviving daughter, with the exception of Cassandra whose "possessed" mind excluded her from consideration). Again Talthybius is the bearer of bad news. He tells Hecuba of Polyxena's death and bids her to bury her daughter. Immediately Hecuba exclaims "O gods, my child! My poor child! Torn from my arms! Dead! Dead. All my children died with you" (*Hecuba* 512–14). Hecuba's on-stage lament of her daughter's death is no less powerful than Talthybius' description of her death to Hecuba: how she died bravely, offering up her half-naked body, holding up her neck to Neoptolemeus, Achilles' son, telling him to strike. This inversion of courage shown by Euripides – a young girl dying without fear before the passive soldiers – suggests that Euripides is calling into question all the accepted ideas about courage then current in Greek society: that women were not as brave as men.[38] But this is not so striking when possibly the most famous passage in the Euripidean corpus is remembered: Medea's bold claim that she would rather stand in battle three times than give birth once (*Medea* 250–51).[39] Together these passages are remarkably consistent.

As in *The Trojan Women*, Euripides is acutely aware of the potential for violence within armies. As Talthybius is about to depart, Hecuba tells him that the Greeks should not touch Polyxena's body:

> for in armies the size of this,
> men are prone to violence, sailors undisciplined,
> the mob gets out of hand, runs wild, worse
> than raging fire, while the man who stands apart
> is called a coward.[40]

Hecuba's remark is telling in several respects. First, it suggests feminine understanding of the dynamics of war and the behavior of men in battle. Skeptics may think that the playwright's gender is only transparent. Yet it is equally plausible that Hecuba's lines reflect women's understanding of the realities of war, realities which affected them so greatly, as Aristophanes noted also in his *Lysistrata*. Second, Hecuba's remark reveals the great potential for violence within an army, how the slightest provocation can incite

---

38 Croally 1994: 78 also notes that Polyxena's death marks a confusion of murder and sacrifice and points again to the breakdown of the model *Self* and *Other*.

39 Cf. also Euripides, *Helen* 1151–54 for a similar sentiment.

40 Euripides, *Hecuba* 606–9. Note also Aeschylus, *Seven Against Thebes* 601–9 for a similar sentiment.

retaliation, or "payback." Also revealed here is an explanation of why Talthybius brought word of Astyanax' death sentence – peer pressure. Euripides calls attention to this view in his remark that the man who stands apart is called a coward or weakling. This sort of pressure – the need to belong to the group and to submit to the decisions and acts of the group – makes many a man commit acts that he realizes are wrong but yet commits. In this analysis, then, Euripides shows himself to be an insightful judge of human character and motivation.

These reversals, the civilized Greeks committing brutal acts upon children and women, suggest that Euripides is posing some fundamental questions about not only "barbaric" and "civilized" conduct, but also the question of commission, i.e. can those who see themselves as *Self* ... the opposite of *Other* ... commit barbaric, reprehensible acts? The issues Euripides raises reflect not only an introspective analysis of the consequences of war and violence, but also a perception that somehow the Athenian community had been perverted by the violence of the Peloponnesian War and that it was guilty of committing some evil acts.[41] Euripides' reflections contrast with the US in Vietnam, which did not begin to approach Euripides' level of self-criticism until late. Moreover, unlike Euripides, US critics never seemed to realize that inversion had in fact taken place – that the US had become the "gook," that it was the *Other*.

Americans and the *Other*

Any living gook is a VC suspect.

Any dead gook *is* a VC.
(GI definition of the *Other*, Vietnam, 1967–)

The American intersection of *Self* and *Other* began with the European discovery of the New World and its inhabitants, was fueled by the importation of African slaves in the seventeenth century, and expanded with Chinese and Japanese immigration in the nineteenth and twentieth centuries. Long before Vietnam, Americans distinguished themselves, and not simply those representing non-white groups, but all those not belonging to the Anglo-Saxon norm – a reality often overlooked or ignored – with descriptive epithets, which if not initially pejorative, came oftentimes to acquire that meaning. Few of the young Americans who served in Vietnam would have known or understood much of this history and background. Most, however, would have been shaped by it in identifying those outside the norm, and so would have fallen into a ready acceptance of the Vietnamese as "gook,"

---

41 See also Croally 1994: 104–6, 110, 115, who argues similarly.

"dink," or one of the other epithets applied to them. In other cases too, when the racial epithet was not used, some Americans referred to the Vietnamese as "the little people," a term lacking the full force of the racial slur perhaps, but still carrying certain paternalistic nuances. J.P. Vann, senior adviser in the Mekong Delta in 1970–71, attempted to curb the practice but without much success.

For their part, the Vietnamese too defined and categorized Americans along racial lines. Black Americans were sometimes looked down upon because they were black, and white Americans were, because of body hair, considered a bit freakish on the one hand, and as one step from monkeys on the other. That said, Vietnamese racial attitudes were certainly much less pronounced than American and only rarely discernible. It should be noted too that not all Americans used the well-known descriptive labels for the Vietnamese, while others did so almost absent-mindedly and without animosity. In these cases it seems fair to wonder just how confirmed the racial attitudes were and if the language adopted did not stem from desires to fit in with the dominant view. Such analysis might well explain why some American GIs who normally would have reacted violently to being called "nigger," "whitey," or "spic" could themselves refer to the Vietnamese by the usual epithets – they simply wanted to be accepted and so conformed to the normative language in use.

It would be tedious to analyze American literature dealing with the "Other" because it is so easily classified – almost generically it refers to the Vietnamese as "gook," or some other epithet. A good example of this treatment is to be found in the novels of Larry Heinemann, *Close Quarters* and *Paco's Story*, both of which convey the brutally realistic perceptions and attitudes of American GIs toward the Vietnamese.[42] Simply they were "gooks": women were there to serve, especially as sex objects and suffer abuse – sexual, verbal, physical. To varying degrees this picture can be seen elsewhere in the literature.

One exception to this is Tim O'Brien's story, "The Man I Killed," which evokes sympathies similar to those of Aeschylus and his *Persians*.[43] The story is a simple one. A young Viet Cong soldier lies dead on a trail, ambushed and shot dead by American soldiers. O'Brien actually refers to the incident in several places, each time suggesting that a different man in his unit, including himself, was the killer. In this way O'Brien is able to universalize the experience so that its pathos is readily transferred. In "The Man I Killed," there are four "voices," two of which are actually silent – those of his killer, Tim, the victim, and two witnesses. The first voice is that of the first witness, Azar, whose response to the killing is enthusiastic amazement, perhaps in part because catching the enemy unawares was not easily done:

42 Especially in Heinemann 1977: 258–61, less so in Heinemann 1992.
43 O'Brien 1990: 139–44.

"Oh man, you fuckin' trashed the fucker," Azar said. "You scrambled his sorry self, look at that, you *did*, you laid him out like Shredded fuckin' Wheat."

Told by another GI to stop and go away, Azar exclaims he was only "saying the truth"; he leaves but not without making a final comment: "Rice Krispies, you know? On the dead test, this particular individual gets A-plus."[44]

Azar's exuberance over the kill reflects first his own youth – probably twenty (if that) and little educated, most likely not past high school. The enthusiasm, however, needs to be placed in context. In his memoir *A Rumor of War*, Philip Caputo tells how one day some of his men acted with particular brutality which he found shocking. One of his sergeants responded, "Before you leave here, Sir, you're going to learn that one of the most brutal things in the world is your average age nineteen year old American boy."[45] Caputo's men had much in common with American soldiers shooting Filipino rebels in 1899 and writing home how "picking off niggers in the water [was] more fun than a turkey shoot."[46] Yet it should not be imagined that such acts of violence were somehow reserved only for non-white *Others*. In his memoir as an infantry officer in World War II, Paul Fussell tells of the "Great Turkey Shoot." One day in the winter of 1944/45, men in his company came upon fifteen to twenty Germans in a deep crater, all wishing to surrender. Fussell tells how,

> perhaps some Germans hadn't surrendered fast enough and with suitable signs of contrition. ... Whatever the reason, the Great Turkey Shoot resulted. Laughing and howling, hoo-ha-ing and cowboy and good-old-boy yelling, our men exultantly shot into the crater until every single man down there was dead. A few tried to scale the sides, but there was no escape. If a body twitched or moved at all, it was shot again. ... the event was transformed into amusing narrative, told and retold over campfires all that winter. If it made you sick, you were not supposed to indicate.[47]

Azar's response, then, should not be imagined as unique or special. It conforms, in fact, to events and attitudes reaching back not only a generation but a century, if one were to include events such as the Sand Creek Massacre of 1864 and similar occurrences elsewhere in the history of US expansion across the western frontiers.

44 Ibid.: 140.
45 Caputo 1977: 129.
46 Miller 1982: 67.
47 Fussell 1996: 124.

The second witness' voice belongs to Kiowa, an American Indian and Tim's friend. His voice is one of consolation, saying "it's a *war*. The guy wasn't Heidi – he had a weapon, right?," then urging Tim, "You got to cut out that staring."[48] All of Kiowa's efforts to console Tim are met silently, and at the end of the story Kiowa is repeating, "Come on, man, talk."[49] Tim's voice, the third, is silent. But the repetitions of Kiowa's efforts to rationalize the experience of having killed suggests that this is not something that can be easily analyzed or dismissed.

The final voice, also silent, belongs to the young dead soldier lying on the forest trail. While he does not speak, O'Brien gives him life, a series of hopes as well as some doubts and reservations. In some ways these reflect O'Brien's own thoughts, and the extension of these argue strongly that he sees this young dead soldier as himself, except that he died defending his native land, killed by an invader.

"The Man I Killed" is striking for the sympathetic portrayal of the *Other*, the enemy. Like Aeschylus' *The Persians*, it reflects the voice of the survivor whose experience with violence allows him to transcend superficial differences and see in the *Other* his own reflection.

Melos and My Lai

> The Melians surrendered unconditionally to the Athenians, who put to death all the men of military age whom they took, and sold the women and children as slaves.
> (Thucydides, *History of the Peloponnesian War* 5.116.3)

> That day in My Lai, I was personally responsible for killing 25 people. Personally. Men, women. From shooting them, to cutting their throats, scalping them, to cutting off their hands and cutting out their tongues. I did it.
> (Vernaldo Simpson, on the My Lai Massacre)[50]

In 416 BC the Athenians completed their siege of the island community of Melos following a campaign that lasted some four to five months. An internal betrayal led to the collapse of resistance and the city's surrender to the Athenians, who then proceeded with the execution of the men of military age and the enslavement of the women and children (Thucydides, *History* 5.116). The Athenian capture of Melos and the destruction of the city and its inhabitants appears to differ from the slaughter carried out by American soldiers in South Vietnam on March 16, 1968. In this attack in

---

48 O'Brien 1990: 141.
49 Ibid.: 144.
50 Testimony cited in Bilton and Sim 1992: 7.

Quang Ngai Province in an area known as "Pinkville" (which included the village of Song My and its constituent hamlets of My Lai 1–4), hundreds of inhabitants, mostly women and children, were killed. Despite the distance in time and the apparent differences in the fates of these two communities, their stories should be considered in the same context, including the treatment of the "Other" as well as the degree of violence visited upon each community.

The island community of Melos was an old Dorian Greek community. This would mean that, while there were similarities between the Melians and Athenians, there were also differences. These would have included language or linguistic differences, not significant perhaps but still noticeable, as well as other cultural and societal variations on the Hellenic ideal. That said, it is also clear that the Melians would not have stood out in an Athenian crowd, other than for some superficial differences, perhaps in dress. Such cannot be said for the Americans and Vietnamese at My Lai. Here the two peoples were radically unlike in every aspect: language, culture, religion, and perhaps most significantly, power. As the preceding discussion has suggested, most Americans in Vietnam would have regarded the Vietnamese as "gooks" or "dinks" and seldom bothered to learn much if anything about the culture and people they saw every day. In this regard, then, the Athenians were certainly closer to the Melians than the Americans could ever be to the Vietnamese. Yet both the Athenians and Americans ended up destroying two communities in much the same fashion. How is this to be explained?

The Athenian attack on Melos should be seen as the result of a failed policy of state to force the Melians to recognize the power of the Athenian Empire and to accept its authority. From its subject states Athens demanded, for example, payment of tribute, use of Athenian coinage, weights, and measures, and acceptance of other aspects of imperial Athenian control. The Athenians seemed to have been little interested in actually possessing Melos. What they really wanted was for the people there to recognize their power and to submit. This much seems clear from Thucydides' account in his "Melian Dialogue" (*History* 5.84–114). The resulting siege must have been an annoyance to the Athenians, who had much grander plans in the offing, particularly the invasion of Sicily, then in preparation. In fact the destruction of Melos seems neither planned nor anticipated. Thucydides' account reveals, among other things, Athenian bewilderment at the Melian stubbornness to see the folly of resistance, which suggests that the final destruction of the Melian population was not premeditated. Rather, spontaneous factors and a desire to inflict revenge led to the destruction of an entire community.

Thucydides' account of the siege suggests that the Athenians had not really anticipated much in the way of resistance from the small community. In the early phases of the siege, the Melians were able to break the Athenian

line, kill some of the attackers, and bring in food stocks to help them withstand the blockade until the hoped for help from Sparta came.[51] Goaded by
these setbacks, the Athenians brought in additional forces, enabling them to
step up their efforts to seize the town both from within and without (*History*
5.115–16). In this they were finally successful, and they were able to force
the Melians to surrender. Thucydides' terse report frustrates any definite or
detailed reconstruction of events. I would argue, however, that it was
precisely at this point that "payback" and an evening of scores must be
considered. The Melians had fought doggedly, much more so than the
Athenians had ever expected. A number of Athenians had died and others
had been wounded in a frustrating operation, and generally the imperial
might of Athens had been embarrassed. At last the Melians were in the
power of the undoubtedly angry and annoyed Athenians. Under these
circumstances the Athenian commander Philocrates, the son of Demeas,
simply made an on-the-spot decision to punish the Melians for their daring
in resisting Athens: men of military age, those aged roughly between eighteen and forty-five were killed, the women and children enslaved.[52]

Plutarch, a Greek writer in the second-century AD Roman Empire, refers
to an Athenian decree endorsed by Alcibiades to execute the Melian men,
but gives no indication of date for this decree.[53] Plutarch's source for this
evidence, Pseudo-Andocides, is a questionable and late authority, and
Thucydides' contemporaneous silence about any such decree at very least
throws some doubt on Plutarch's account.[54] A way out perhaps is to see the
decree as authorizing the sale of the Melian women and children, which
would explain Plutarch's reference to Alcibiades' support for the decree, and
approving or legitimizing the deaths of the Melian men, which had already
taken place. In this sequence of events the Athenian destruction of Melos
would have been spontaneous, arising from the decision of the commander
Philocrates to inflict the maximum penalty on Melos – literally its death as
a community.[55] In this light, the destruction of Melos would have provided

---

51 Thucydides 5.104.2 implies that the Melians hoped for help from the Spartans. The
    Athenians, better judges of the chances of this aid than the Melians, correctly predicted
    that such assistance was so much Melian wishful thinking. Thucydides' reference to it,
    however, suggests that the subject probably did come up in the discussions.

52 Lattimore 1998: 301, n., points out how Thucydides provides the name and patronymic
    of the Athenian general, "Lover of Might, Son of Populace [or Democracy]," so as to
    emphasize the brutality of the Athenian decision to suppress the entire community of
    Melos.

53 Plutarch, *Alcibiades* 16.5–7, seems more interested in Alcibiades' Melian concubine who
    gave birth to a son.

54 See Gomme *et al.* 1945–81: 4, 190–1, for discussion of Pseudo-Andocides.

55 After the Athenians destroyed the population, they brought in five hundred colonists to
    resettle the community. This last detail of Thucydides is noteworthy, as this would have
    been occasion for a decree, which Alcibiades could easily have supported, and which
    Plutarch has confused with the execution of the Melian men.

both theme and stage background to Euripides' *The Trojan Women*, which Athenian audiences would see within a matter of months.

Conversely, the American attack on My Lai was premeditated, as it was a combat operation ostensibly against an entrenched enemy in his own back-yard: stiff resistance was anticipated, casualties could be expected to be significant. Additionally, adding to the high anxiety levels of the troops participating in the action was another factor – revenge. The men making up the attack force had taken numerous horrific casualties from an unseen enemy that was yet paradoxically highly visible – the farmer in the field, the young girl carrying a basket of fruit down the trail, the young boy herding water buffalo all seemed harmless, yet all were potential enemies.[56] Now an opportunity for "payback" was at hand, and those who were to participate in the attack were told by their leaders that the moment for revenge had finally arrived. After the excitement of the initial landing it became clear that there was in fact no enemy, no resistance at My Lai.[57] Yet there would be death on a grand scale. Why? It stemmed in part from the actions and directions (to call it leadership would be perverse) of Lieutenant William Calley, who seemed intent on restoring his diminished status in the eyes of his men and commander. Calley did incite or otherwise provoke the men around him in his platoon to kill unarmed civilians. And though he would later be court-martialed and found guilty there were other officers who were no less culpable, including his company commander, Ernest Medina, and other officers in his company.[58]

But there were other factors at work too. What happened was in part a contagion of violence not unlike that described by Paul Fussell in the "Great Turkey Shoot," a mob-like frenzy in which there is no control or order, and scared men begin striking back at perceived enemies. Others were yet motivated by "payback." They had lost friends to unseen enemies, and now they had an opportunity to strike back and even the score. The fact that it was women and children who paid the price mattered little. Their deaths could be easily rationalized with the conclusion that they were quite possibly the unseen enemy who had indeed planted those booby traps and if not, then they were probably related to someone who did and so now paid the price. Someone must.

Paradoxically, then, the massacre at My Lai was both premeditated and spontaneous. Premeditated because an attack was planned on an unseen and hated enemy; spontaneous in that, once combat was refused by the enemy,

56 For a description of the village life in Vietnam, and the actual combat roles of children, see Hayslip 1990: 42–8.
57 For detailed treatment of what happened in My Lai March 16, 1968, see Bilton and Sim 1992 and Olson and Roberts 1998 (the latter a collection of documents). For analysis of the issues see Anderson 1998. The human dimensions of the tragedy of My Lai have been explored by O'Brien 1994.
58 See Bilton and Sim 1992: 126–7,128–9.

more than enough pretexts could be found for releasing long-contained emotions of fear, revenge, and hatred. In this, American perceptions of the Vietnamese as *Other* can only partially explain the deaths of so many people. What has to be seen is that the psychological factors of hate, fear, and stress exerted as much if not greater influence than that of *Otherness*. An argument in support of this view may be found in the nickname for the area generally including My Lai – "Pinkville." This area, one feared and hated by those American units required to conduct operations in it, was not called "Gookville," but "Pinkville" on account of its political allegiance to the Viet Cong and National Liberation Front. Had it been called "Gookville," then the slaughter at My Lai would be much easier to explain along racial lines – that it was simply the product of *Otherness*. But the politics intrinsic to a name like "Pinkville" makes it difficult to accept this view, which then throws us back to the alternative, that anger heightened by fear and stress had as much, if not more, to do with what happened at My Lai as blind, racial hatred.

Melos and My Lai show that both Athenians and Americans regarded their enemies as not quite like themselves, though it is readily apparent that the degree of difference was greater for the Americans in Vietnam than the Athenians at Melos. Both could inflict violence on their enemies with little scruple or restraint, and this included women and children as well as men. In both cases again it would appear that emotional factors – anger, fear, and stress – were greater inducements to carry out brutal acts of violence than racially or culturally based perceptions of the "Other." One major difference, however, is that the Athenians Euripides and Thucydides appear to have been distressed, if not shocked, at the violence visited on the Melians and expressed their misgivings in their work. Other than the Vietnam veteran authors of poetry and prose, where are the American authors who have been so influenced?

7

THE HISTORIOGRAPHY AND
LANGUAGE OF VIOLENCE

It became necessary to destroy the town to save it.
(US Army officer, in Ben Tre, Vietnam,1968)

To fit in with the change of events, words, too had to change
their usual meanings.
(Thucydides, *History of the Peloponnesian War* 3.82.4)

Like so many other things associated with violence, language too changes as
a result of the situations and the contexts to which it is applied. This
Thucydides noted when he wrote his *History of the Peloponnesian War*. As he
lived through the conflict he recorded, he had the opportunity to reflect on
the events and on the nuances of their implications and consequences. This
is revealed in the passage cited as epigraph to this chapter, a part of his analysis of the violence that destroyed the *polis* of Corcyra – not only its
humanity but its sense of community – in vicious civil strife that erupted in
427 BC. Thucydides plainly states that the events literally created a new
language, a language of violence in which words changed or acquired new
meanings in order to conform with the realities brought by violence-induced
change.[1] Much the same thing occurred in Vietnam, where, as Michael Herr
relates,

All in-country briefings, at whatever levels, came to sound like a
naming of the Parts, and the language was used as a cosmetic, but
one that diminished the beauty. Since most of the journalism from
the war was framed in that language or proceeded from the view of
the war which those terms implied, it would be as impossible to

---

1 The standard translation since Crawley's 1874 edition, followed by e.g. Warner (Penguin
ed. 1954: 209), Blanco 1998: 130. Finley 1959: 296, translates "words had to change
their ordinary meanings and to take that which was now given them." On Thucydides'
language and its translation here see below nn. 25, 30.

know what Vietnam looked like from reading most newspaper stories as it would be to know how it smelled.[2]

These disparate efforts at writing about the past, whether it is the distant past or only the recent past, show the varied meanings of the words "history" and "historiography," the act of writing about the past. History can refer simply to the past, or it can be used to mean the activity or discipline of inquiring into the past. History can mean the record of past events, particularly as these relate to individuals and human society; it can refer to drama, as when applied, for example, to Shakespeare's "Histories."[3] Thucydides' account is a work of inquiry in that it attempts to understand what happened when the Athenians and Spartans went to war. This inquiry may be seen in the causal explanation that Thucydides gives (*History* 1.22), and also, as scholars since the Enlightenment have seen, in his positivist or fact-laden reporting of events. But then there are the psychological and sociological analyses, which are much less positivist and more literary and dramatic in both their scope and telling. These include the debate over Mitylene, the revolution in Corcyra, and, possibly the best-known, the "Melian Dialogue."[4] In these passages Thucydides attempts to go beneath the surface of events to try to understand the nature of human motivation in a literary and psychological fashion. When considered from this perspective, all directed toward an understanding of events, then Michael Herr's *Dispatches* can be placed alongside Thucydides and a productive comparison made.

Michael Herr and Thucydides saw that violence had a way of influencing language as well as the thoughts of those who were exposed to it. It might be argued that any sort of a comparison between these two authors ignores some very real differences. One was a newsman, a journalist who wrote "popular" stories about a nasty little war, while the other was a historian who recorded the events of a "great" and significant conflict. Such distinctions as these are plainly superficial. They ignore, first, that Thucydides "wrote up" (*xynegrapse*) the war that we now call "the Peloponnesian," reducing him to a sort of "official" historian. This actually distorts his whole persona, ignoring his role in the conflict itself and making him much more like the modern researcher working out of his study, divorced from the goings-on of the world.[5] Actually Thucydides' interests in writing up this war might be closer to Michael Herr's reasons for writing about Vietnam: to attempt an understanding of what was going on in this mad, vicious conflict. Moreover, both writers make it plain that violence shaped the

---

2 Herr 1977: 92–3.
3 See e.g. any dictionary definition or for further discussion Marwick 1971.
4 Thucydides 3.37–48, 81–4, 5.84–113 respectively.
5 Noted by Orwin 1994: 3.

minds and words of those who were confronted by it, whether as observers or as participants, and this too brings them together. What they show us, then, in much the same way is the historiography, the literature and language of violence.

Students and general readers often find Michael Herr's *Dispatches* a perplexing and difficult read. There is little that passes for order and sequence in the stories he tells, and there can be little doubt that one aim is to convey to the reader a sense of the mind-numbing confusion and unreality of life and violence that was Vietnam.[6] Similar reactions may be found in reading the two great historians of ancient Greece, Herodotus and Thucydides. Once, while I was reading Thucydides in graduate school, another student and Vietnam veteran remarked to me that Thucydides must have had a bad conscience about something to write such convoluted prose.[7] More than a quarter century earlier, R.G. Collingwood had said nearly the same thing in his famous study *The Idea of History*:

> The style of Herodotus is easy, spontaneous, convincing. That of Thucydides is harsh, artificial, repellant. In reading Thucydides I ask myself, What is the matter with the man, that he writes like that? I answer: he has a bad conscience. He is trying to justify himself for writing history at all by turning it into something that is not history.[8]

Collingwood then proceeded to critique Thucydides on the grounds that he wrote psychological history, which in his view was not proper history. While a full exploration of Collingwood's argument is not possible here, a brief response might be noted. Historians in fact must often "venture into the realm of psychology" in order to explain the motives and actions of men and societies, and this appears to be a primary concern of Thucydides'.[9] Now on reflection, some twenty years later, it seems to me that these critics sensed that Thucydides' style of writing history had been shaped by some circumstance. Neither seems to have realized what that experience in Thucydides' past might have been or how it might have influenced his *History*. Experiences in the Peloponnesian War, the experiences of the survivor of violence, influenced him in composing the structure, language and goals of his *History*.

That Thucydides served as *strategos* or general in the Peloponnesian War is well known. He recorded his own failure in losing to the Spartans the strategic town of Amphipolis in the northern Aegean in the eighth year of the war; rather than face his fellow Athenians afterwards, he chose a life of

---

6   For a discussion of *Dispatches* see Herr's interview in Schroeder 1992: 33–50.
7   Stephen Ruzicka, now teaching at the University of North Carolina, Greensboro.
8   Collingwood 1946: 29.
9   As argued e.g. by Marwick 1971: 141.

exile and perhaps never returned to Athens.[10] Unknown, though not to be doubted, is Thucydides' earlier service in the War, during 431–424 BC, which seems likely on account of his subsequent election to the office of general. Additionally, his connections with the famous family of Miltiades, the victor in the Battle of Marathon, and his son Cimon, who carried the war to the Persians after 480 BC, argue that Thucydides from youth would have emulated his famous relations. The horrific experience of the battlefield that Thucydides, as other Greek soldiers, faced cannot be ignored when attempting to understand the mind of the historian. This military past seems to have shaped "General" Thucydides' writing, as seen in his terse style – the result of writing dispatches – and his attention to military affairs.[11] Additionally, Thucydides survived the plague that swept Athens early in the war, and this experience of survival must also be taken into account in understanding the disposition of the historian (*History* 2.48.3).

The outlook of Thucydides the survivor finds counterparts in survivors of other conflicts, such as Aeschylus. In several instances, the impact of violence on individuals has been expressed by reference to Michael Herr's interview with a veteran LURP who enigmatically tells him of the "lost patrol" (see pp. 4, 66). This story has been used to illustrate the essence of the violent wartime experience that can be related only in cryptic and elusive language. The LURP's story, however, has an antecedent from the American Civil War, a story told by Praxiteles Swan, a captain in the Confederate Army: "We all went up to Gettysburg, the summer of '63: and some of us came back from there: and that's all except the details."[12] Vietnam veteran William Broyles cites this story as an example of the survivor's cryptic tale meant to exclude, to convey to the listener that as you did not share in the experience, you must remain an outsider to it.[13] Broyles's interpretation may not catch all the nuances of Captain Swan's statement. I would argue that the reason for such language, as in the case of Herr's LURP, like the Spartan survivor of Sphacteria, is that the violence itself has inflicted such trauma that, in order for the survivor to cope, the event must be reflected on obliquely rather than directly. The need to establish barriers between participants and non-participants might follow, as Broyles notes, though this may well be defensive in nature, the result of a perceived lack of understanding by the survivor of violence. A further effort will be made later to examine language's adaptation by these survivors.

Language is also contorted so as to fit or otherwise make sense of a new

10 Thucydides 4.104.4–116.
11 Hornblower 1987: 40–1, 109, refers to Thucydides as "Colonel," but he was in fact a general, as used here. On his connections with the family of Miltiades, see Cawkwell 1997: 2.
12 Cited in Broyles 1990: 75.
13 Ibid.

place or situation as well as surroundings. Herr tells of a young Marine who, strangely it seems, is unable to get on the airplane out of Khe Sanh that will take him home.

> Something more was working on the young Marine, and Gunny knew what it was. In this war they called it "acute environmental reaction," but Vietnam has sponsored a jargon of such delicate locutions that it's often impossible to know even remotely the thing being described.[14]

Not only does language adapt to describe the environment, as here, but also adapts to new and varied circumstances of political conflict, as Thucydides relates so well, notably in the case of Corcyra to be examined in this chapter.

Finally there are those cases in which language is manipulated or shaped by higher authorities, whether it be the product of governmental deceit, "Big Brother" power, or bureaucratic malaise. From Vietnam there are any number of examples of this manipulation of language, including such terms as "friendly fire" (nothing friendly about it), or "collateral damage," the term used to refer to civilian casualties. Hollywood mimicked this sort of language in *Apocalypse Now*, in which Martin Sheen's character of Captain Willard is required to "eliminate with prejudice" Marlon Brando's Colonel Kurtz. While this particular example is Vietnam-inspired rather than Vietnam itself (perhaps), there are enough genuine examples to explain the cinematic imitation. An institutional manipulation of language seems evident too in Thucydides' "Melian Dialogue." This famous text certainly demonstrates Thucydides' dramatic talents and flair. His arguments of power and expediency, however, reflect more than just the intellectual climate of fifth-century Athens. These are also expressions of imperial might and the belief that the subject states and intended subject states of Athens were but slaves expected to submit whenever demanded.[15]

Violence and language

> But war is a violent teacher; in depriving them of the power of easily satisfying their daily wants, it brings most people's minds down to the level of their actual circumstances.
> (Thucydides, *History of the Peloponnesian War* 3.82.3)

---

14 Herr 1977: 91.
15 On the Greek Enlightenment see Solmsen 1975, for the Athenian empire see Gomme *et al*. 1945–81:163.

When Thucydides wrote "war is a violent teacher," he was speaking from experience and not merely as an observer of the greatest and most violent war ever fought by the Greeks.[16] In the war's early phases Thucydides served as soldier and commander, and it was in the latter capacity that he "lost" the city of Amphipolis to the Spartans.[17] This occurred in 424/3 BC, the eighth year of the war, during which Thucydides had served in a number of campaigns. His service as general attests further the active role he played: he was then a witness to the violence that increasingly characterized the prolonged conflict that, as he remarks, brought people down to the level of their circumstances. Like Aeschylus, Thucydides too was a survivor of war's violence, an experience that heightened his awareness of its toll. What he learned of events such as the massacres at Plataea and Mitylene in 427 BC, to name but two, would have set him to thinking on the nature of violence. But the horrors that occurred in Corcyra in the same year gave a new meaning to the realities of war and impelled Thucydides' creation of a new language of violence, one inspired by reports of atrocities previously unknown to the Greeks.

Corcyra was one of the flashpoints that ignited the Peloponnesian War in 431 BC. A powerful and unattached maritime state off the western coast of Greece, Corcyra entered into a defensive alliance with Athens after becoming embroiled in a bitter dispute with Corinth, her much-hated mother city.[18] Several naval engagements resulted in the capture and detention of a large number of Corcyraeans in Corinth. The Corinthians won these captives over to their side and then released them homewards with the idea that they should detach Corcyra from her alliance with Athens.[19] This Corinthian ploy took shape in 427 BC, when these men returned home and quickly challenged the democratic pro-Athenian party led by Peithias.[20] A prosecution for subversion failed to topple Peithias, who retaliated against five of his opponents with charges of sacrilege. His plans not only miscarried

---

16 Thucydides 1.1–2 refers to the war as the greatest ever fought by the Greeks. This and other passages (e.g. 3.82.1, 7.30.3) suggest that Thucydides lived through the Peloponnesian War and was revising the entire history when he died (the *History* ends abruptly in 411/10 BC). For more detailed treatment see Hornblower 1987: 136–54.

17 Thucydides 4.104–108. Thucydides possessed ample wealth that enabled him to go into exile rather than face the wrath of the Athenian people for Amphipolis' loss, a failure that could have cost his life.

18 Thucydides 1.24–55. The dispute between Corcyra and Corinth broke out when a third city, Epidamnus, located on the Adriatic coast, appealed to Corinth for aid after Corcyra had refused help in fending off native attacks from the interior. The Corcyraeans were angered at this Corinthian intrusion into their backyard and so went to war. On the enmity between Corcyra and Corinth, see e.g. Salmon 1984: 282–93

19 Corinth had a long-standing grudge with Athens dating back some twenty years to a particularly nasty Athenian massacre of a group of Corinthian soldiers. See Thucydides 1.103, 106 and the discussion on p. 7, n.13.

20 Thucydides 3.71–2.

but proved disastrous: the opposition attacked him and his political allies in council chambers and killed over sixty of them with knives in a particularly brutal scene. Within a short time Corcyra was in an uproar – street fighting erupted between democrats and conservatives. Thucydides relates how women on the democratic side joined in, hurling down roof tiles and "standing up to the din of battle with a courage beyond their sex."[21] Euripides' Hecuba and Tim O'Brien's Mary Ann would have been in good company here!

The presence of allies, Athenians for the democrats and Peloponnesians and Spartans for the conservatives, both compounded the violence and stress and inflamed the passions on both sides. This rapidly growing community rupture then exploded in a seven-day paroxysm of violence. The democrats were able to gain the upper hand, and the resulting violence, as Thucydides relates, must have resembled the recent killing fields of Bosnia. He tells how men were killed under pretense of trials and truces, asylum seekers in temples committed suicide rather than be killed by their enemies. Sometimes charges of conspiracy were mere ruses to kill those hated on personal grounds or on account of holding debts. The anarchic scene worsened, and soon

> there was death in every shape and form. As it usually happens in such situations, people went to every extreme and beyond it. There were fathers who killed their sons; men were dragged from the temples or butchered on the very altars.[22]

Thucydides' narration and description of the savage encounter in Corcyra is but a prelude to his much deeper psychological analysis. He begins with the reference to how the revolution in Corcyra was only the first of many that shook the Greek world. This statement tells us that he lived to see the end of the war which enabled him to reach such conclusions as this. He notes the divisions into pro-Athenian and pro-Spartan factions in the Greek cities and how these became regular political features. His observations then take a broader analytical look at human nature, arguing that the tragedies that occurred at Corcyra will always happen, "while human nature is what it is, though there may be different degrees of savagery, and, as different circumstances arise, the general rules will admit of some variety."[23]

This explanation is one that some modern readers will find objectionable, owing to what they perceive as Thucydides' appeal to "human nature,"

21 Thucydides 3.75.1.
22 Thucydides 3.81.4. It is interesting to note that Eurymedon, the Athenian commander, and his squadron of ships took up a station off Corcyra while this slaughter took place, providing perhaps moral and material support. It is likely that Eurymedon himself, as well as some of the other Athenians, told Thucydides of the events he recorded.
23 Thucydides 3.81.5.

particularly the fixed notion he suggests. Such criticism, however, fails to recognize just what prompted him to reach this conclusion. In two places in his analysis he refers to revenge. He refers to the extravagant plans that were made for seizing power and of the "unheard of atrocities in revenge" that accompanied them (3.82.1). Then he states that "revenge was more important than self-preservation" (3.82.3). Jonathan Shay has isolated revenge as one of the attributes of the berserk warrior who fights with no regard for his own life but is determined to make others pay for the loss of friends. Revenge, Shay notes, "denies helplessness, keeps faith with the dead, and affirms that there is still justice in the world, even if this is manifested only in the survivor's random vengeance."[24] Revenge or payback is a psychological response to trauma that follows from natural biochemical and physiological changes. Human chemistry then dictates the predictable range of responses, which culture will follow rather than guide. Thucydides' reference to the dominance of revenge, then, points to the very real presence of trauma and its consequences influencing the actions of the Corcyraeans and those other Greeks also caught up in the savage cycle of violence.

The violence unleashed by the civil war in Corcyra, the payback that led to the "unheard of atrocities" that Thucydides alludes to, produced the deterioration of moral values that could allow people to transgress religious scruples and kill on sacred ground and worse. This amorality is also reflected in his language and how "to fit in with the change of events, words too, had to change their usual meanings."[25] In analyzing the civil strife in Corcyra, Thucydides writes that "irrational recklessness" became "courageous commitment," "hesitation" and concern for the future was seen as cowardice, while "senseless anger" defined a true man, and the intriguer who succeeded was intelligent, yes, but not nearly so as one who detected a plot. The casual reader of Thucydides might well pass over these definitions and word changes without realizing the forces that have shaped these views. But it seems worthwhile to reflect on these within a context of violence and the experience of a survivor – Thucydides – as well as the cultural context of the Greek Enlightenment.

To ignore the contortion of language that took place in Vietnam is to miss an essential dimension of the "Experience." The first level of word change is that which occurs on the superficial level, i.e. terms that are descriptive of violence, so much so that they can only be expressed sardonically. Terms like "crispy critters" to describe napalm casualties and dead, or a detached limb as the result of "response-to-impact" fall into this cate-

---

24 Shay 1994: 90.
25 Thucydides 3.82.4. Translating and interpreting this passage has troubled critics since the investigation of Dionysius of Halicarnassus in the late first century BC (see Hornblower 1992–96: 1, 477–9). The Greek is not easily deciphered, but note the translation of Rhodes 1994: 133, "words normally used to evaluate deeds were changed to fit what was justified." See further n. 30 below.

gory.[26] Michael Herr mentions soldiers of the 173rd Airborne Brigade refer-ring to the "KIA [Killed in Action] Travel Bureau," when describing the processing home of the bodies of the dead. Much more sinister, however, is "payback," the term that evolved to describe the revenge visited on the enemy. Perhaps the best definition of this is to be found in Gustav Hasford's *The Short Timers*, the work that became the Stanley Kubrick film *Full Metal Jacket*. Here Hasford's character "Animal Mother" gives a brutally lucid statement of what motivated combat soldiers in Vietnam.

> You think we waste gooks for *free*dom? Don't kid yourself; this is slaughter. ... Yeah, you better believe we zap zipperheads. They waste our bros and we cut them a big piece of payback. And payback is a motherfucker.[27]

Payback is simply revenge, which as Thucydides and Hasford both show, inflicts "unheard-of atrocities" that themselves induce payback in an unending cycle of violence.

But perhaps the most telling of all the word changes to come out of Vietnam is the paradoxical "It don't mean nothin'." This phrase can be found in the literary works of Vietnam veterans as well as the discussions of their therapists and counselors. Jonathan Shay refers to it as "the Vietnam combat soldiers' mantra, spread out to engulf everything valued or wanted, every person, loyalty, and commitment."[28] Vietnam veteran William Broyles refers to it as meaning "everything, it means too much. Language overload."[29] Taken together, both definitions explain what processes are at work in creating such language: experiences so brutal and extreme that they lie outside normative language and represent events that run counter to every principle, value, and right one has been taught.

Now it is true that the meanings and nuances of words change over time. Words like "jury" and "bourgeois" are well-known examples of this sort of ordinary adaptation of language. But it seems clear, as Thucydides shows in the Spartan survivor of Sphacteria, that violence exerts its own impact on language. It is impossible to know, for example, when and by whom "crispy critters," a new fast-food version of the french fry in the late 1960s, was first used to describe napalm casualties in Vietnam. So too with the terms that Thucydides introduces in Book 3 of his *History*. Since he wrote after the end of the Peloponnesian War, he could introduce terms and innovations in terms that had emerged in the course of the revolutions that swept the

---

26 Herr 1977: 18. "Crispy critters" began to appear in 1967/8 and is a term often found in Vietnam writings.
27 Hasford 1979: 136.
28 Shay 1994: 38.
29 Broyles 1990: 75.

Greek world during the conflict. In both Vietnam and ancient Greece, terms were selected that had the opposite meaning, or nearly so, of that which they described. This should be seen as a means of coping with trauma, of putting distance between subject and object, between that which the observer sees and attempts to understand. To cope with such trauma, then, language adapts and so changes to conform to the transformed reality that the survivor of that event has experienced.[30]

It is in this context that Thucydides' new definition of violence should be understood. He states (*History* 3.82.4–5) that daringly wild aggression (*tolma ... alogistos*) was now seen as brotherly commitment (*philetairos enomiste*). Concern for the future (*mellesis ... promethes*) was cowardice (*deila euprepes*), while moderation, one of the great Greek virtues handed down from Apollo (i.e. "the golden mean"), *to ... sophron*, had become unmanliness, or within the Greek scheme of things, womanly (*anandrou*). The circumspect or careful individual (*to pros apan xuneton*) was really the inactive one (*epi pan argon*), and the violent man (*ho chalapainon*) was always trustworthy (*pistos*), and anyone who spoke against him was suspect (*hypoptos*).[31]

Thucydides' definitions reflect his survivor's instincts to see things in a different way than the non-survivor and with a rather sarcastic and bitter edge. Without this sarcasm and bitter irony, as in the aforementioned "crispy critters," or in the designation of Vietnamese dead as "believers,"[32] it is difficult to understand how Thucydides could imagine the moderate man, for example, as womanly. From the bitter standpoint of the survivor, however, the formation of such words and the ideas they represent becomes comprehensible.

Another factor that influenced Thucydides here was the intellectual development current in Athens when he wrote, the so-called "Greek Enlightenment." This was one of the great intellectual "booms" of all time and saw the flowering of drama, both tragedy and comedy, philosophy with such thinkers as Socrates and the Sophists, rhetoric and history, the latter including Thucydides.[33] This was a great mixing of ideas and it comes as no surprise to see Thucydides experimenting with various ideas and approaches in his "inquiry" or history of the war between Athens and Sparta. It is in this context that his experimentation with language and word changes, his use of the dialogue form later made famous by Plato, is to be placed. His

---

30 Wilson 1982: 18–20 (followed e.g. by Hornblower 1992–96: 1, 483 and Lattimore 1998: 169) argues that the usual translations of Thucydides 3.82.4 are inaccurate, that the "words" did not change their meaning as much as acquired new meanings as situations themselves changed. But then does this not mean that the words acquired new connotations – essentially meanings?

31 For discussion of the language see Hornblower 1992–96: 1, 483–5, Gomme *et al.* 1945–81: 2, 374–6.

32 Herr 1977: 42.

33 On the Enlightenment, see the sources cited in n. 15 above.

experiences in war, however, predisposed him to interpret these developments differently. The impact of these experiences can be seen by way of contrast with Herodotus, his great predecessor in the birth of historical writing. Herodotus wrote in the generation before Thucydides when the era of the Enlightenment was just underway. Yet his writing does not show the same sort of language experimentation and contortion as Thucydides', and the explanation may well rest in the differences in their experiences ... one was an exiled citizen of the world, the other a failed and exiled general. It was noted above that Aeschylus, another survivor of violent conflict, emerged from that experience to become a cultural leader in the development of drama as the art form and the teacher of the Greeks that we associate in the modern world. In the same way Thucydides, another survivor, also put his experiences, reactions, and survivor mentality into his work. In doing so he too would become influential in the formation of the emerging genre of historical writing.

The intellectual climate in which Thucydides composed his history is not to be discounted here, nor should the survivor experience be made into the single greatest factor in his formation as a writer and a thinker. Yet it remains true that Thucydides was impressed by the horrors of war he saw and had reported to him. One such case was the destruction of the city of Mycalessus in central Greece in 413 BC. Here Thracian mercenaries under Athenian command attacked an unsuspecting and relatively obscure place and destroyed it. Thucydides writes:

> The Thracians burst into Mycalessus, sacked the houses and temples, and butchered the inhabitants, sparing neither the young nor the old, but methodically killing everyone they met, women and children alike, and even the farm animals and every living thing they saw. ... Among other things, they broke into a boys' school, the largest of the place, into which the children had just entered, and killed every one of them.[34]

The scene that Thucydides evokes here is what any modern reader of the My Lai massacre would see in the photographs taken there – animals killed, women and children cut down wherever encountered. In creating this portrait Thucydides clearly intends this incident to serve in an exemplary fashion, to convey the horror of the war he served in and lived through. This can be seen in the details of the slaughter in the cited passage, but other points could be made. Among these is the use of the verb *katakoptein*, to butcher, a verb that is close in meaning to *kreokopein*, to butcher or literally, "cut meat." Thucydides also stresses the non-combatant casualties,

---

34 Thucydides 7.29–30. For a recent discussion see Quinn 1995: 571–3.

mentioning the killing of women once and that of children twice.[35] As in the discussion of Corcyra and how it served as a paradigm for revolutionary violence, so it appears that Thucydides took Mycalessus as the paradigm for what befell a town taken by storm. This seems evident in his closing sentence, "Mycalessus lost a considerable part of its population. It was a small city, but in the disaster just described its peoples suffered calamities as pitiable as any which took place during the war."[36]

The slaughter of the innocents at Mycalessus, however, was matched by a growing ferocity on the battlefield as well, events that also shaped Thucydides' writing in an even more personal way. Accounts of these battles would have evoked in him the same sort of reaction as Odysseus to the tale of Troy and how he took a great cloak "dyed in sea-purple, drew it over his head and veiled his fine features, shamed for tears running down his face."[37]

Odysseus' reaction is mirrored by that of eighty-year-old World War II veteran Ralph Berke, who after seeing *Saving Private Ryan* said, "'I hope I don't have nightmares again,' wiping away the tears."[38] Thucydides' description of what occurred on the battlefields of the Peloponnesian War reveals too the increase in the war's bloody toll. At the battle of Delium in 424 BC, Thucydides tells of the Thespians, fighting against the Athenians, who were surrounded and cut down, along with some Athenians, killed by their own men who did not recognize them – an example of "friendly fire" in the ancient world.[39] What Thucydides omits here is not so much that these Athenians were killed by accident, as that they were killed on account of the terror and confusion of battle. Ron Kovic in his *Born on the Fourth of July* tells of killing another Marine in much the same way: "I think I might have … I think I might have killed the corporal. … It was very confusing. It was hard to tell what was happening."[40] The Athenian victory over the Thespians, however, was of little help as elsewhere the Athenians failed to defeat the rest of the Boeotian army and so lost the battle and the field. The Boeotians stripped the corpses of the Athenian dead, a battlefield ritual that would have been a brutal business accompanied by both humiliation and mutilation of the dead.[41]

Even more chilling, however, is Thucydides' account of the slaughter of

---

35 Thucydides 7.29.3 (women and children), 7.29.5 (attack and slaughter at the boys' school). Cf. Herodotus 7.181, Euripides, *Cyclops* 359.

36 Thucydides 7.30.3.

37 Homer, *Odyssey* 8.84–6.

38 Reported in the *Los Angeles Times*, July 27, 1998, p. F10.

39 Thucydides 4.96.3, who uses *katakoptein*, to butcher, in describing how the Thespians were cut down.

40 Kovic 1976: 193.

41 Thucydides 4.97.1 (on the Boeotian treatment of the Athenian dead), with Tritle 1997a: 135.

the Athenian army retreating from its failed effort to capture Syracuse in
413 BC. What began as an orderly withdrawal degenerated into a rout, with
the Syracusans and their Peloponnesian allies ripping into the battered
Athenians again and again. Exhausted and near mad from thirst, the
Athenians plunged in utter confusion into the Assinarus River, where they
were destroyed. Thucydides describes how,

> the Syracusans [hurled] missiles down at the Athenians as they were
> drinking thirstily ... And the Peloponnesians descended and did
> the most butchery when they were in the river. The water immedi-
> ately turned foul but was drunk just as much as when full of blood
> along with the mud but fought over by most of them.[42]

The language of terror employed by Thucydides reveals clearly the
slaughter that befell the Athenians. The verb describing the Peloponnesian
massacre of the Athenians is *sphazo/sphazein*, which can be used to describe
sacrificial slaughter as in the cutting of throats, or just plain murder. In
either sense the act described is particularly brutal and bloody, and
Thucydides' use of it conveys vividly the idea of battle. Elsewhere he uses a
participle form of *phoneuein*, another strong word for slaughter or the taking
of life. Taken together these passages present war on the battlefield as no less
violent than the events Thucydides describes in the case of the revolutions
that wracked Corcyra and so many other places in the Greek world. Study of
Thucydides and his language of violence alongside that of Michael Herr (and
other Vietnam era writers) demonstrates convincingly that the violence
encountered on the battlefields carried over into the language of those
caught up in it.

The state and the language of violence

> some correspondents [wrote] their stories from the daily
> releases and battlegrams, tracking them through with cheer-
> crazed language of the MACV Information Office, things like
> "discreet burst" (one of these tore an old grand-father and two
> children to bits ...), "friendly casualties" (not war, not fun),
> "meeting engagement" (ambush), concluding usually with 17
> or 117 or 317 enemy dead and American losses "described as
> light."
>
> (Michael Herr, *Dispatches*, p. 222)

---

42 Thucydides 7.84.2–5.

Michael Herr demonstrates with remarkable artistry the manipulation or "spin" applied to language by political and military officials in Vietnam. These include the usual well-known euphemisms, "friendly fire" and its corollary "friendly casualties," like the Athenian hoplites killed at Delium. Before proceeding with a further examination of this issue, however, brief explanation needs to be made of the idea of the state mentioned here, in order to clarify the grounds for the comparison. The Athenian *polis* did not have a "government" in the sense of a modern state such as the US today or in the 1960s. The Athenians were a self-governing community of citizens who took turns performing political, judicial, and military functions (religious functions, too, but lacking in the US counterpart) on behalf of their fellow citizens. It was consequently difficult for an ancient Athenian, for example, to become agitated by a notion of "fighting city hall," where officialdom or the bureaucracy ran according to its own rules, usually intended to frustrate or make life difficult for the average citizen. It is for this reason that the term "government" for ancient Athens does not convey a true picture of its democracy.[43] There were then no official "organs" that stated policy or could somehow shape language to fit certain political needs or manipulate policy. Nevertheless, Pericles' "Funeral Oration," a speech delivered in 430 BC on the occasion of the first year's dead, makes clear that a "vision" of the Athenian *polis* existed that provided it with an identity and ideology that was projected abroad. This vision was certainly subjective and selective in its language and vocabulary. In much the same fashion the modern American democracy projects its own ideology and values too. Both communities, then, were capable of manipulating language to suit their ideas about themselves and their world-views. Thus there is little that separates the Athenian and American states when it comes to matters of language or, as will be seen, to expressing violence in that language.

Herr makes clear the origins of the often contorted language emanating from MACV, the American military headquarters in Saigon. Part of this resulted from the isolation and detachment that characterized the headquarters as it attempted to satisfy the needs and demands of the press and the expectations of official Washington. Such efforts were bound to fail and sink into cynicism, as Herr relates:

> nothing so horrible ever happened up country that it was beyond language fix and press relations ... You'd either meet an optimism that no violence could unconvince or a cynicism that would eat itself empty every day ... These men called dead Vietnamese "believers," a lost American platoon was a "black eye," they talked

43 Sealey 1993: 271–2 has argued the point previously; the view is not mere pedantry, but really essential to understanding how different ancient democracy was from its modern counterparts.

as though killing a man was nothing more than depriving him of his vigor.[44]

Herr's description here of language change and manipulation reflects a "Saigon" viewpoint, a sarcasm that lacks the veneer of both violence and bitterness that attempts to conceal the trauma and hurt of the language of the field. But then there really was a difference in the attitudes of those who served in "safe" areas like Saigon or the big bases like Da Nang or Cam Ranh Bay. A good example of this is found in Gustav Hasford's *Short Timers*, with an exchange of contempt between these two groups that follows a screening of John Wayne's *The Green Berets*, a film that most combat soldiers in Vietnam found hugely hilarious.

> The grunts laugh and whistle and threaten to pee all over themselves. The sun is setting in the South China Sea – in the East – which makes the end of the movie as accurate as the rest of it ... Most of the Marines in the audience are clean-shaven poges who never go into the field ... After the screen loses its color and the overhead lights come on, one of the poges says, "Fucking grunts ... they're nothing but animals ... ". The grunts turn around. One grunt stands up. He walks over to where the poges are sitting. The poges laugh and punch each other and mock the grunt's angry face. Then they are silent. They stare at the grunt's face. He's smiling now. He's smiling like a man who knows a terrible secret. The poges do not ask the grunt to explain why he is smiling. They don't want to know.[45]

The explanation for the "poges"' or "REMFs"' hostility and contempt for the grunts (and of the grunts for the REMFs it should be noted) lies in their isolation and detachment from the violence of the battlefield. In the same way, those who worked in MACV headquarters in Saigon or with the press were also insulated from the action of the front. These disparate reactions, mirrored here and elsewhere in the language contortions, follow from the violence encountered in Vietnam, just as Thucydides tells of the people of Corcyra and elsewhere in the fifth-century BC Greek world.

In the case of Vietnam, however, we see these reports resulting from official or quasi-official pronouncements to the media and reports to Washington and the Pentagon. A stunning example of this may be seen in the official press release following the battle of the Ia Drang between the US

44 Herr 1977: 42.
45 Hasford 1979: 32–3.

1st Cavalry Division and the NVA in November 1965.[46] In the second and deadlier phase of this battle, the Division's Second Battalion of the 7th Cavalry (ironically General Custer's old outfit of the Little Big Horn defeat of 1876!) walked into an ambush. Entire platoons of thirty to forty men were cut down, some reduced to a single survivor. Total losses amounted to 121 wounded, 155 dead.[47] Shortly afterwards came the official description of this action as a "fierce firefight" (no ambush having occurred) that resulted in "light to moderate casualties" for the Cavalry (in fact they amounted to roughly 50 per cent, hardly light or moderate). Eight days after the battle, General Westmoreland visited the survivors over their Thanksgiving Day dinners and congratulated them on their "distinguished victory," leaving the men left to wonder "if he had any idea of what [they had] just been through."[48] This is but one example of the hundreds that could be cited to illustrate how the state, in this instance MACV and the US Army, manipulated the language of violence.

Similar examples of the abuse of language could be found in the statements and writings of Secretary of Defense Robert McNamara. McNamara's orchestration and defense of the Vietnam War earned him and his creation the not entirely neutral, or undeserved, description "McNamara's War." A reading of McNamara's *In Retrospect: The Tragedy and Lessons of Vietnam* would bring to light some of his number-crunching assumptions which, when applied by the generals on the ground, created a dimension of violence that he could not have anticipated nor understood then any better than he does now. Foremost among these is his shaping of policy around the principle of "attrition" that led to the formula of body-count as the indicator of victory or success. In explanation of this formula, McNamara states that "things you can count, you ought to count. Loss of life is one."[49] McNamara, granted, had little idea how his quantitative analysis and his near messianic belief in numbers would become reality in the violent, surreal war in Vietnam.

This sort of analysis in part explains the first official reports of the day's action at My Lai – the 128 Viet Cong guerillas killed, the three weapons captured. Such a report might sound ludicrous today: who could really

46 For an account of the battle see Moore and Galloway 1992, and also the NBC News *Day One* program, "They Were Young and Brave," broadcast June 29, 1995 (and available from NBC News).

47 See Moore and Galloway 1992: 215–302, Herr 1977: 5, 95 (the latter a reference to a belief among the survivors that the number of dead was actually much higher but suppressed). The intensity and brutality of the fight are evident in the disproportionate number of wounded to dead: usually the number of wounded is higher by a factor of two or three than that for the dead.

48 The references to the supposed victory come from the official US Army Newsreel that reported on the Ia Drang battle, including the references to "firefight," "light to moderate casualties," and Westmoreland's victory message, the latter reported by survivor L. Gwin, a young lieutenant in the ambushed battalion.

49 McNamara 1995: 237–8, cf. 211.

believe that you could kill 128 of the enemy and recover just three weapons? Yet this sort of thing happened repeatedly. I still recall the briefing given by J.P. Vann, the senior adviser in IV Corps in the area of the Mekong Delta, upon arriving there for my tour of duty. Vann told us how some years before, the US 9th Infantry Division had conducted a month-long operation into the Delta and had killed something like 700 Viet Cong, but recovered only twenty or so weapons. The official explanation for the "shortfall" in the number of weapons was that the dying enemy soldiers had managed to hide their weapons before expiring! This same attitude extended in other ways and resulted in the deaths of many peasant farmers killed while working in their fields in areas that lay in "free fire zones" unbeknownst to them.[50] McNamara could not imagine, as he had no combat experience and was ignorant of the US military's reliance on firepower, how the philosophy of "attriting" the enemy could produce disastrous consequences and unimaginable brutalities. In short, the language of violence adopted by official channels in Saigon and Washington produced results more heinous and tragic than could be imagined.

This language of violence was created as much by ignorance as by the reality of a war where 25 per cent of the casualties came from booby traps and land mines, singularly nasty instruments of death and mutilation. Such distinctions were lost on MACV command in Saigon which, as Michael Herr says, "rode us into attrition traps on the back of fictional kill ratios, and an Administration that believed the Command [created] a cross-fertilization of ignorance."[51]

The air-conditioned trailers that senior officers above the rank of colonel enjoyed, along with the other perks of rank, only insulated them further from the war's realities. Their detachment was little different than that of the French monarchy on the eve of revolution in 1789, and there were probably senior officers who thought that the troops were eating and generally faring as well as they were, just as Marie Antoinette thought the Parisian poor had cake. In their ignorance and isolation, it is small wonder that

> spokesmen spoke in words that had no currency left as words, sentences with no hope of meaning in the sane world, and if much of it was sharply queried by the press, all of it was quoted. The press

---

50 On the first reports on the action at My Lai see Bilton and Sim 1992: 182–3. In November 1970 I met and spoke with a young widow whose husband had been killed by a helicopter crew in Hoa Tu district of Ba Xuyen Province. His only crime was that he was farming in a "contested" area that had been designated a "free fire zone" where aircraft were freely permitted to kill anyone who looked at all suspicious. Usually being Vietnamese and wearing black "pajamas" (they were not really pajamas, but looked like it to Americans) were all that was required.

51 Herr 1977: 214.

got all the facts ... but it never found a way to report meaningfully about death, which of course was really what it was all about.[52]

Herr's point then is that the state's use of a language as bankrupt of meaning as it was rich in images of violence, beguiled not only the agents of the state but even the media. So it was that

conventional journalism could no more reveal this war than conventional firepower could win it, all it could do was to take the most profound event of the American decade and turn it into communications pudding ...[53]

As one who experienced the violence of those inflicting and suffering it, Herr saw both its destructiveness on bodies and its employment by the state and/or its agents. In this way, then, violence exerted yet additional casualties, those of mind and spirit. Many Vietnam veterans so troubled today are distressed because they see themselves as betrayed by their own state, which manipulated them through language, assured them that what they were doing was "ok," only to realize or learn that this was not the case. In this regard, then, the violence of language is no less destructive than normative violence, the kind of violence inflicted in war and conflict. Michael Herr's account of Vietnam is the more remarkable because it shows how he recognized the impact of the destructiveness and, in the case of language, the arrogance of power that led the American state and its military into deceit and deception. The manipulation of language to express violence and to reduce it to simplicity and deceit was just one example of this.

The manipulation Herr saw is mirrored in the earlier work of another veteran who also recognized in his state the expression of power and violence in language – Thucydides in his "Melian Dialogue." As discussed above, the Athenians decided in the summer of 416/5 BC to right a trifling affront to their imperial might and suppress the freedom and autonomy of a rather minor (if that) state, the island community of Melos (pp. 119–21). Through the Peloponnesian War Melos had followed a neutral course, though it seems to have had some contact with Sparta, something which is understandable as Melos was a Spartan colony. The Athenians decided, however, that an independent Melos could no longer be tolerated and set out to bring it to heel. But the Melians did not prove compliant. They had long enjoyed their freedom and accordingly declined the Athenian invitation to submit, resisting to the end (at least temporarily) of their existence as a community. All of this Thucydides related in what is probably his most fascinating piece of writing. Presented in the same dialogue form that Plato would make

52 Ibid.
53 Ibid.: 218.

famous, the "Melian Dialogue" examines a number of issues of interest to Greek intellectuals in the later fifth century BC, including the idea of justice and a key concept of intellectual discourse, the idea of *nomos*, law, versus *physis*, nature. Another dimension to the intellectual background in the "Dialogue" is the eristic or sophistic discourse, a form of debate in which an opponent was trapped in a series of questions and answers.

While the intellectual roots and nuances are of great interest, the "Melian Dialogue" is about power and the dispensing of justice. The Athenians tell the Melians that their "right" to force their will upon the Melians is essentially a matter of power and not some abstract notion of justice. Justice is tied in fact to one's power: the strong do what their power allows them while the weak accept what they must. Thucydides' analysis of power appears to be the result of his reflections on the course of the Peloponnesian War, as he alludes to Athens' potential loss of empire, which did occur. The emphasis on power, however, follows from so many expressions of it during the Peloponnesian War, including the incident at Melos, the suppression of the Mitylenians, the destruction of Scione, and the failed attempt to conquer Sicily. Each in its own way was a reflection of Athenian power and the conviction that Athens had the right or was justified in so doing because it possessed the power to do it. Elsewhere in the "Melian Dialogue," Thucydides has the Melians identify themselves as potential slaves of the Athenians. The comic playwright Aristophanes, in his drama *The Birds*, uses similar, though not exact, terms to refer to Athens' allies, calling them "subjects" or *hypekooi*. His comedy, however, makes it clear enough that the Athenians regarded their allies as inferiors, even if it was only by a matter of degree, and so felt justified in dominating them.

Michael Herr's MACV and Washington "spin artists" and the Athenian speakers in Thucydides' "Melian Dialogue" demonstrate forcefully and clearly the manipulation of language by the powerful. Both would appreciate perhaps the lines of Allen Ginsberg's "Wichita Vortex Sutra,"

> Time Mutual presents
> World's Largest Camp Comedy:
> Magic in Vietnam
> Flashing pictures Senate Foreign Relations Committee room
> Generals faces flashing on and off screen
> Mouthing language
> State Secretary speaking nothing but language
> McNamara declining to speak public language
> The President talking language,
> Senators reinterpreting language
> General Taylor *Limited Objectives*
> Owls from Pennsylvania.[54]

54 Ginsberg 1996: 165–6 (Pt. II, ll. 157–9, 163–71); Ginsberg wrote the poem in February 1966.

8

REMEMBRANCE, RHETORIC, AND MEMORY

[Achilles] tossed from one side to the other in longing for
Patroklos, for his manhood and his great strength and all the
actions he had seen to the end with him, and the hardships he
had suffered ... Remembering all these things he let fall the
swelling tears, lying sometimes along his side, sometimes on
his back, and now again prone on his face; then he stood
upright, and paced turning in distraction along the beach of
the sea ...

(Homer, *Iliad* 24.6–12)

Homer relates how after the funeral and memorial games he had arranged for
his companion Patrocles, Achilles remained distraught over his friend's death,
unable to sleep or do much of anything else. Achilles' experience is not
unique. For combatants, coping with the death of friends in battle is a painful
experience becoming a life-long process of remembering. For a society at
large it is no less difficult. In various ways that will be explored below,
survivors remember the nature of their suffering and pass that experience on
to others. On a broader level, societies and cultures do the same thing:
erecting monuments and creating other memorials, employing literature as a
vehicle to remember these events. In the Peloponnesian and Vietnam Wars,
the societies of ancient Greece and the US experienced numerous violent
events that would have been remembered and memorialized in diverse ways.

Thucydides relates the aftermath of a series of engagements between the
Ambraciots, a western Greek people, and their Acarnanian enemies allied
with Athens during the Peloponnesian War (426/5 BC). After suffering a
defeat, an Ambraciot herald came to ask for the return of the bodies of his
dead countrymen in the customary way. Surprised at the amount of equipment taken from the bodies of the slain, he stumbled into the horror that in
fact two Ambraciot armies had been destroyed. On learning of this, he cried
out loud, Thucydides tells, "overwhelmed by the extent of the disaster [and]
went away at once without doing what he came to do and without asking

143

any more for the recovery of the bodies."[1] The twin defeat suffered by the Ambraciots was crushing: Thucydides does not cite complete statistics here, but something like a thousand men were killed, and the Ambraciots were effectively knocked out of the war.[2] It was, Thucydides notes, the greatest disaster that fell upon any Hellenic city in a comparable number of days.

In a similar stretch of time, three days in November 1967, the 173rd Airborne Brigade attacked entrenched and stubborn NVA defenders near Dak To at a place known simply as Hill 875. The 173rd suffered terrible casualties, the worst since the Ia Drang fight of the 1st Cavalry two years before. During the fighting two battalions, including the 2/503rd which led the assault and became completely surrounded by the North Vietnamese, would be severely mauled. Many men who might have lived died, as medivac helicopters could not land. To make matters worse, an airforce fighter-bomber providing air support dropped a 750-pound bomb on top of the embattled paratroopers, killing thirty and wounding another fifty. The relief battalion, the 4/503rd, finally fought its way to the top but in doing so suffered heavily. Lieutenant Larry Moore began the assault up the hill with a platoon of thirty-eight men – when he reached the top he had seven left.[3] In *Dispatches*, Michael Herr conveys the trauma these men went through, like the soldier who could not keep a cigarette lit: "I couldn't spit for a week up there, now I can't stop."[4] Herr also describes the memorial service for the Brigade's dead:

> When the 173rd held services for their dead from Dak To the boots of the dead men were arranged in formation on the ground. It was an old paratrooper tradition, but knowing that didn't reduce it or make it any less spooky, a company's worth of jump boots standing empty in the dust taking benediction, while the real substance of the ceremony was being bagged and tagged and shipped home through what they called the KIA Travel Bureau. A lot of people there that day accepted the boots as solemn symbols and went into deep prayer. Others stood

---

1   Thucydides 3.113.5. This event occurred toward the end of the sixth year of the Peloponnesian War (426/5 BC), when the struggle between Athens and Sparta and their respective allies focused in western Greece.

2   Thucydides 3.113.6. He adds that the Athenians and their allies in this victory divided the spoils into thirds, with the Athenians taking back home 300 sets of armor (3.114.4). This would place the number of Ambraciot dead at minimally 900–1000, as others reportedly drowned attempting to escape.

3   See Murphy 1993: 252–326. Later Captain Moore served as the company commander of the officer candidate school class I trained in at Fort Benning, Georgia (1968/9), and it was here that he told me of this action (also Murphy 306–7, 310). His experience at Dak To (and elsewhere in Vietnam) led him to set such a demanding course that of the 250 men in the class, half failed to graduate.

4   Herr 1977: 23.

Plate 12 US Marines salute fallen friends, 1969. Ceremonies like this were intended to memorialize the dead, but sometimes they became opportunities for commanders to encourage their men to seek revenge, "payback," for those who had fallen. Thus the cycle of violence is intensified, the wounds deepened.

Photo: United States Marine Corps Historical Center, 127-N-A193052.

around watching with grudging respect, others photographed it and some just thought it was a lot of bitter bullshit.[5]

What is involved in the act of remembrance, and how is it related to memory – both the memory of individuals and the larger "cultural memory?" The Greeks seem, at first glance, to be much more limited in the ways in which they could remember the dead, honor them, and commemorate them than a modern society like the US in the 1960s or as a contemporary society remembers and reinvents memories. In Athens there were many monuments, some of which survive today, as any tourist knows. The Parthenon, the great Temple of Athena, sits impressively over the city, but there were many others that commemorated Athenian achievements: the Temple of Athena Nike, the paintings in the Stoa Poikile (Painted Stoa) and the many statues of brave Athenians in the agora.[6] There are also a number of battlefield monuments of which the *soros* at Marathon and the Lion of Chaeronea commemorate great events. Though the remains are pitiably few, most Greek communities built their own monuments, which also remembered signal events and great figures. These include the inscribed marble slabs found at Thebes commemorating dead warriors, the "Monument of the Shields" in the Macedonian city of Dion, as well as the little-known "Circular Pedestal" in Corinth.[7] Delphi, the famous international shrine of Apollo, housed many monuments that not only preserved memory of the Greek defeat of the Persians, but also of Spartans over Athenians, etc. Fragments all, but they show that what was practiced in Athens was done throughout the Greek world. The Athenians, however, also established the "Funeral Oration," a commemorative speech that was pronounced over the honored dead before the assembled community. Both the monuments of Athena's city (see Chapter 9) and the rhetoric provide a glimpse into the heart of the Greek community and how it remembered the sacrifice of the dead and memorialized them.

But what is memory? "Cultural memory" as distinct from "personal memory" consists of a number of discrete parts: memorials and monuments,

5   Ibid. Casualties for the two battalions in the four days of fighting totaled 122 dead and 255 wounded; for the entire brigade in November 1967 around Dak To, casualties in the rifle companies were 51 percent. See Murphy 1993: 326, 328–9.
6   The Temple of Athena Nike commemorated victories over the Persians as well as Peloponnesian enemies of the 420s BC; see Hurwit 1999: 213–14. Dating to c. 475–450 BC, the Stoa Poikile housed the famous paintings of Polygnotus, Micon, and Panaenus as well as various objects taken in military campaigns; see Camp 1986: 66–72. On the statues in the Agora see e.g. the discussion on Chabrias (pp. 46, 157).
7   An example of the inscribed slabs in Thebes, that of the warrior Athanias, may be found in the J. Paul Getty Museum in Los Angeles (see Plate 17). On the monuments in Dion and Corinth see Ginouvès 1994: 100 and the *Blue Guide to Greece* (4) 1981: 242, respectively.

Plate 13 The *stele* of Dexileos in the Kerameikos, Athens. Dexileos was a nineteen- or twenty-year-old cavalryman when he died fighting in the Corinthian War (394/3 BC). Monuments like these would have helped the Athenians to remember the past and the heroic actions of fellow citizens.

Kerameikos Museum, Athens. *Photo*: Foto Marburg/Art Resource, New York, B & W Print, S0044254, 1.019.166.

147

public art, popular culture, literature, as well as physical objects. In modern society some authorities argue that the camera image, followed by film, has replaced the monument as a means of remembering.[8] All of these enable a society to construct memories and to change or modify them. Remembrance and memory then combine to provide a cultural history as well as a sense of identity. "Cultural memory," however, should not be imagined as static. Rather memory and forgetting are "co-constitutive processes," and each is essential to the other. In effect what happens is that memories are generated in new forms, a process that appears to be forgetting.[9] In much the same way that history, our views and ideas of the past, "changes," so too do cultural memories change as the present and past intersect to recreate the past.[10] The act of remembering and memorializing those who died in battle bears a distinctly Greek mark, as can be seen in Homer's *Iliad* as well as in the development of rhetoric in the Greek world of the classical era.

Rhetoric and remembrance

> I shall begin by speaking of our ancestors ... In this land of ours there have always been the same people living ... and they, by their courage and virtue, have handed it down to us, a free country. They certainly deserve our praise. Even more so our fathers deserve it. For to the inheritance they had received they added all the empire we have now, and it was not without blood and toil that they handed it down to us of the present generation.
>
> (Thucydides, *History of the Peloponnesian War* 2.36.1–2)

Pericles' famous "Funeral Oration," the speech that proclaimed Athens the "School of Hellas," was actually a speech composed to commemorate and remember the Athenian dead from the first year of the Peloponnesian War.[11] As Thucydides informs us, this speech was an annual custom that the Athenians had long followed so as to remember and memorialize their war

8 Sturken 1997: 1–12, 19.

9 Ibid.: 2.

10 Ibid.: 17. See also Bentley 1999: 154–5, who discusses memory and its relationship with history the discipline. Bentley notes rightly that the idea of memory as a "social construct," i.e. influenced and shaped by society, can be misleading. I would agree, too, that combining history, commemoration, and individual memory should be treated cautiously, but would emphasize that its results can enrich our understanding of culture and society.

11 Thucydides 2.34.7–8. Pericles undoubtedly gave such a funeral oration, but the speech as we have it is Thucydidean in structure. For sake of convenience, it is simply referred to here as Pericles'.

dead. The custom would survive into the fourth century BC (and later), though there would be several modifications. First, the funeral oration as a type of speech would itself become an object of intellectual curiosity and experimentation. In his dialogue *Menexenus*, Plato invented a funeral speech, ostensibly composed by Aspasia, Pericles' courtesan lover, in which Socrates ironically praised Athenian achievements.[12] Cicero reports that this speech was quite popular and frequently recited at public gatherings.[13] The other development that occurred followed several devastating battlefield defeats with corresponding loss of life. The occasions of these include Philip of Macedon's defeat of the Athenians (and their Greek allies) at Chaeronea in 338/7 BC, and that by the Macedonian regent Antipater following the Lamian War (322/1 BC). In both instances speeches over the fallen were delivered shortly afterwards. On both occasions, too, the Athenians commissioned leading public figures and orators, Demosthenes and Hypereides respectively, to address the people.[14] Demosthenes' speech has survived in its entirety, though some scholars find it inferior to his other speeches and doubt its authenticity.[15] That of Hypereides, long known only by title and a few fragments, became better known after discovery of a papyrus text in Egypt. From these and other surviving funeral orations, but especially that of Pericles, we have considerable information regarding the views conveyed by the speakers as well as their reflections on the nature of remembrance and memory.[16]

The funeral oration seems to be an Athenian and democratic invention, though the point should probably not be pressed. Since Homeric times the Greeks had remembered or commemorated the dead with funeral games, of which those of Patroclus described in the *Iliad* are perhaps the greatest example.[17] Even in the Homeric world, one can see in the spoken elements the origins of formal funerary oratory of later settled and urbane times. Possibly people began to realize that games, as distracting as they were on the one hand and honorific on the other, were still not satisfying emotionally in terms of providing a sense of closure. Homer suggests as much in the thoughts of Achilles following the completion of the games he had organized

---

12 Noted by Parker 1996: 137.

13 Cicero, *Oration to M. Brutus* 151. Cicero had studied in Athens in the early first century BC, and his report suggests that he might have heard the speech delivered at some recital.

14 The scholarly literature on the fourth-century Greek struggle with Macedon is immense. For brief but thorough accounts see Heskel 1997: 167–88 and Heckel 1997: 189–227.

15 See the comments of N.W. DeWitt and N.J. De Witt, p. 4, in the introduction of their Loeb edition of Demosthenes' *Funeral Oration*.

16 Additional funeral orations are known by Lysias (speech 2 in his corpus of works), while that of Gorgias is fragmentary. For text and translation of Gorgias' speech see Wills 1992: 257–9, Diels and Kranz 1961: 2, 285–6.

17 Homer, *Iliad* 23.

for Patroclus. Achilles, unable to sleep, kept turning over in his mind his friend's accomplishments and their time together, "remembering all these things he let fall the swelling tear" and was so upset that he did not even note the rising of the sun. As he dwelt on Patroclus' life and death, the recollection of which the ceremonial games had done nothing to ease, the anger and pain at his death grew correspondingly. It was this pain that led Achilles to take the corpse of Hector and in a rage drag it around Troy, submitting it to fearful vengeance.[18] It is here in this treatment of the enemy that we can see one dimension of an inadequate remembrance of fallen friends – the hateful fury of the survivors who dishonor and otherwise humiliate their enemies.

Some Vietnam veterans tell of similarly empty memorials, or no memorials at all, for friends killed, which left them enraged ever after. One veteran tells of a friend's death that was simply ignored, and the sense of rage is plainly evident:

> They didn't even have a fucking stand-down for the fucking kid. They had a fucking stand-down for all the fucking pothead mother fucking dope-stuffing mother fuckers. [Stand down] is when guys in the outfit get killed, they'd bring the whole unit back, and they'd set his rifle up and put his helmet or his boonie cap on, and play taps and shit. Pay him fucking respect. They do all this for these mother fucking junkie mother fuckers around here. They can't do it for a fucking kid who did every fucking thing he was asked to do. Fucking kid never complained about nothing.[19]

Remembering the dead began as a battlefield ritual which then, possibly with the emergence of the *polis*, became communal or civic in dimensions. This seems to be the case in Athens by the early part of the fifth century BC. Thucydides remarks on the anomalous burial of the heroes of Marathon on the battlefield itself rather than in the Kerameikos, the public cemetery of Athens, and this suggests that public funerals were an institution of some standing (see below, p. 166).[20]

The Athenian remembrance of the dead took on a regular and ritualized process that Thucydides outlines clearly. For two days before the funeral oration, the bones of the fallen were laid out in a tent where people could bring whatever offerings they wished. Then the bones were placed into ten coffins, one for each tribe with an eleventh and empty coffin for the missing

---

18 Homer, *Iliad* 24.15–22.
19 Shay 1994: 66–7.
20 Thucydides 2.34.5. The Kerameikos may be thought of as similar to Arlington National Cemetery in Virginia. For discussion see Jacoby 1956: 260–315, and below, p. 166.

or unrecovered dead. The procession then proceeded to the Kerameikos with the people following; there the female relations of the dead could make their lamentations at the tombs. Afterwards the speaker chosen for the occasion delivered his speech at the end of which he dismissed the people to their homes.[21]

Thucydides relates that the speech's primary intent was to praise the dead. By the fourth century funeral speeches followed a much more conventional format dictated by tradition and the similarity of circumstance. In addition to the idea of heroic sacrifice, the standard and time-honored themes included civic praise of Athens, including her cultural preeminence and political institutions. In Pericles' speech praise of Athens emerges in three main points: the patriotism of Athenians, the greatness of Athens and unequalled excellence of Athenian life. This part of the speech constituted that known today as the "School of Athens." His second theme evoked an image that would have found much favor with the Spartan poet Tyrtaeus – that dying for your country, as Horace and Wilfred Owen put it, was "sweet and proper." Lastly Pericles spoke to the survivors and offered comfort rather than condolences.

Pericles' speech has been studied intently by generations of scholars, but what might be mentioned and emphasized here is the connection of remembrance and memory made possible by rhetoric. As Pericles begins to conclude his second main point before closing with his words of comfort, he states that these dead have "won praise that never grows old," as

> famous men have the whole earth as their memorial: it is not only the inscriptions on their graves in their own country that mark them out; no, in foreign lands also, not in any visible form but in people's hearts, their memory abides and grows.[22]

In these words of Pericles we have all the essential components for the creation of memory, not just individual memory – that of the survivors and their fellow citizens hearing the dead praised – but also cultural memory that leads to the creation of accepted patterns of behavior for the citizen. Such an example has already been noted in Xenophon's reminder to the Cyreian army that they should emulate their ancestors who had famously beaten the Persians (p. 105): like the grandfathers, so the grandsons. From this combination of rhetoric and memory emerges the notion that to die for your country is not only brave and honorable, it is the right thing to do. The ideas presented here also lead to the invention of belief in the greatness of Athens and its historical mission. Marita Sturken has explored the

21 Thucydides 2.34.3–6.
22 Thucydides 2.43.3.

convergence of these concepts, noting that "the forms remembrance takes indicate the status of memory within a given culture. In acts of public commemoration, the shifting discourse of history, personal memory and cultural memory converge."[23]

Pericles' Funeral Oration illustrates the connections of remembrance and memory linked by rhetoric, to create not only cultural memory but also values and a shared perception of a common past or history. Demosthenes echoes Pericles' views in his own funeral oration over the Athenian dead of Chaeronea (338/7 BC). Again this is to be expected, as by this time tradition had shaped both the themes and structure of the funeral speech, leaving only to the orator linguistic or artistic elaboration and historical example to compose his speech (see Demosthenes 60.1). The reader of Pericles' and Demosthenes' speeches will find much in common: the claim that the Athenians were "autochthonous" (i.e. inhabitants of Attica from time immemorial (60.4)) the defeats of the invading Persians (60.10), and praise of the democratic institutions and ways (60.25–6).[24] This last point Demosthenes elaborates into praise for the Athenian *demos* as a whole, as he recalls a mythical legend for each of the ten Attic tribes that tells of heroic self-sacrifice for the common good (60.27–31). This theme of self-sacrifice provides the transition to the consolation, in which Demosthenes – much like Pericles – tells the survivors that these heroes have gained ageless fame (60.32) and that the world and not just their own country mourns their deaths (60.33). In conclusion, Demosthenes speaks of the heroic fame linking the fallen with their forebears and surviving parents and children, who can find their respective honor in being either the parent of a hero or the child of one (60.35–7). This brief summary of Demosthenes' speech reveals the same intersection of remembrance, rhetoric, and memory as in Pericles' speech.

There can be little doubt that rhetoric was a powerful tool for remembrance. For the survivors, rhetoric provided a rationale that proved to them that their loved ones had died in defense of a fatherland inhabited from time immemorial and whose democratic values made the community unique. These same concepts occupy much the same place in US history of the later nineteenth and twentieth centuries. This is seen most notably and clearly in Lincoln's Gettysburg Address. This famous speech reveals the same themes as the speeches of Pericles and Demosthenes, albeit with a different structure.[25] Lincoln's Address, delivered November 19, 1863 on the dedication of

---

23 Sturken 1997: 44.
24 On this idea of autochthony, cf. Loreaux 1986: 284, who argues that this myth of autochthony provided Athenian men with a rationale to exclude women from citizen status.
25 For a thorough discussion of the speech see Wills 1992.

the cemetery at Gettysburg, illustrates effectively the impact of the "Greek Revival" on American culture and society. Not only were houses, like Lincoln's own, built in this style, but also Greek ideas informed the language and thought of the time. Gary Wills, in his *Lincoln at Gettysburg: The Words that Remade America*, shows the influence of the Greek Revival on Lincoln's speech, including the use of symbol and contrast, the latter seen in the *men–de* construction.[26] More broadly, however, Lincoln's Address accomplished two goals of the funeral oration, as noted by Plato, "to extol the dead and to exhort the living." In this Lincoln succeeded, and in doing so, "created a political prose for America." [27]

Lincoln, like Pericles and Demosthenes, speaks on the greatness of the Union then fighting for its survival: "a new nation, conceived in liberty and dedicated to the proposition that all men are created equal." Again like Pericles, Lincoln aspired to make the butchery of battle intellectual, with "abstract truths ... vindicated."[28] This idea evokes the Periclean image of Athens as the "School of Hellas." Like the Athenians killed in the first campaigns of the Peloponnesian War or at Chaeronea, the men who died at Gettysburg gained an undying fame. Their achievement in death exceeds anything that the living can ever attain: "The world will little note, nor long remember, what we say here, but it can never forget what they did here."

The whole of Lincoln's Address might appear to be a consolation, as seen in the concluding message emphasizing how the dead did not die in vain. But as Wills and other commentators have noted, "the basic elements at work in the whole speech are life and death."[29] Lincoln clearly intended to show that the men (and here note the generic, as also in the Greek funeral oration) who "here gave their lives that that nation might live" enabled a government by, for, and of the people not only to survive but to grow.[30] In this instance life emerges from death, which would seem to accomplish at once consolation and exhortation to the survivors.

Lincoln's speech is typical (though perhaps not in terms of its brevity!) of nineteenth-century American political leaders, who were educated in and influenced by the classical tradition.[31] Moreover, after Lincoln, probably few American presidents or statesmen would have been as eager to speak as he had over the "hallowed dead" and be compared with him. This factor, the

---

26 *Men–de* constructions mark strong and weak contrasts of various kinds and are sometimes translated as "on the one hand ... on the other hand."
27 Wills 1992: 51–62.
28 Ibid.: 37.
29 Ibid.: 62.
30 Ibid.
31 Wills (1992: 180–1) also notes the Thucydidean quality of Lincoln's 1854 criticisms on the abandonment of the Compromise of 1850, how violence only incites greater violence.

tense political situation, and the unsophisticated education of Lyndon Baines Johnson may explain why during his wartime tenure, Johnson spoke little publicly on the subject of American dead in Vietnam. Johnson was timely in sending messages of moral support to the troops in Vietnam and reminding the public of what he saw as their sacrifices. His *Public Papers* frequently record occasions of this concern for the lives and safety of the troops, as seen in his Proclamation 3686, designating a "Day of Dedication and Prayer" for those serving in Vietnam (November 9, 1965). This was followed on Thanksgiving Day 1965 by a "Message to Members of the Armed Forces" that wished them well. It alluded only briefly to fallen comrades and noted as fleetingly that "our thoughts are with you." This message, however, came only a matter of days after the 1st Cavalry Division had lost 240 killed in its battle with North Vietnamese troops in the Ia Drang valley, to which the President's message omits mention, presumably out of concern for the domestic political agenda.[32] In a Memorial Day Speech at Arlington National Cemetery, May 31, 1966, Johnson spoke publicly on Vietnam, and in view of the day and place, his speech may appear to be a "funeral" oration. Yet in this address the President's intent was primarily to explain and justify US policy in Vietnam as seen in the numerous references made to Cold War hotspots (i.e. Greece, Korea, and Berlin) and the willingness of Americans to defend the causes of freedom and peace, whatever the cost.[33] Johnson made it clear, by quoting John Kennedy, that the US aim was altruistic: "We want the war to be won, the Communists to be contained and the Americans to go home." At the end of his speech, Johnson returns to a familiar theme, one that may be seen in the speeches of Pericles and Abraham Lincoln:

> On this Memorial Day it is right for us to remember the living and the dead for whom the call of their country has meant much pain and sacrifice. And so today I remind all of my fellow countrymen that a grateful nation is deeply in their debt.[34]

The brevity of Johnson's public statements concerning the loss of life contrasts with the private remarks and anguish that Johnson felt over American casualties. In February 1965 he was angered at a VC night attack on the Pleiku air base that killed eight US advisers: "They are killing our men while they sleep in the night."[35] This reaction led him to approve of a

---

32 Johnson 1965: 2, 1108, 1125–6.
33 This theme also characterizes Johnson's other speeches such as his State of the Union addresses. See e.g. his first three addresses to Congress in which he emphasized defending freedom against communist aggression, in Israel and Schlesinger 1966: III, 3160, 3164, 3171, 3176, 3178–80.
34 Arlington Cemetery Address, reported in the *New York Times*, May 31, 1966.
35 Dallek 1998: 248.

Plate 14   Memorial of the Ia Drang Valley Association, 1st Cavalry Division, the
Vietnam Veterans' Memorial, "The Wall," Washington, D.C. Associations
such as these, modern-day "Marathon-fighters," enable veterans to
remember the past and pass that legacy on to others.

Photo: © Larry Powell, Image number 89 from *Hunger of the Heart: Communion at the Wall.*

retaliatory strike against North Vietnam. Additional air strikes, however,
did not follow, as the President still hoped for an alternative to a wider war.
Later when that expanded war came, Johnson looked on American casualties
personally, saying on one occasion, "I lost 320 of my boys this week," while
military personnel around him used the much more impersonal "body
count."[36] These remarks show that he was heartsick at the loss of American

36 Ibid.: 283. Cf. the similar remarks of Lady Bird Johnson at this time.

lives, which he believed the media downplayed to emphasize Vietnamese casualties, as well as the atrocities committed by the Viet Cong during the war. Still he chose not to speak publicly on the subject of American dead in the two biggest battles that occurred during his Presidency, those of the Ia Drang and Dak To in November 1965 and 1967 respectively.

While it is clear that privately Johnson felt keenly the deaths of American servicemen in Vietnam, this sorrow was not effectively conveyed to the public. There are instances recorded during press conferences when he addressed this subject, but what is missing is a substantial speech to the families of the dead, the survivors, that would have offered some sort of an explanation. Only the President's 1966 Arlington Cemetery address comes at all close to being a "funeral oration," but even here his primary focus is political. In short, Johnson essentially failed to give a "funeral oration" like that of Pericles, Demosthenes, or Lincoln. It has already been shown how these speeches placed the deaths of soldiers into the historical context of society, how they were shown to have died upholding the ideals of the democracy, and how the parents, wives, brothers, sisters, and children could be proud to be connected with such men. In short the survivors would have heard that the deaths of these men meant something, that their deaths, as Lincoln said of those at Gettysburg, had not been in vain (the "truth" or reality of this is entirely another – political – matter). The popularity of the Athenian funeral oration, the fact that Plato composed such a speech for its educational value, that Cicero heard these recited in his own day, suggests that they were powerful speeches that brought comfort to the survivors, both families and fellow soldiers. The impact of such rhetoric can be measured in the reactions of many Vietnam veterans who still mourn the unrecognized deaths of their friends and comrades. The same might be said for the parents and families of these men, who received only a telegram and flag and very little else that would explain or at least begin to explain the death of a son, husband, or father.

Remembrance and memory

The last part of the painting consists of those who fought at Marathon. The Boeotians of Plataea and the Attic contingent are coming to grips with the barbarians ... at the extreme end of the painting are the Phoenician ships and Greeks killing the barbarians who are tumbling into them ... Of the combatants the most conspicuous in the picture are Kallimachos, who was chosen by the Athenians to be polemarch, and of the generals Miltiades.[37]

37 Pausanias 1.15.1–4.

Pausanias' description of the Athenian "Stoa Poikile" (the "Painted Stoa," or Porch) came six hundred years after the artists Polygnotus, Micon, and Panaenus decorated it with scenes of Athenian military exploits spanning the mythological wars with the Amazons, that at Troy, and the very real epic struggle against the Persians.[38] Such a place, and other nearby monuments, would have served as a gathering place for Athenians to reflect on the words of the orators who spoke the funeral orations just delivered. In fact one can imagine the Athenians, the men that is, not returning home but rather withdrawing to the agora to discuss what they had only just heard.

The Athenians then gathered and reflected on the "sacrifices" of the dead as well as on the orators' words that praised them and the community. This act of public commemoration and remembrance led to public reflection that would then become memorialized in one of several ways. These included public festivals, perhaps the most visible form of public memory. An example of this would include the public celebration of the victory over the Spartans in 376 BC by the general Chabrias. This was celebrated annually on the sixth of Boedromion with the free distribution of wine provided by Chabrias himself to encourage celebration and remembrance of his victory![39] After his heroic death in battle in 358/7 BC (during the Social War), an honorific statue was set up in the agora which included reference to his many victories on behalf of Athens (see Plate 4). This monument assured that his name and achievements would remain part of the Athenian memory.

The Panathenaic Festival may have also served as an occasion to celebrate the memories of fallen heroes, possibly depicted as the riders on the frieze of the Parthenon itself. John Boardman has argued that these figures represent the 192 Athenians who fell fighting the Persians at Marathon. These men were subsequently heroized or memorialized on the frieze and, it might be said, mythologized.[40] Boardman's views have been criticized on several grounds; for example the number of "riders" is not certain, nor is it clear that they would have been visible from the ground, which calls into question the idea as a whole. But there were other events in the Festival in which veterans in particular might have had occasion to recall their experiences on the battlefield. Among the competitions at the Panathenaia were those of rhapsodists, "singers," who presented celebrated songs, including tales of the Trojan War, but also lighter fare such as racy stories of the illicit love affairs of the gods.[41] For the veterans, however, the impact of hearing stories of war and the deaths of friends recited, as remarked above of Odysseus on hearing

38 Camp 1986: 66–71.
39 Plutarch, *Phocion* 6.7.
40 Boardman 1977: 39–49, and 1984: 210–15. Boardman's views have been criticized. See e.g. Hurwit 1999: 224–5 for discussion and reference to other views on the identity of the riders on the frieze. Regardless of the identity of the riders, it remains that the men who died at Marathon were memorialized by posterity.
41 Shapiro 1992: 72–4.

Demodocus' song of Troy (p. 86), could well have had an emotional impact and served as the catalyst for remembering lost friends. The similar reactions of veterans in 1998 to viewing *Saving Private Ryan* calls to mind the powerful appeal of story and song to the memory and emotions. Festivals such as the Panathenaia and that of Chabrias, then, would have provided occasion to remember past events and friends, and to celebrate their memory – to remember too what their sacrifice had meant to the democratic community of Athens.

Such celebration would also appear to be the ultimate aim of the funeral oration, or a painting or sculptural relief preserving memory of an individual or event. But memory is an elusive thing, subject to loss as well as revision, and even metamorphosing into something even greater, myth. The rhetoric of the funeral oration not only praised the dead and the living alike, it also established, perhaps even created, the ideas and values of the Athenian citizen community. This may be seen in the speeches of Pericles, Demosthenes, and Hypereides in ancient Athens. In nineteenth-century America, Lincoln's Gettysburg Address achieved the same effect in shaping the beliefs of the US at a critical moment in its history.

The funeral speech, then, created more than simply a record of life and loss. It also founded a whole system of beliefs that Athenians of the classical era, just like Americans of the nineteenth and early twentieth centuries, treasured almost as a way of life. Ideas intrinsic to the rhetoric also established a collective cultural memory that was selective and occasionally utilitarian. One can think, for example, of Xenophon appealing to the surrounded Greek soldiers of the Cyreian army – hundreds of miles from home – to be brave and resist the Persians, just as their forebears who had beaten them a hundred years before. Rhetoric's power in the contemporary world seems to have waned. An example of this may be the events and trauma of World War I that daily recede into the past and are accordingly poorly understood. During the eightieth anniversary celebrations of the end of World War I in the autumn of 1998, a fifteen-year-old French schoolgirl could only comment that the war had been "stupid." A CNN reporter referred to "memories disappearing into history" as the last survivors of that war die.[42] What the CNN reporter does not understand is that the memories in fact remain, but in a changed form and structure as they become the possessions of others who share a different version of the event. This sort of thing also occurred in ancient Athens.

An example of the intersection of memory, myth, and what constitutes the "Past," and how the Athenians might have understood this, may be found in Edith Hall's discussion of Aeschylus' *Persians*. Hall claims that "Aeschylus' audience could not tell the difference between the battle of

42 CNN [Europe] broadcast, November 11, 1998.

Salamis and the mythical siege of Thebes by the Seven."[43] One could, just for good measure, throw in the Trojan War too. Hall's argument is really no argument at all, as it does not take into account the nature of memory, how memories can change, be revised or even recreated, or, on the other hand, how objects such as relics or trophies can preserve memory. Moreover, her argument also ignores the very people, the Athenians, in question. The best example of this would be the famous "Marathon-fighters" themselves. Aristophanes in his comedies several times makes fun at their expense, but clearly they seem to be a recognizable group, and the term may have become proverbial for veteran. In this, then, the "Marathon-fighters" were similar perhaps in stature to World War II vets in the US, or even to groups of Vietnam veterans today, who still meet regularly in group and divisional associations to remember and commemorate the past.[44]

Would not these veterans be able to recognize the difference between what Aeschylus, himself a "Marathon-man," depicted on stage in *The Persians* and the mythic conflict staged in *The Seven Against Thebes*? Like Aeschylus, they *knew* they had been in the fight of their lives with the Persians, and, like veterans of other conflicts, it was something they talked about. There is only a bit of evidence to this effect but it is telling. According to Herodotus, Epizelus, the "blindman" of Marathon, was apparently famous for talking about his battlefield experience – probably to anyone who would pause long enough to listen! Epizelus recalled just at the moment he went blind, seeing the man next to him struck down and killed by the giant shadow warrior. In the aftermath of war, veterans often find themselves drawn to the families of their friends who died in battle. One can easily imagine the talkative Epizelus – a man trying to live with the trauma of battle – visiting the family of that man who died next to him, telling them how nobly their son, husband, father died, fighting a giant warrior. In this passage, memory, the heroic ideal, heroic myth-making, and trauma intersect as nowhere else in Greek literature.

Similar accounts figure in the newspapers of modern America, most notably around Memorial Day and Veterans Day – the only times that veterans are generally remembered – and report veterans visiting graying parents of sons lost in war. Such visits not only provide some comfort to the families, but also provide a tangible connection to the events themselves.[45] This would seem to apply as well to Epizelus and Aeschylus as to American veterans today.

Aeschylus and Epizelus might not have been able to vouch for the historicity of the Seven or the heroes of Troy. But they knew that the fights

---

43 Hall 1996: 9, also noted by Hurwit 1999: 212, who adds that the line between real and heroic was "not clear."

44 Aristophanes, *The Acharnians* 181, *The Clouds* 986, *Lysistrata* 317–18. The Greek lexicon of Liddell, Scott, and Jones defines it as "proverbial of a veteran."

45 As an example see the *Los Angeles Times*, May 31, 1999, A1, 25.

at Marathon, Salamis, and Plataea were real – Aeschylus had the memory of his dead brother Cynegirus to live with, as did Epizelus of the man who died beside him. The sharing of these memories was but one way that the reality of the Persian Wars would become substantive. There are dimensions to the nature of cultural memory that lend additional weight to this view. First among these is the role of objects, in which Marita Sturken has noted "memory is often embodied."[46] Herodotus tells us, for example, that after the Battle of Plataea, the Greeks took vast quantities of booty from the Persian dead as well as their camp.[47] So much loot was taken that there were probably few homes in Greece that did not have a Persian souvenir that became an heirloom, passed down through the generations. This may be seen in many American families today passing down objects from the Civil War or another conflict (in my own family there are such objects from the Civil War, both World Wars and even the Napoleonic campaigns). The point here is that such objects are more than simply interesting curiosities. They are objects that help in fixing or setting memory and bringing a tangible reality to the past. Aeschylus and Epizelus and the other "Marathon-fighters," then, could have passed along such objects as these to their families, and failing that to friends, or made them dedications to the gods. In this way the community as a whole would have seen that (unlike Troy and Thebes of the Seven) Marathon, Salamis, and Plataea were real places of glory as well as death.

In the generations after Aeschylus and Epizelus, the Athenians continued to collect such objects, and modern archeologists have even found some in their excavations. One such example is the Spartan shield recovered from a well in the agora and now to be seen in the Agora Museum in Athens. Its inscription reads "The Athenians from the Lacedamonians at Pylos," and it hung for years for passersby to see. One of these was the traveler Pausanias, who six hundred years after the Spartan shields from Pylos were hung, saw and recorded them.[48] A detail of this description needs to be emphasized. Pausanias adds that the shields were smeared with pitch to protect them from rust and the elements. This care suggests that the Athenians valued them not merely as trophies; they also wanted to maintain the shields so as to remember the event and what it meant to the community. Objects, then, need to be seen not only as "souvenirs," but also as tangible links to the past that provide memory and so history.

Cultural memory then resides in objects as well as public celebrations,

---

46 Sturken 1997: 19.
47 Herodotus 9.80–81.
48 Pausanias 15.5, and Camp 1986: 71–2. Camp notes that the shield now on display in Athens had actually been dumped into the well in around the third century BC where modern archeologists found it. Four hundred years later, Pausanias saw one of the approximately two hundred others taken by the Athenians, still preserved and on display.

literature, and funeral oratory. In the case of Athens, Aeschylus' *The Persians*, the poetry of Simonides, and the Stoa Poikile would have provided the Athenians, as well as other Greeks, with a concrete connection to the Persian Wars. In contrast, the Trojan War and the war of the Seven against Thebes lacked a tangible reality. Undoubtedly there were Athenians who believed in the historicity of these early mythological battles. But just as philosophers such as Xenophanes rejected belief in the gods, so there would have been Athenians who regarded the accounts of Troy and Thebes simply as entertaining stories. But in the streets and homes of Athens, as well as the rest of Greece, there were to be found mementoes and other reminders of real conflicts that brought home memories of war and violence.

Memory and myth in Vietnam "past"

Images have the capacity to create, interfere with, and trouble the memories we hold as individuals and as a nation.
(Marita Sturken, *Tangled Memories*, p. 20)

The Athenian audience of Aeschylus' *The Persians* and *Seven Against Thebes* might not have been as confused as to the images conveyed by the playwright as Edith Hall has suggested. In fact, there is reason to think that survivors of the Persian Wars like Aeschylus and Epizelus would have been able to help their families and friends, their neighbors generally, in making the distinctions between historic past, as in *The Persians*, and the mythic past, as in *Seven Against Thebes*. It might be thought that a modern society such as that of the US would not have such problems in looking on the past, that myth would not figure in the reconstruction of ideas about the past. Yet in some ways it may be that the issues of myth and memory in the two societies are not entirely dissimilar – that modern society is as burdened as ancient society by an overload of images and stories of the past. This seems particularly true in regard to modern American society and its imagining of the Vietnam War in film.

Discussions of film and Vietnam are many and varied in the approaches they take. Studies vary in quality from Michael Lee Lanning's superficial and apologetic *Vietnam at the Movies* to the academic though politicized study of Dittmar and Michaud, *From Hanoi to Hollywood: The Vietnam War in American Film*.[49] Yet films relating the Vietnam Experience fill a critical void in American culture, providing an exposure to the issues and nature of the War that few bother to learn about by reading either the extensive body of

49 Lanning 1994, Dittmar and Michaud 1990.

fictional literature or its historic counterpart.[50] In some ways, then, it might seem that those viewing *Apocalypse Now* – particularly if the flamboyant claim of its director Francis Ford Coppola, "This *is* Vietnam!" has been seen or heard – could as easily confuse mythic and historic Vietnam as Edith Hall's Athenians on the Persian and Theban wars. Film images have been extremely powerful and influential with both American and world society, creating such storied myths and stereotypes as the psychotic "Vietnam Vet," and inventing others, most notably perhaps the heroic "Rambo," the noble but betrayed warrior.

Already in the later 1960s it was becoming clear that returning Vietnam veterans were, or so it seemed, not always adjusting as well to civilian life as their fathers had in 1946. This was noticed particularly by the Veterans Administration, which in many instances was identified by the veterans as an extension of the military and equally untrustworthy. Years of lengthy congressional hearings finally yielded the Vet Center program, store-front centers where veterans could meet away from the institutions of government and, in effect, heal themselves. Some of these veterans became caught up in the anti-war movement, either joining existing groups and their activities on college campuses, or forming an independent organization, the VVAW (Vietnam Veterans Against the War).[51] Names familiar today in modern American society and culture – poet W.D. Ehrhart, Senator John Kerry (D – MA) and writer-activist Ron Kovic – are just a few of the veterans who participated in these activities.[52] In the winter of 1970/71, members of the VVAW organized local investigations, the "Winter Soldier" hearings (taking their name from American Revolutionary War patriot-writer Thomas Paine, who said only real patriots stayed through the hard winter months), at which accounts of American war crimes in Vietnam were reported. Shortly afterwards, VVAW organized a major demonstration, "Dewey Canyon III," which saw hundreds of veterans descend on Capitol Hill for four days of protest in April 1971. Toward the close of the demonstrations, veterans threw their decorations back at the government in contempt.[53] Then there were the veterans who because of unemployment and lack of opportunities, drug or alcohol addiction, committed some celebrated crimes and either

---

50 In 1997 my student David Urbach investigated what college-age Americans knew about the Vietnam War. Nearly all admitted that most of what they knew came from film and only a small percentage could name a book they had read on the subject of the Vietnam War. See Tritle 1998: 1.

51 See Stacewicz 1997 for a thorough discussion, including statements of VVAW members on their reasons for participating in the organization.

52 For accounts of activities for these see e.g. Ehrhart 1986, Stacewicz 1997: 232, 235, 240, Kovic 1976 respectively.

53 Stacewicz 1997: 233–51; the "Winter Soldier" hearings were later published by the VVAW 1972.

were killed themselves or, at very least, ended in police cells or prison.[54] All of this was so much grist for Hollywood, which already in the late 1960s was producing films that depicted Vietnam veterans as violent, psychotic, and generally antisocial. These include the four "Billy Jack" films, starting with *The Born Losers* (1967), and other films such as *Angels from Hell* (1968) and *Taxi Driver* (1976).[55]

In the background, meantime, forces were at work that would to some extent change these perceptions. Many of the veterans, in fact the majority who returned from Vietnam, did so silently – returning to work and school, raising families, in effect returning as their fathers had after World War II. These organized in other ways: to raise money for the construction of the Vietnam Veterans' Memorial and to participate in the political process.[56] These activities coincided with the "Reagan Revolution" and the conservative swing in American politics. This gave impetus to a reinterpretation of Vietnam best seen in the *Rambo* films (1982–8) that made Sylvester Stallone an international star (as "Rambo" an international "hero" and icon) and also the *Missing in Action* (1984–8) films that did not quite the same for Chuck Norris. These films have been properly termed "right-wing revisionism," but the same should not be said (though it has) for other films made at roughly the same time *Platoon* (1986), *Hamburger Hill* (1987) and *Full Metal Jacket* (1987).[57] While it is possible to critique these latter films on various grounds, to term them "right-wing" fails fundamentally to understand them. Oliver Stone's defense of violence in his films may actually provide a rationale for these three films, which offer a cinematographic account of the violence of war no less authentic than the more celebrated *Saving Private Ryan* of 1998: "I've been to war and it's not easy to kill. It's bloody and messy and totally horrifying, and the consequences are serious."[58]

This brief excursus on film, myth, and memory in Vietnam "Past" shows that the camera image, whether it is still or motion, has exerted a powerful force in creating myths and shaping memories. Social thinker Roland Barthes, a long-time student of semiotics and other forms of communication, argued in 1981 that the photographic image had replaced monuments in constructing cultural memory.[59] This view, however, is at best uncertain and seemingly contradicted by hundreds of thousands, perhaps even millions, of feet. For the most-visited monument operated by the U.S.

---

54 Many such stories are known, but see e.g. Terry 1984: 89–108, which tells the story of a young vet turned bank-robber. His story would be dramatized later in the 1995 film *Dead Presidents*.

55 Dittmar and Michaud 1990: 4.

56 On the organization to build the Vietnam Veterans' Memorial, see below, Chapter 9.

57 Studlar and Desser 1990: 104.

58 O. Stone, in *Newsweek*, "Quotes for the Week," October 13, 1997.

59 Barthes 1981: 93, cf. also Sturken 1997: 11.

National Park Service is "the Wall," the Vietnam Veterans' Memorial in Washington D.C., a monument that shares much with its numerous counterparts in Athens and the rest of ancient Greece.

9

THE VISIBLY DEAD

Monuments and their meaning

There is also a painting here of the deeds of the Athenians
when they were sent to help the Spartans ... [T]he picture
shows a cavalry battle in which the outstanding figures are
Xenophon's son Grylus on the Athenian side, and
Epaminondas of Thebes in the Boeotian cavalry. Euphranor
painted these pictures.

(Pausanias, *Description of Greece* 1.3.4)

Remembering the past is a complex affair that involves forgetting as well as
remembering. The invention or creation of new traditions or beliefs, sometimes including myths, also becomes a part of remembrance and memory. A
vital dimension to this process is the role played by monuments to
commemorate the triumphs (individual and group) as well as the defeats of a
society. Modern Western society – whether on the eastern or western shore
of the Atlantic – is replete with monuments and memorials and these have
been a part of Western culture since the earliest days of the Greeks. Even in
Mycenaean times the warlords or barons of the Peloponnese erected
reminders of their achievements which came to light in the first excavations
of Heinrich Schliemann at Mycenae. These seem to have been largely
personal in nature. With the rise of the *polis*, monuments and memorials
became community expressions, and nowhere are these in greater evidence
than in Athens, though clearly all the Greek communities constructed trib-
utes of various kinds to ensure the survival of the past.

Athens: city of monuments

The dead from the sea-battle of the Hellespont have graves
here and those who fought against the Macedonians at
Chaeronea, those who marched with Cleon against
Amphipolis, those that died in Tanagra, those Leosthenes led
against Thessaly, and the men who sailed with Cimon against
Cyprus, as well as the dead from among Olympiodorus'

companions when he threw out the garrison, not more than 13 men.

(Pausanias, *Description of Greece* 1.29.11)

So in about AD 150, the tourist author Pausanias described some of the monuments that he saw in the Athenian *demosion sema*, or National Cemetery, in the Kerameikos district of Athens, as he made his grand tour of the city.[1] In addition to the graves and accompanying markers such as these, he recorded the tombs of famous Athenians such as Pericles, Chabrias, Phormio, and Thrasybulus which were also to be seen here.[2] Among the other tombs in this precinct was the *polyandrion*, or multiple burial, of the Spartans who died in 403 BC assisting Thrasybulus in the restoration of the Athenian democracy. The Athenians considered the Spartan sacrifice no less inferior than their own, hence their burial near men they had been fighting against only a short time before.[3]

Pausanias describes not only the actual burials of fallen soldiers, but also the casualty lists that were inscribed with their names. These were set up in richly ornate frames, and the accompanying inscriptions identified for the viewer the places where these men died. Perhaps surprisingly for a democratic community, the dead were distinguished by rank. For example, generals and other officers were set off from the rank and file in the listings that were grouped according to the tribes in which Athenian citizens were organized. Numerous fragments from these lists have been found in excavations in and around Athens. While these provide valuable information regarding the demographics of ancient Athens for modern scholars, more importantly they demonstrate the sacrifices that Athenians were called upon to make for the community.

In addition to making distinctions by rank, the Athenians also distinguished the kind of soldier a man was, whether or not he had fought bravely and adhered to the heroic virtues. In describing another group of monuments, Pausanias refers to the inscriptions that recorded the dead in the ill-fated Sicilian Expedition of 415 BC. The reference earlier (p. 87) to Aristophanes' play *Lysistrata* makes clear the collective pain of the Athenians after the virtual destruction of their army fighting in Sicily. The inscription that Pausanias saw reveals that the painful memory was no Aristophanic

---

1   The Kerameikos, or "Potters' Quarter," lay outside of the archaic city of Athens. Construction of the Themistoclean walls divided it in half, one within the city, the other without. It was the site of the famous assassination of Hipparchus carried out by Harmodius and Aristogeiton (Thucydides 6.57.1) and also the staging area of the Panathenaic Festival in honor of Athena. I refer to the *demosion sema* simply as the Kerameikos, as most travelers to Athens today will learn of it by this name. On the excavations see further Knigge 1991.

2   Pausanias 1.29.3.

3   *Blue Guide* (4) 115 for a description of the tomb.

Plate 15 An Athenian casualty list, c. 450 BC. This fragment, one of many found
in excavations in Athens, lists the names of the war-dead in tribal order.

Photo: American School of Classical Studies: Agora Excavations.

invention. In describing the list of the Sicilian dead, Pausanias discusses
Demosthenes and Nicias, the two generals who commanded the expedition
in its final days. He states that Nicias' name was deliberately left off the list
of the heroic dead.[4] While his account of the final agony of the Sicilian expedition is rather general, Pausanias accurately relates how the Syracusans
steadily pushed and hemmed in the Athenians until they broke in half, each
meeting its separate fate. The first half to surrender was that commanded by
Demosthenes. The Athenians believed that Demosthenes had at least
attempted a defense, but more importantly, he had attempted suicide upon
his capture. Nicias, however, the Athenians believed, had surrendered too
willingly, though he too, as Demosthenes, was killed by his Syracusan

4   Pausanias 1.29.9.

captors. Accordingly, Nicias' "was despised as a willing prisoner and a man unfit for war," and his name was not placed on the list of the expedition's dead.[5] This suggests that Athenian soldiers who did not serve heroically and who died might have been omitted from casualty lists.

Today it may seem difficult to imagine what effect these tombs and inscriptions, sometimes listing hundreds of names, might have had on the Athenian viewer, the families of those who died fighting far from home. It is possible, however, to create a picture and image of what the Kerameikos may have been like in the fifth and fourth centuries BC when it would have served as a meeting point for all Athenians.

First, Thucydides (*History of the Peloponnesian War* 2.34.5) in his account of the annual burial of the war-dead, describes the Kerameikos as "the most beautiful quarter outside the city-walls." It seems likely that this would have been a precinct filled with trees and plants (in some ways it is like this today) that would have created a pastoral setting where one could find the tranquility essential to a visit with the dead. A frieze relief of the goddess Athena suggests that visits of this kind to the Kerameikos did occur. In the relief the goddess is shown looking down on a low slab of stone, probably a casualty list. Known as the "Mourning Athena," the frieze suggests that this was something that the Athenians themselves did.

Thucydides' description of the funeral procession allows for this sort of remembrance during the course of the year. While lamentations for the dead, crying out and pulling of the hair, and other dramatic acts, seem to have been rather regulated, there were various festivals, particularly the *Genesia*, where the dead were remembered annually. The *Genesia* was an annual celebration in Athens, held on the fifth day of Boedromion. It was a state celebration for the dead that seems to have been reorganized and in some ways democratized by Solon in the sixth century BC. Some modern commentators have referred to it as a sort of Remembrance Day or *Volkstrauertag* on which the community at large honored the dead. While this was a public occasion, there seems no reason to think that families did not go privately to the tombs of relatives with offerings on the anniversaries of their deaths.[6] There is also evidence of a night-long festival called the Nemeseia held in honor of the dead.[7] Such times and occasions would invariably have brought families of the war-dead into the Kerameikos where they would have, like "Mourning Athena," looked on the names of their men and remembered them.

5 Pausanias 1.29.9. Gomme *et al.* (1945–81: 4, 463–4) accept Pausanias' report as credible, but also note that by the fourth century BC Nicias' reputation had improved. At the time the casualty list was put up, there were many Athenians who blamed him for the disaster that befell them in Sicily.
6 See further Parke 1977: 53–4, after Jacoby 1956: 241–59, and most recently Parker 1996: 48–9.
7 Noted by Garland 1985: 105.

Plate 16 "Mourning Athena," relief carving c. 460 BC. Just as the goddess Athena
mourned her citizens who fell in battle, so too would the Athenians come
out to read the lists of the dead and remember them.

Acropolis Museum, Athens. *Photo*: FotoMarburg/Art Resource, NY, B & W Print, 50079950,
134152.

Families of the dead came to view the lists of names, decorate the tombs
and leave tokens of love and remembrance, and offer food and oil. Much of
what is known of mortuary practice is revealed to us on so-called *lekythoi*,
white-ground vases with black figures that were the Athenian grave-gift par
excellence into the late fifth century BC. Fragments of these can sometimes
be seen in the area of the Kerameikos today.[8] In his study of Greek mortuary
practice, Robert Garland describes the decorating of tombs, but more

8   Ibid.: 107–8.

importantly the various kinds of gifts that were carried to the tombs in baskets called *kaneon* or *kaniskion*. Scenes on vases show that tomb gifts included such objects as the discus and lyre, perhaps intended for an athlete, and swords, possibly indicating dead warriors.[9] Garland observes that the meanings of these gifts resist interpretation. In the same way, only the visitors who bring the many objects to "the Wall" understand their gift's message, a secret shared only with the dead. Visitors to the Vietnam Veterans' Memorial in Washington D.C. would likely see the same sort of mourning as in classical Athens.

These offerings are reminiscent of the many items left at "the Wall" by family and friends, so many that the National Park Service must collect and remove them daily. By 1993 more than 250,000 objects had been left at "the Wall" by some of the 10 million visitors. From the very beginning, rangers of the National Park Service collected these and kept them in a warehouse in Maryland, sensing that they were valuable reminders of past and present. These "offerings at the Wall," now comprising the Vietnam Veterans' Memorial collection, have been placed on display in the Smithsonian in Washington D.C., where the public may now view them too. At "the Wall" one can watch families making rubbings of the names listed or, as Plate 11 shows, simply sitting before a name on the wall and remembering. Numerous efforts by the Athenians over the years to restrict public expressions of grief should tell us, then, that Athenians remembered their dead in much the same way visitors to "the Wall" do today.

Remembering the dead at the Kerameikos was one way in which the Athenians commemorated those who sacrificed their lives for the community. There were other reminders, however, of this. Chief among these were the monuments erected in the agora, the center of life in the Athenian *polis* as for other Greek communities. Among the monuments that a visitor would have seen here was the statue set up to honor the Athenian general Chabrias, a veteran of many wars. Chabrias' generosity made him a popular figure among the Athenians, but as John Buckler's convincing reconstruction of the fragments shows, it was for his valor that they remembered him.

Heroism's focal point in the agora undoubtedly lay in the Stoa Poikile, the "Painted Porch," that would later provide the Stoic philosophers with their name. The great paintings of Micon, Polygnotus, and Panaenus commemorated the victory over the Persians at Marathon (and over the Trojans in that famous war of the past), but it was not the only painting that

---

9   Ibid.: 108, 115–16. Garland also discusses the offerings of drink to the dead (commonly honey, milk, water, wine, and oil) and food, including the honey-cake called *melitoutta* mentioned in Aristophanes *Lysistrata* 601 (pp. 110–13). In the discussion cited gifts have been emphasized.

Athenians could look upon in the agora.[10] There were other paintings and monuments there, including the Stoa of Zeus Eleutherios ("the Deliverer"). The Athenians built this stoa c. 430 BC in an effort to weaken Spartan claims that they were the real liberators of Greece (i.e. from Athenian tyranny).[11] As in the Stoa Poikile, famous paintings, including Euphranor's of the Battle of Mantinea, adorned its walls.[12] Also as in the Stoa Poikile, there were mementoes of Athenian heroism on display here too, particularly the shields of men who died in battle. One of these was the shield of Cydias, who was killed fighting the Gauls in 279 BC. The inscription on his shield carried a dedication composed by his family:

> Here I am dedicated, yearning for the young manhood of Cydias, the shield of an illustrious man, an offering to Zeus, the first shield through which he stretched his left arm, on the day when furious war against the Gaul reached its height.[13]

The family's dedication is interesting as it shows that Cydias was fighting his first battle, which probably would make him eighteen to twenty years old. The dedication also reveals the family's sense of loss, as the shield is seen "yearning for the young manhood of Cydias." This familial grief is reflected in the numerous offerings at "the Wall" in Washington D.C. These range from photographs of the dead and living to items brought home from Vietnam as souvenirs and gifts for the dead, things that they might have talked about wanting to have upon returning home. Such items even included a Harley-Davidson motorcycle that appeared one morning, parked in front of "the Wall."[14]

In addition to the paintings that commemorated glorious accomplishments and individual items such as the shields of soldiers who died for the community, there were also the numerous statues erected by the community. Near the Royal Stoa, for example, statues of the general Conon, his son Timotheus the general, and the Cypriot king Evagoras (Pausanias 1.3.2), Demosthenes (1.8.3), and the statues of Harmodius and Aristogeiton (1.8.5)

---

10 See Camp 1986: 66–72, and the discussion on pp. 156–7. As noted above, the Stoa Poikile also displayed numerous trophies of Athenian victories, most notably perhaps the shields taken from the Spartans at Sphacteria.

11 Camp 1986: 106–7 places the Stoa in a context of the post-Persian War era. Raaflaub 2000 notes its construction to counter Spartan claims.

12 Camp 1986: 105–7.

13 Pausanias 10.21.3–4. By the time of Pausanias' visit to Athens, Cydias' shield had been taken away to Rome as booty, seized in Sulla's sack of Athens in 86 BC. Pausanias actually refers to an inscription that recorded the dedication. Pausanias 1.26.2 records another heroic warrior's shield hung here, that of Leocritus, who died fighting the Macedonians with Olympiodorus c. 295 BC.

14 Rawls 1995.

were all to be seen.[15] Like the other monuments in the *agora*, these would have conveyed powerful images of civic responsibility and obligation, not to mention heroism. The young Athenian clearly would have realized his duty.

Monuments outside of Athens

> Stranger, go tell the Spartans that here we lie obedient to their laws.
>
> (Simonides, quoted in Herodotus, *Histories* 7.228.2)

Perhaps of all the epitaphs that have survived from the ancient Greek world, Simonides' for the Spartan dead at Thermopylae is best known. The three hundred Spartans and their king Leonidas had shown spectacular courage and obedience, holding back the Persians while their Greek allies could withdraw safely from what had become a death-trap. Simonides actually composed two other epitaphs, one for all the Greek dead and another for the seer Megistias. These were inscribed on *stelai* by the Amphictyons along with that for the three hundred Spartans. A stone lion honoring Leonidas was also erected on the site.[16] The simplicity of Simonides' epitaph for the Spartans is matched only by the heroism it proclaims. So well known is the epitaph that the Greek tourist board has placed a modern text there for visitors to the site to see today.

The epitaph also provided the title and theme to the 1978 film *Go Tell the Spartans* which some critics regard as one of the better films depicting the Vietnam War. Set prior to the massive post-1965 build-up, *Go Tell the Spartans* successfully brings out the ambiguities of the war, the anonymity of friend and foe, all placed within a context of American arrogance and sense of mission in reshaping the world. Simonidean heroism and obedience, however, also figure in the drama. The elderly Major Barker, played by Burt Lancaster in a memorable performance, does his duty even when the mission makes little sense. When a young draftee reveals that he volunteered for Vietnam because he wanted to see what a war was like, Major Barker tells him it was too bad he could not have seen a real war like Anzio or Bastogne, because Vietnam was a "sucker's tour, going nowhere." Like the Spartans at Thermopylae before, the Americans and their Vietnamese allies are finally annihilated on the site of an old French fort, where the cemetery carried the

---

15 After Athens came under the influence of the Hellenistic empires, monarchs of these states frequently commissioned their statues in the Agora as well. These, however, reflect personal megalomania and the power of the particular figure and have little to say about monuments and meaning as discussed here.

16 Herodotus 7.228.2, 225.2. Mulroy 1992: 136 notes that Simonides' epitaphs cited by Herodotus are generally regarded by scholars as authentic.

Simonidean epitaph at its entrance. Nearly all are killed, and as he dies, the old major gasps, "Oh, shit." The words may not seem heroic but they ring true. Herodotus' description of the final stand of the Spartans at Thermopylae offers a graphic parallel: "[The Spartans] resisted to the last, with their swords, if they had them, and, if not, with their hands and teeth."[17]

No amount of heroic description by Herodotus can obscure this otherwise grim scene. While the Spartans may not have said, "Oh, shit," some of them, on watching the Persians approach, surely thought something similar.

Writing in the early second-century AD Roman Empire, Plutarch turned Herodotus' use of inscriptions against him. In his account of the Battle of Salamis in 480 BC, Herodotus characterized the actions of the Corinthians as unheroic, reporting that at the battle's beginning their commander Adeimantus sailed away in panic, followed by the rest of his contingent (*Histories* 8.94.1). A mysterious boat divinely sent persuaded them to return to the fight. Herodotus recounts this as an Athenian story, which the Corinthians repudiated. He added that the rest of the Greeks supported the Corinthian contention of having fought valiantly (8.95.1). Herodotus' disclaimer, however, did not save him from Plutarch's wrath, or research.

Plutarch's anger with Herodotus' "malice" stemmed from parochial pride. From Chaeronea in Boeotia, Plutarch came from an area of Greece whose loyalties in the great war with the Persians had been subverted by Persian might. Some Boeotian towns, primarily Thebes, had even fought with the Persians against their kindred Greeks (*Histories* 9.31.5). Plutarch took up the cause of those maligned by Herodotus and mounted an all-out attack on the historian. In his defense of the Corinthians, Plutarch applied Herodotean methodology, consulting several inscriptions on Salamis island – Athenian territory – testifying to Corinthian valor. These inscriptions, erected over the dead as the Athenians had allowed them to be buried near where they died, demonstrated the loyalty of the Corinthians to the Greek cause.

> Stranger, once our home was Corinth's spring-fed town;
> Now Ajax' isle of Salamis holds us.
> Here ships of the Phoenicians, Persians, and Medes
> We took, saving sacred Greece.[18]

Plutarch also learned of Adeimantus' reputation outside of Athens, including his epitaph:

> This is Adeimantus' grave, on account of whom

---

17 Herodotus 7.225.2.
18 Plutarch, *On the Malice of Herodotus* 871e. See also the discussion in Bowen 1992.

All Greece wears the crown of freedom.[19]

The investigations of Herodotus and Plutarch show that the Greeks, not just the Athenians, honored their dead with honorific inscriptions and grave markers. These particular examples show too that the Greeks early in the fifth century BC tended to bury their dead on the field where (or at least near to where) they died. Epitaphs and monuments marked the graves. It is not clear from Herodotus' or Plutarch's remarks that the names of the dead were listed, as is known to have been the Athenian practice in the late fifth and fourth centuries BC. It is likely that the remains of the dead were simply interred in mass graves over which stood a monument with a dedicatory epitaph. The Lion at Chaeronea, believed to stand over the elite Theban "Sacred Band" killed in the Battle of Chaeronea (338/7 BC), is an example of this sort of burial.[20] Later in the fifth century it appears that the Greeks attempted to repatriate their dead when possible. A variety of inscriptions and fragmentary remains of burials from such places as Olynthus, Tegea, and Chaeronea suggests that the dead were recovered and brought home.[21] Aeschylus, no stranger to war's terror, relates such journeys in the *Agamemnon*, and how

> Ares, money-changer of dead bodies
> Held the balance of his spear in the fighting,
> And from the corpse fires at Ilion
> Sent to their dearest the dust
> Heavy and bitter with tears shed
> Packing smooth the urns with
> Ashes that once were men.[22]

Recovery of the dead and observance of proper burial rituals, however, has always been a concern for soldiers as well as societies. Xenophon tells how a group of Arcadians in the Cyreian army, as it marched on Byzantium, was surrounded and cut to pieces by the Thracians. When the Arcadians were finally relieved, the Greeks were able to recover their dead. Xenophon relates that these had lain out five days and could only be covered where they lay and a cenotaph raised to the missing.[23]

In the months after these burials, families might set up a monument to a dead warrior at their own expense, to remember him as well as to celebrate his life and sacrifice for the community. Examples of these may be seen in the incised reliefs (once painted as well) in the J. Paul Getty Museum in Los

19 Ibid.: 871f.
20 Pausanias 9.40.10.
21 Pritchett 1971–91: 4, 125–39.
22 Aeschylus, *Agamemnon* 437–444. For discussion of this passage see Garland 1985: 92.
23 Xenophon, *Anabasis* 6.4.9.

Angeles and the small but interesting museum in Thebes. These reliefs, respectively depicting Athanias (Plate 17) standing ready to do his duty and Mnason heroically advancing against the enemy, reminded their countrymen of their sacrifice.[24] In the years following Leonidas' death at Thermopylae, the Spartans erected a bust in his memory. Scattered elsewhere in Sparta were small funerary inscriptions that listed a man's name and showed that he died "in war."[25] These monuments, like that of the Athenian cavalryman Dexileos (see Plate 13), proclaimed to all a man's heroic sacrifice and death.

Recovery and proper burial of the dead are no less important in the modern era. Since 1990 reports out of Russia have detailed the surfacing of the 6th Army outside of Stalingrad (now Volgograd), exposed in their shallow (or non-existent) graves of nearly sixty years.[26] The controversy over what to do has rocked the political and cultural climate of Germany no less than the on-going debate over the MIAs of Vietnam in the US.

Monuments and their meaning to the Greeks

> War memorials are collective symbols. They speak to and for communities of men and women.
>
> (Jay Winter, *Sites of Memory, Sites of Mourning*, p. 51)

In her study of memory and its forms, Marita Sturken argues that "monuments are not generally built to commemorate defeats; the defeated dead are remembered in memorials."[27] Whether this is done for the Memorial of the Royal Artillery at Hyde Park Corner (and the many monuments elsewhere in France from World War I), or for those of ancient Greece, to distinguish between monument and memorial seems neither helpful nor necessary. In the Greek world, the first purpose of the monument was simply memory – to preserve heroic achievement and identity – as in most instances only the leaders and bravest would be so remembered. This is shown, for example, in Herodotus' account of the bravest at Thermopylae: of the three hundred, the historian names only Leonidas and three of his men, Dieneces and the

---

24 Listed in the *Blue Guide* (4) 369. In the sculpture garden outside the museum in Thebes numerous monuments of cavalrymen may also be seen.

25 Leonidas' bust in the Sparta Museum is well known, though attribution is not completely certain. See Pritchett 1971–91: 4, 244–6, who discusses the local inscriptions in Sparta recording men who may either have died abroad or from wounds upon coming home.

26 Numerous sources attest the recoveries of Gettysburg and World War I dead in the year(s) afterwards. On Stalingrad see T.W. Ryback, "Stalingrad: Letters From the Dead," *New Yorker* February 1, 1993: 58–71.

27 Sturken 1997: 47–8.

Plate 17 Detail of Boeotian grave *stele* of Athanias, c. 425–375 BC. He stands ready to meet the enemy. In doing so, he died for his country and was memorialized by his family.

Photo: J. Paul Getty Museum, Los Angeles, accession number 93.AA.47

brothers Alpheus and Maron (he identifies also Dithyrambus as bravest of the Thespians).[28] Of the other 297 Spartans, only Aristodemus and Pantites, the two survivors, are known by name. The rest are anonymous in death.

Leonidas' lion monument, however, stood as a reminder not only of the king's heroic death and sacrifice, but of all of those who stood at Thermopylae. The selection of the lion then conveys not only a heroic ideal for the king, but for all those who died with him. The lion of Thermopylae as a symbol of heroism would be followed by others, such as those of Amphipolis, Chaeronea, which the visitor may see today, and, in slightly more dramatic fashion, that of Lucerne commemorating the Swiss guardsmen who died defending the Bourbons. All project images of heroism, but obedience too.

Heroism and obedience – two themes that we have followed from Simonides' opening epitaph on the Spartan dead of Thermopylae – dominate Greek views of the monument. These surely reminded viewers of what was expected of them: to stand in the battle line, obey the commands and fight bravely onto victory or death. Elsewhere in the city, citizens and their sons were daily reminded of their obligations and visually stirred to acts of heroism. Kurt Raaflaub has observed how an Athenian, as he walked through the city, would be likely to see monuments like that of Chabrias and the ten Eponymous Heroes. Quickly the Stoa Poikile and the Stoa of Zeus Eleutherios would come into view, both decorated with gallant pictures of heroic moments and trophies of Athenian triumphs over enemies, Greek as well as barbarian. These simply underscored the personal and family monuments visible in the Kerameikos. Raaflaub's conclusion that the Athenian young were in this way prepared for war is difficult to refute.[29] While Athens is the great example of the power of monuments in shaping attitudes and forming beliefs, enough survives from the Greek communities as a whole to see that others did the same.

The monuments, then, enforced and expanded the ethic that was expressed elsewhere in the community. The pronouncements of the orators on the occasions of the funeral orations laid out the idea that the state was, as Raaflaub has observed, the "father of all and the destroyer of all."[30] Other acts affirmed this ideology: state support of war orphans, who received in the theater of Dionysus a complete set of armor and weapons upon reaching age eighteen, dramatically underlined the state's role in preparing the young for war. Athenian viewers of the monuments would have been inspired both to emulate the deeds of the heroic dead and to live up to their sense of obedience to the law, just as Simonides says of the Spartans.

28 Herodotus 7.226–227.
29 Raaflaub 2000.
30 Note the title in Raaflaub 2000.

Monuments, America and Vietnam

> They charged within 10 paces of the Wall ... The men of the
> 26th Regiment would dress on their colors in spite of the World.
> (State of North Carolina battlefield marker at Gettysburg,
> erected 1986)[31]

The casual visitor to Gettysburg today might miss it. Just below and to the
right of "The Angle" sits a small plaque noting where Pickett's heroic yet
arrogant charge against Meade's line failed on the last day of Gettysburg.
Only eight weeks before at Chancellorsville, pickets of the 18th North
Carolina Regiment had mistaken the returning Stonewall Jackson for Union
cavalry and fired on him and his staff, mortally wounding the brilliant
commander. This delivered an equally fatal blow to Lee's staff, from which it
never recovered. The collective guilt felt by the North Carolinians
compelled them to right the wrong with some act of heroism, which they
performed on the afternoon of July 3rd, 1863.[32] In the end they were only a
little more successful than the rest of Pickett's Division, but what is of
interest here is once again the now ambiguous distinction between monument and memorial. For this small marker is no less a monument to heroism
and obedience than the other markers around Gettysburg or the stone lion
and inscriptions that once located Greek bravery at Thermopylae. In the
earlier discussion of Lincoln's Gettysburg Address (p. 153), we have seen
how Lincoln turned the heroism and self-sacrifice of those who fought into a
political statement. In the years that followed his speech, the field at
Gettysburg received the many monuments that today draw thousands of
tourists and, on the anniversary of the battle, "re-enactors" as described
recently by Christopher Hitchens.[33] The same can be said of other Civil War
sites, and memorials ranging from Lexington and Concord to the Soldiers'
and Sailors' Memorial of the Spanish–American War at the entrance to the
Los Angeles National Cemetery, passed daily by thousands of motorists.

Heroism and obedience were themes that in the nineteenth century made
a certain amount of sense to viewers of such memorabilia, and the "Greek

---

31 My thanks to Matt Atkinson (of Houston, MS) of the National Park Service's staff at the
Gettysburg National Military Park, who confirmed my rather hazy recollections of the
North Carolina marker's wording.

32 The pickets of the 18th had received the order to fire from Major John Barry, who
survived the war but died in 1867 at age twenty-seven. His family believed his death
resulted from the depression and guilt he suffered as a result of having given that fateful
order. The homepage of the Virginia Military Institute (which houses some of the
Jackson papers) provides this as a response to the frequently asked question, "Who shot
Stonewall Jackson?"

33 C. Hitchens, "Rebel Ghosts," *Vanity Fair* July 1999: 34–44.

Revival" so popular and influential in that era provided a context and idea. These classical themes, however, were shattered ... like so much else ... by the tremendous losses of World War I. It seemed to many that

> the bombast of the imperial Roman monuments, of Napoleonic triumphal arches or Prussian victory columns hardly seemed to speak of the memory of four years in the trenches.[34]

In the four years after World War I, a more humanist design of memorials was adopted. The British architect Sir Edwin Lutyens took the lead in introducing such designs as that at Ypres (and elsewhere), where the listing of the names of the missing became the substance of the memorials, what Thomas Laqueur called "venues for names."[35] In the villages of Britain and Germany, however, local memorials have tended to remain heroic. This remains so into the 1980s, as George Mosse relates of the discussion in the Bavarian village of Pocking over a design for a village monument. Given the choice between an abstraction intended to warn of the horrors of war and a traditional and heroic recumbent soldier, the village overwhelmingly chose the latter.[36] In most British and German villages, however, the listing of the dead, a form of memory and remembrance since the fifth century BC, may also be seen.

In the United States, however, memorials of the "Great War" remained patriotic, celebratory, and very often practical. Memorials were broadly conceived, particularly "as part of civic beautification projects or to provide meeting places and other services for veterans."[37] To this end, civic centers and auditoriums were constructed, though many of these were not completed until shortly before the outbreak of World War II. With the end of that war the functional approach to the construction of memorials expanded, with the building of bridges, roads, and many other public structures that benefited the community at large. This occurred as recently as 1996 in Los Angeles County, where a highway interchange was named after a Japanese–American soldier, killed in battle in France in World War II.[38]

One exception to this approach to memorials was the Iwo Jima Memorial, built in 1954. President Eisenhower refused to attend the memorial's dedication, believing that it excessively extolled Marine Corps valor.[39] As one who had witnessed the sacrifice of the US Army on Omaha Beach, in the Huertgen Forest, and at Bastogne, he was entitled perhaps to his annoyance at this expression of Marine hubris. Vice President Nixon substituted, and

34 Curl 1980: 317.
35 See further the discussion in Hass 1998: 55–6.
36 Mosse 1990: 102–5.
37 Ibid.: 58.
38 The Sadao E. Munemori Interchange, located near Los Angeles International Airport, at the junctions of the 405 and 105 freeways.
39 Cited in Hass 1998: 59.

his inaugural remarks focused on the future and the fulfillment of the American dream of the post-war era. The dead were remembered chiefly as a means to a better future.

The Iwo Jima Memorial, the numerous public structures such as the Veterans' Memorial Building in Culver City, California, and the cemetery at Gettysburg, all provide the background to the construction of the Vietnam Veterans' Memorial in Washington D.C. (dedicated 1982). Previously, however, smaller community memorials had already begun to appear in cities across the United States. One of these was the Westchester Memorial, dedicated in November 1970 "by grateful citizens" and listing the names of twenty-six men "who gave their lives while serving their country during the Southeast Asian Conflict" (see Plate 18).

The photograph shown here is typical of the monument's appearance on Veterans and Memorial Days, the two occasions that it receives formal attention. Dedicated twelve years before the Memorial in Washington, the Westchester Memorial marks a return to the tradition of a community

Plate 18   A community honors its heroic dead. An American casualty list, Westchester (Los Angeles), California; Veterans Day, November 11, 1997.

Photo: L. A. Tritle.

paying tribute to the sacrifices of its members that is familiar to us from ancient Athens. It is but one example of many local memorials built before and after that in Washington.

The story of the building of the Vietnam Veterans' Memorial, the controversy surrounding its design and its designer, Maya Lin, has been much discussed. The result of a grass-roots campaign initiated by veteran Jan Scruggs, it was organized by a broad coalition spanning the political spectrum in just two years. Bob Hope, Gerald Ford, and George McGovern were among those who lent their names and endorsements to the project.[40] No less surprising was the identity of the architect, released only after the award for the design had been made. Maya Lin was young – only twenty-one – a woman and Asian-American, all facts that surprised and angered not a few people, including veterans, for a variety of transparent reasons.[41] The design, which disappointed (and disgruntled) veteran and competitor Tom Carhart described as "a black gash of shame," has proved to be stunningly classical in its effect.[42] The V-shaped memorial individualizes the dead by listing them in the order that they died during the war's course (1961–75). Men are listed with those who died alongside them and without notation of rank, meaningless in death. In this the Vietnam Veterans' Memorial deviates from Athenian lists and effectively democratizes the dead. Otherwise the list of names resembles an Attic casualty list of the campaign at Samos in 440 BC or some other place, organized only a little differently.

Maya Lin's "venue of names" does not heroize the dead as much as it remembers them. The addition of two inscriptions subtly alters this:

> In honor of the men and women of the Armed Forces of the United States who served in the Vietnam War. The names of those who gave their lives and those who remain missing are inscribed in the order they were taken from us.

and

> Our nation remembers the courage, sacrifice and devotion to duty and country of its Vietnam veterans. This memorial was built with private contributions from the American people.

These added texts established a theme of obedience and devotion to the community, ideas that the classical monuments of Greece evoke as well. With these additions, the reinforcement of heroism would and did come shortly.

40 Ibid.: 9–11.
41 Ibid.: 12–14.
42 T. Carhart, "Insulting Vietnam Vets," *New York Times*, Oct. 24, 1981.

Visitors to "the Wall" today will inevitably be drawn into its expression of grief – both in the intrinsic design as well as through the constant offerings of families and friends – which intrigues and invites the viewer to participate in the mourning and remembrance. The highly polished Indian black granite (from Bangalore) draws the viewer "in" too, reflecting you as potentially "them." The design and its startling effect appeared too untraditional and particularly unheroic, and this impelled further additions to the site to bring about the "heroization" of "the Wall." This was effected by the introduction of three bronze statues cast by sculptor Frederick Hart, himself a critic of the Maya Lin design, in 1984.[43] These figures, representing a white, black, and "other" soldier, provided the heroic touch that conservative, heroic-minded veterans see whenever they reflect on the Iwo Jima Memorial, or more likely, the exploits of John Wayne and Audie Murphy. As visitors to "the Wall" know, these figures attract little notice, while Maya Lin's design continues to be the main attraction. Contrary to these critics, Maya Lin's design was not simply democratic in that it placed all the dead on the same level, it also imparted the classical ideal of obedience to the law – of accepting the community's decision to serve.[44] This acceptance of social obligation is itself heroic, especially when the object was so obscure and unpopular. While the Hart sculptures may make the Wall's heroism clearer, it was already there for the informed viewer to see.

The building of the Vietnam Veterans' Memorial seems to have generated support for other memorials. In 1986 authorization was won for the Korean War Memorial, and its design was approved in 1989. Now constructed, it sits opposite the Vietnam Veterans' Memorial on the Reflecting Pool of the Capitol Mall. Fifty years after their victory, the surviving veterans of the Second World War will soon see their memorial, currently under development and also to be placed on the Mall. These plans suggest that there was a previously unrecognized and possibly repressed desire for recognition on the part of Korean War and World War II veterans, one that the building and naming of public roads and highways did little to assuage. Other memorials that followed include that to the California Veterans of the Vietnam War, built in 1987. Unlike its prototype in Washington, this lists the names and ranks of those who died, as well as their towns. The California Memorial also includes a series of bronze reliefs depicting various commonplace scenes – wounded soldiers cared for by nurses and various combat poses. Viewed overall, the California Memorial is essentially classical in its depiction of the themes of heroism and obedience.

These twin themes also characterize memorials that have been set up in

43 In 1993, another sculptural group, composed by Glenna Goodacre, and representing the nurses and women generally, was added to the Memorial. See Hass 1998: 18–19.
44 See also Bodnar 1992: 9, who notes also that "the Wall" can be read at once "as an embodiment of the ideals of patriotism and nationalism and as an expression of comradeship with and sorrow for the dead."

Vietnam. Some critics have noted the absence of references to the Vietnamese dead of the war, and it seems unlikely that many visitors to Washington, absorbed in the transparent imagery of "the Wall," reflect on the millions of Vietnamese dead. It has been observed, for example, that if a wall were constructed to carry the names of the Vietnamese dead, it would be sixty-nine times the size of the Vietnam Veterans' Memorial and stretch from the Washington Memorial to the Lincoln.[45]

Even during the war the Viet Cong had already founded cemeteries for their war dead. In November 1970 I spent a week with a South Vietnamese reconnaissance platoon, composed of *chieu hoi*, or ex-Viet Cong who had rallied to the Saigon government under amnesty, reconnoitering in Hoa Tu district, a still contested part of the province. During our operations we passed through an old Viet Cong, possibly even Viet Minh, cemetery in this old enemy heartland. Numerous graves were to be seen, in fact the site was so large that it had been marked on our maps, though its identity was unknown. Many of the graves had cement markers detailing names, dates of birth and death. This visit left an impression on me of heroism and obedience to a cause, the latter especially lacking in many of the South Vietnamese with whom I served – possibly the reason for the recollection even now. Since then the Vietnamese have built their own memorials and in many of these Americans figure, as both the "Imperialist enemy" and as the *Other*.[46] These representations are seen in absent apposition to the heroic poses given the Vietnamese heroes, but also as the depicted killers of women and children at My Lai.[47]

Memorials of the ancient Greeks, like those in modern America, honor the victorious, the brave, the dead, yet give little inkling of the terror and shock of battle. What of those who survive, not as heroes but shattered in mind and body?

45 Ibid.: 129, n.24.
46 M. Frey of Cologne has told me that the former "American War Crimes Museum" of the 1980s became the "War Crimes Museum" in the early 1990s as Vietnam opened up, and is now called simply the "War Remnants Museum" (e-mail, March 26, 1999).
47 For further discussion see Tatum 1996, who also examines some of the classical themes discussed here.

10

THE UNANCHORED DEAD
Mental cases and walking wounded

The strongest mind can not but break under misfortune's blows.

(Sophocles, *Antigone* 563–4)[1]

These are men whose minds the Dead have ravished.
(Wilfred Owen, "Mental Cases," l. 10)

Like Sophocles before him, Wilfred Owen's poetry reflected his battlefield experiences. In "Mental Cases," Owen combined his reading of Dante with those experiences, clarified by the weeks recovering from his "shell shock" at Craiglockhart in Scotland. Both poets convey images of the fearful toll exacted on the mind, and how "the unanchored dead," as Shay describes them, always seem to hang over the living.[2] This grip of the dead on the living was related to me also by Emma, the mother of a Vietnam combat veteran. She told me of talking with her son soon after his return from Vietnam, where he had once been the sole survivor of his ambushed platoon. As he recounted one horrific incident after another, sometimes confessing his own brutalities, Emma thought to her herself, "This isn't my son." As he continued his confessions, she began to look for birthmarks and childhood scars, to prove to herself that the man sitting before her was an imposter. Quickly her son sensed what she was doing and, like many another veteran, "went off," as he realized that his own mother did not believe or trust him. Emma's story reveals not only the change of character as a result of trauma, but also how the dead are never far from the minds of the living.

There are certainly fewer accounts that show us veterans talking about their wounds and their service from the ancient Greek world than for the modern era, but they can be found. Herodotus' story of Epizelus shows that he clearly talked around Athens of his "vision" at Marathon and surely much

---

1   The translation is E.F. Watling's in the Penguin edition (1974), which comes closer to Sophocles' meaning than the Chicago translation of D. Grene.
2   Shay 1994: 7, after Scarry 1985.

else. Aristophanes' references to the "Marathon-fighters" supports Epizelus' talkativeness, but later generations of Athenians heard similar stories too.[3] In his *Memorabilia*, Xenophon introduces an Athenian citizen-soldier named Nicomachides, who complains to Socrates about the Athenian electorate preferring an untried businessman, Antisthenes, to him for the office of general. Nicomachides goes on to recount the many wounds that he had received in the line of duty, which he believed demonstrated his courage and suitability for office. Xenophon's concern is to discuss in Socratic fashion what makes a good commander, and in the following discussion Socrates tells Nicomachides that surely Antisthenes' business skills qualify him for the command.[4] Xenophon notes, even though incidentally, a veteran soldier talking about his service, listing his wounds, and how all this is seemingly little appreciated by his fellow citizens. Epizelus and Nicomachides, separated by a century, are just two examples that could be cited of soldiers who returned home bearing physical and mental wounds of war.

Similar examples can be found following every war. The Spartan inscriptions discussed above record wounded Spartans who lingered for some time before dying. The earthquake that struck Los Angeles in 1970 completely destroyed the veterans' hospital in the San Fernando community of Sylmar. When rescuers recovered the injured and dead, more than fifty were found to be World War II veterans, some of them patients at the facility since 1946. John Keegan in *The Face of Battle* tells of a British officer of the Foot Guards, who lost his jaw and tongue at Waterloo and who died two years later of malnutrition.[5] These cases, ranging from ancient Greece into modern times, are alike in illustrating the problems shared by all societies in treating and caring for their war wounded, the casualties of both the mind and the body.

Mental cases

If someone posed the question, which would you choose?
To grieve your friends while feeling joy yourself,
Or to be wretched with them, shares alike?

(Sophocles, *Ajax* 264–6)

The chorus' answer to Tecmessa's question – an effort to locate the pain from which Ajax suffers – is clear: "the last, lady, is twice as bad a thing."[6]

---

3   Aristophanes, *The Acharnians* 181, *The Clouds* 986.
4   Xenophon, *Memorabilia* 3.4. The discussion is philosophical but the individuals Xenophon identifies are authentic. The date is uncertain, but probably c. 370s BC. See Develin 1989: 291, who cites sources attesting Antisthenes.
5   Keegan 1976: 205.
6   Sophocles, *Ajax* 267.

Sentiments such as this are timeless. Paul Baumer's *joie de vivre* in leaving his dying friend Kemmerich finds its counterpart in Michael Herr's *Dispatches*: "A dead buddy is some tough shit, but bringing your own ass out alive can sure help you to get over it."[7] Tecmessa's question reflects too Sophocles' own experiences as a general and soldier. He is known to have held the office of general in 441/0 BC with Pericles and again with Thucydides, either in the same decade as with Pericles or in the 420s. His record of public service makes it more than likely that, as argued by R. Develin, "a number of *strategiai* [generalships] cannot be ruled out for him."[8] This service, which certainly included the Athenian war with Samos in 441/0 BC, argues forcefully that Sophocles was all too familiar with the brutalities of war and explains how he could describe in his *Eurpylus* Argive hoplites tramping over the bodies of the dead and laughing. Samos, where he had served with Pericles, had been a particularly bitter campaign and was capped by a final bit of nastiness. When the Athenians gained control of Samos, captured Samian trierarchs and marines were bound to posts in the market place and left for ten days. Afterwards Pericles gave orders that they should be taken down and their heads smashed with clubs, their bodies to remain exposed.[9] Sophocles, like Oliver Stone, had been to war and knew that it was terrifying and the consequences were serious. His experiences clearly influenced his writing and choice of topics, just as Tecmessa's question – also written about this time – suggests.

Tecmessa's dilemmatic question, its theme of the living reflecting on the dead, is an old *topos* in Greek literature. Already we have heard of Odysseus' pain on hearing Demadocus' "Song of Troy" and how it reduced him to tears. Again in the *Odyssey* Homer tells of Odysseus' visit to the Land of the Dead. Here the hero visited his fallen companion Elpenor, left behind unburied when the hero and his surviving companions fled Circe (*Odyssey* 11.52–3). Odysseus then spoke with the spirits of other fallen friends – Agamemnon, Achilles, and even Ajax (11.467–9). Odysseus' abortive effort to appease Ajax reveals clearly the survivor's guilt. Odysseus remarks that he wished he had never won Achilles' armor, depriving Ajax of the prize. Odysseus says to Ajax, "Ajax, son of Telamon, could you then never in death forget your anger against me." Odysseus continues, praising Ajax and telling him how much the Achaeans felt his loss, finally asking him to ease his

7   Remarque 1929: 32–3, Herr 1977: 26.
8   Develin 1989: 89, 104. Sophocles also served as a "treasurer of the Greeks" (i.e. *hellenotamias*) in 443 BC and then as *proboulos* or "adviser" after the Athenian disaster in Sicily in 412. There were two men named Thucydides with whom Sophocles could have served: the politician Thucydides, son of Melesias, active in the 440s and the historian Thucydides who served in the 420s. Sophocles was born c. 496 BC and his service as general in the 440s, when he would have been in his fifties, seems more probable than twenty years later.
9   Plutarch, *Pericles* 28.2. See Stadter 1989: 258–9 and Meiggs 1972: 191–2 for discussion.

anger and pride (11.548–62). Ajax gives no answer, but merely walks away into the darkness. Odysseus' visit with the dead, especially that with Ajax and his tearful reaction to hearing of Troy, points to how the dead have, as Wilfred Owen describes, ravished his mind.

Sophocles' *Ajax* is a drama about more than simply "madness," its usual characterization.[10] It is a play that explains the nature of the human mind under duress and how it eventually breaks. Ajax' "madness" should not be regarded as divine but as human in its origins and placed within the context of a society that knew violence and conflict. Ajax' raging frenzy is first explained by the betrayal of his own comrades in arms, the very men he is or should be closest to, namely Odysseus and the Atreidae. Jonathan Shay has discussed the consequences for the individual soldier who is betrayed, how this destroys the fiduciary bond between himself and those around him, and how this, amid combat, can change character.[11] Moreover, for the soldier who has been exposed extensively to combat, whose emotions are compromised, it is more likely that an act of betrayal will have even deadlier consequences.

For Ajax, however, the loss of the armor only compounds what he feels in the death of Achilles. While Sophocles' drama is fixed in the world of Homeric heroes, its concern is rather with the emotions and psychology of the men with whom he served in places like Samos. As Tecmessa's question shows, the burden oppressing Ajax follows from his efforts to cope with the dead, particularly Achilles and his prized armor. Ajax' reaction to Achilles' death and the loss of his armor to Odysseus broke Ajax and led him to the seemingly mad slaughter of the flocks of sheep and goats.

Ajax' crazed reaction finds a parallel in a story told by Tim O'Brien in *The Things They Carried*. One day two GIs, Curt Lemon and Rat Kiley, were relaxing, playing a game of "chicken," – tossing back and forth a smoke grenade, the pin of which had been removed. The idea was to catch the grenade before it popped; if you didn't, you'd be covered in smoke and everyone would stand around and laugh – an example of GI humor. Suddenly, Lemon stepped on a hidden booby-trapped artillery shell and in an instant was blown to pieces. As his body parts were pulled out of the tree, another GI began singing the folk song "Lemon Tree" – his way of coping with the trauma. Not long after, Rat Kiley, Curt Lemon's best friend, expressed his reaction. He "captured" a VC baby water buffalo. That night he began shooting the animal,

---

10 Most discussions of the *Ajax* emphasize or highlight the title character's crazed conduct. See e.g. Kirkwood 1958: 102, Winnington-Ingram 1980: 20, and Segal 1995: 18. I would accept that Ajax is indeed "mad," but would argue that what prompts Sophocles' exploration of such madness lies in his own experiences at war as much as the intellectual background of the Greek Enlightenment.

11 Shay 1994: 14–20.

not to kill; it was to hurt. He put the rifle muzzle up against the mouth and shot the mouth away. Nobody said much. The whole platoon stood there watching, feeling all kinds of things, but there wasn't a great deal of pity for the baby water buffalo. Curt Lemon was dead. Rat Kiley had lost his best friend in the world.[12]

Rat Kiley kills on account of his personal loss and grief for the dead. Is it not possible that what drives Ajax to slaughter the flocks of sheep is more complicated than simple "madness"? Could it not be that Sophocles' tale of Ajax' mad slaughter is symbolic of loss – Ajax' loss of Achilles rather than the armor – and his consequent suffering? At one point Ajax states before Tecmessa and the chorus that had the choice been Achilles', the armor would have been his (*Ajax* 441–5). This suggests that Sophocles was actually exploring the connections between friends and what happened when death separated them. This would provide a plausible explanation to Ajax' otherwise mad behavior.

It has been argued that Sophocles deliberately obscures Ajax' claim with Agamemnon's rebuttal that it was not his decision to award Achilles' armor to Odysseus, but the vote of many.[13] This view, however, actually supports the position advanced here that Sophocles is exploring broad issues in human psychology. When he takes the decision out of Agamemnon's hands and places it in the hands of the many, he looks broadly at the trauma of loss and its impact on the survivor. In his drama of Philoctetes, Sophocles notes also the reflections of the living upon the dead, which suggests that this was a subject in which he was experienced personally and interested intellectually.[14]

Sophocles' Ajax is literary fiction. Within the context of the injured warriors discussed here, however (Clearchus, Xenophon's wasted mercenaries, and the blind Epizelus), it may be seen that what Sophocles describes is reality. His drama of Ajax suggests that there were Athenian veterans who had survived battle, but because of what they had done and seen had difficulty living in peace. These themes and figures recur in the literature of other times. Wilfred Owen's poem "Mental Cases" quoted earlier reflects this, and Sassoon's poem "Survivors" tells of,

> [the boys] "longing to go out again," –
> These boys with old, scared faces, learning to walk.
> They'll soon forget their haunted nights; their cowed
> Subjection to the ghosts of friends who died …[15]

John Mulligan, a Scot from Glasgow who served in the Air Force in

12 O'Brien 1990: 77–8, 85, 89.
13 Kirkwood 1958: 72.
14 See Sophocles, *Philoctetes* 427–30 and the discussion in this chapter.
15 Sassoon 1983: 97 (ll. 3–6).

Vietnam, takes up the same issue in his autobiographical novel *Shopping Cart Soldiers*. Homeless and sometimes vagrant veterans have been part of the American landscape since the "hobos" of post-Civil War days. From the 1970s, a new generation of hobos, created in Vietnam and numbering nearly 300,000, has tramped across America pushing their worldly possessions in shopping carts.[16] Familiar sights on American streets and freeway onramps, many of these are men also living with the burden of dead friends. One of these was Mulligan, who spent ten years on the streets homeless and drunk. His novel relates powerfully his own battlefield trauma and loss of friends, and how this left him simply "empty" – of emotion, of any sense of direction.[17] During his years on the streets he relates the murder of other veterans by street toughs and of alcohol-induced visions or dreams of the dead.[18] It is these dreams that in fact brought Mulligan back. In one place he relates his alter-ego Finn's conversation with his friend Johnny, killed years before in Vietnam:

> Some of the other guys are pissed-off. Ye gotta be prepared for that Finn. They're pissed off 'cause you lived an' they didn't, an' you're wastin' your life, killin' yourself with the booze. Ya can't blame them either.[19]

Like the "bush-vets" living in the mountains of Washington state's Olympic Peninsula and the forest recesses of Hawaii (and elsewhere), the shopping cart soldiers are burdened by their memories of the dead, which they cannot shake off. Sophocles' Ajax, however, reminds us poignantly that men also snapped in the classical age. It may be, however, that this comparatively (to the modern) simpler time in fact had an advantage in its simplicity and, more importantly, its rituals.

Rituals, as E.R. Dodds notes, are "usually older than the myth by which people explain [them] and [have] deeper psychological roots."[20] In such rituals, dance plays a key part, and this appears to be a phenomenon shared by all cultures. Well-known examples of ritual dance include the Greek Corybantes, Muslim "whirling dervishes," the Jewish Hasidim, and the

---

16 Newspaper accounts of homeless veterans in the US appear frequently. See (e.g.) *Los Angeles Times*, May 30, 1999 (*Westside Weekly*, pp. 1, 7) for the number of homeless veterans cited here. The *Los Angeles Times*, September 17, 1997 (A1, 16), also published a story on train-hopping transients known as the FTRA (Freight Train Riders of America), which began with a core of Vietnam veterans now subsumed by a younger group of white racists responsible for scores of murders.
17 Mulligan 1997: 116–18.
18 Ibid.: 130–4, 33.
19 Ibid.: 171, again at 181–4.
20 Dodds 1960: xiv, citing Huxley 1937: 232, 235. See McNeill 1995: 13, who discusses dancing as a human ritual.

Lakota Sun Dancers. Greek initiation rituals, for example, involved dancing; those performed in divine sanctuaries such as those of Idean Zeus and Athena were especially elaborate.[21] Rituals expressed in dance and accompanying music seem able to induce calming and joyful emotions in dancers and audiences, as a number of anthropologists have observed.[22] Depending on the occasion, dancing can induce a sense of possession – it can also become infectious and, as Euripides says in *The Bacchae*, can spread "like fire" (*Bacchae* 778). William McNeill has examined the physiology of dance and suggests that sympathetic and para-sympathetic nervous systems are involved, along with various hormones, primarily endorphins, in creating a "diffused state of excitement that is definitely pleasurable at the conscious level."[23] McNeill adds that an explanation of what induces the emotional high that dancers describe defies exact analysis. Whatever the exact cause, the widespread nature of reports from various cultures around the world confirms Radcliffe-Brown's account of warrior-dancers from the Andaman Islands "able to perform prodigies of exertion."[24]

For the Greeks, dancing and music were inseparable and included group dancing, not only for young boys, girls, and women, but also warriors.[25] The most widely performed warriors' dance was the *pyrrhic*, a war dance that emerged from sacrifices associated with hunting and war, activities requiring identical ritual needs. Plato described this dance in the *Laws* and showed that it combined a series of movements, dodges, and jumps, all in imitation of defense against attack as well as strikes on the enemy.[26] The *pyrrhic* celebrated at the Athenian Panathenaia was competitive and performed by three age-classes of men. Aristophanes refers to it in his drama *The Clouds*, where he pokes fun at the younger generation unable to perform the dance as well as their elders.[27] In the Athenian version of the *pyrrhic*, young men danced nude in imitation of the divine birth of Athena from the brow of Zeus. In the dance, warriors carried the heavy shield of the hoplite and performed a series of maneuvers in which they raised and lowered the shield, all the while keeping it out from the body at a right angle.[28]

In *The Persian Expedition*, Xenophon reported a variety of *pyrrhic* dances

---

21 Burkert 1985: 102.
22 See e.g. McNeill 1995: 7–8. Radcliffe-Brown 1922: 252, notes that Andaman Islander warriors danced before battle to induce the anger necessary to fight, and then later to enter into peace and reconciliation. Interestingly, Radcliffe-Brown was a student of W.H.R. Rivers, the Cambridge psychiatrist who worked with Siegfried Sassoon.
23 McNeill 1995: 6–7, at 6.
24 Radcliffe-Brown 1922: 252–3.
25 Burkert 1985: 102.
26 Plutarch, *Laws* 815a 1–7.
27 Aristophanes, *The Clouds* 985–9. *Lysistrata* 21.1 also refers to the dance, particularly in competition.
28 See the discussion in Kyle 1992: 94–5, including a frieze relief from the Athenian acropolis c. 330–320 BC that depicts the dance.

performed by the soldiers in the Cyreian army.[29] These included a war dance in full armor by some Thracians, a dance called the *Karpaia* performed by some Thessalians, and finally a Mysian, who topped his own performance by bringing in a young girl who danced a *pyrrhic* carrying a light shield. These performances show clearly that the *pyrrhic* was a dance known virtually to all the Greeks, though each community had its own interpretation of movements. The dances Xenophon described were performed at a feast and celebration in Paphlagonia after the mercenary army had fought its way out of the interior of Anatolia. The celebration, then, came at the end of a harrowing march in which hundreds had died and every man had been tested to the limits of his endurance. Like the funeral games held for Patrocles in the *Iliad* and by Alexander the Great on several occasions, these games should not be seen as purely festive (or commemorative) or military in nature, but as possessing a religious and ritual dimension too.[30] This suggests that such dances, with their deeply rooted religious component, had a therapeutic or healing effect on both the dancers and their audiences. Through the dance, warriors were able to cleanse themselves in a sense of the trauma of battle and leave the violence behind. W.K. Pritchett has noted that purification rituals were sometimes held after mutinies and other disorders.[31] The performance of other rituals involving actual religious sacrifices would also facilitate the warrior's return home to civilized society.

The modern warrior has little opportunity to be so cleansed. On several occasions the so-called "Boots" ceremonies held in Vietnam to remember and honor the dead have been mentioned (see Plate 12). Michael Herr described that held by the 173rd Airborne Brigade after the battle at Dak To and the diversity of the reaction to the ceremony itself. While some accepted the boots symbolically and prayed, others watched "with grudging respect, [some] photographed it and some just thought it was a lot of bitter bullshit."[32] There is little in this account that suggests that the participants, including those who prayed, could have somehow been "cleansed" of the trauma they had experienced, unlike those Greek warriors who danced the *pyrrhic* and had the opportunity to act out their fear and trauma.[33]

29 Xenophon, *Anabasis* 6.1.5–13.
30 See Homer, *Iliad* 23.257–897 for the games after Patroclus' funeral, and Arrian 3.6.1, 6.28.3 for games celebrated by Alexander (after the successful siege of Tyre and passing through the Gedrosian desert respectively). Pritchett 1971–91: 3, 183, adds that such games were also celebrated in Athens on occasion of the burial of war casualties in the Kerameikos.
31 Pritchett 1971–91: 3, 196–202, at 202.
32 See pp. 144–6.
33 Since the early 1980s American Indian Vietnam veterans have adopted ceremonies from a number of tribes (e.g. the Kiowa *Tiah-piah*, or Gourd Dance) and made them available to all veterans. Silver and Wilson 1988: 337–54 discuss the cathartic value of these as well as "sweat lodge" rituals. Holm 1996: 189–97, notes that American Indian Vietnam veterans have told how performing tribal rituals and dances enabled them to ease the trauma of death and loss.

Walking wounded

> When you cross [the river Eurotas] you come to the shrine of
> Asclepius the "Belly" built by Heracles; he gave Asclepius the
> title "Belly" because he was cured of the wound he received in
> the belly he got in his first battle with Hippocoon and his
> sons.
>
> (Pausanias, *A Description of Greece* 3.19.7)

The dead could be recovered, buried, and honored. The lucky could return
home and rejoice in their fortune with their families while also bearing a
sense of guilt in having survived. But the wounded would live every day
hence with their scars and, in cases like Epizelus of Athens and Philip of
Macedon, their handicaps.[34] The prospect of receiving a severely traumatic
wound, one involving the loss of a limb for example, has haunted soldiers
since antiquity. In his description of Sparta, Pausanias provides the above
reference to the Spartan shrine of Asclepius' "Belly."[35] Pausanias uses the
word *kotyle* for belly, which means generally anything hollow, but Greek
physicians beginning with Hippocrates adopted it to define the hip-joints
when describing human anatomy. What Pausanias described, however, and
what the Spartans feared, can be detected by drawing a line from hip-joint
to hip-joint.[36] The line so drawn crosses the lower abdomen or belly just
above the groin. It is a groin wound, and not one in the hip, that not only
worried the Spartans, but scared them as well – as any soldier from whatever
era. Hoplite warfare was violent and the wounds it yielded were as horrific as
any.[37] If an opponent were able to drive his spear upward under your shield,
the thrust would most likely enter the lower belly or groin and the results
would be frightful to say the least. Richard Holmes comments that "it
requires no great feat of mental gymnastics to connect the powerful pres-
sures of *machismo* which spur on so many soldiers."[38] (It is not just soldiers
who are so worried. Observe the posture of soccer players on a penalty kick
and you will see the same fears acted out!)

More horrific but probably not more frightening were the fears of similar

---

34 During his reign as king of Macedon (360/59–336 BC), Philip II suffered wounds to his
   leg and thigh which left him nearly crippled, and lost the sight of an eye, taken by an
   arrow (see Demosthenes 18.67, Didymus in Demosthenes 12.64, Isocrates, *Letters*
   2.1–12, Diodorus 16.34.5 respectively). His son Alexander the Great suffered an even
   greater number of wounds, some of which were nearly mortal. Cf. Lazenby 1991: 102,
   who suggests that the sources say little about the wounded.
35 See Hippocrates, *Places in Man* 7 (ed. E.M. Craik) for an anatomical description.
36 See Hippocrates, *Places in Man* (ed. E.M. Craik), App. II (p. 238), for illustration.
37 Anderson 1991: 32–4, discusses some of the other wounds known to have occurred in
   battle.
38 Holmes 1985: 182.

wounds in Vietnam. An American GI, speculating on the fate of casualties from "Bouncing Betties," commented that "they explode and get your thighs, take your penis, your rectum ... So big deal, you get a guy to the hospital and you save his life, but if he's not a quadriplegic, he's got a colostomy, he can't have sex, he can't have kids."[39] Asclepius of the "Belly" and fears of "Bouncing Betties" illustrate powerfully the universal fear of catastrophic wounds that has haunted soldiers over the last two thousand years. I remember upon arriving in Vietnam the dread of booby-traps that would leave you without legs or arms, but yet alive, wondering how life could still be lived. Hardly less worrisome were concerns for receiving some kind of care.

Such care for wounded veterans is well known in several instances. It is possible that in the great empires of the Ancient Near East prominent individuals might have received some sort of bounty from a grateful king. Disabled Roman soldiers received the privileges of those discharged upon completion of their service, but later generations of soldiers were seldom as fortunate.[40] In 1671 Louis XIV ordered the establishment of the Hôtel des Invalides in Paris that would care for the seriously injured and disabled. By the end of the seventeenth century, Les Invalides housed four thousand disabled soldiers, but these represented only a small percentage of those eligible for residence.[41] After the Civil War, similar hospitals were established throughout the US to care for Union veterans. Out of these "Soldiers' Homes" would grow the US Veterans Administration, which today operates a vast complex of hospitals and clinics on a billion-dollar annual budget.

Veteran care, then, has a long history of its own, but the earliest appearance of bureaucratic procedures for assisting the war wounded seems to have been in Athens in the later fifth century BC, right at the time Sophocles was composing his dramas. In his life of the Athenian statesman Solon, Plutarch reports that he "added laws, one of which is that the maimed in the wars should be maintained at the public expense; this Heracleides of Pontus records, and that Pisistratus followed Solon's example."[42]

---

39 Baker 1981: 276; see also Murphy 1993: 305, Holmes 1985: 182–3 for other examples.
40 Roman soldiers incapacitated by battle were eligible for discharge by *honesta missio*, but those who had become mentally or physically unfit were discharged without privileges. See Watson 1969: 124, citing relevant sources.
41 The Hôtel des Invalides is today a curious museum and monument. It is fully "heroic" in its exhibition of nineteenth- and twentieth-century warfare and images of "glorious" death, mostly from the Napoleonic era. Unless one were to look closely – and the casual tourist or observer would miss it altogether – at some of the literature, it could be easily missed that this vast structure was originally built to care for bodies shattered in war. One might reasonably expect to see some sort of an exhibit, a room set up as the "*Invalides*" lived, but there is nothing at all like this. The current display of heroic imagery calls to mind those of classical Athens or the battlefield at Gettysburg and omits altogether any mention of the real horror of war.
42 Plutarch, *Solon* 31.3–4.

Plutarch's statement that Solon had provided veterans with state subsidies in the early sixth century BC has received little support.[43] In the late fifth century BC, as Athenian democrats and oligarchs battled for leadership of the community, they tended to describe laws as "Solon's" in order to empower their own political views and platforms. Some scholars even argue that the phrase "Solon's laws" is an Athenian shorthand for simply an "old" law, the author of which had been forgotten.[44] Moreover, it seems unlikely that until the establishment of the Athenian Empire in the mid-fifth century, Athens would have had adequate financial resources to fund such payments, or that there would have been so many crippled veterans to demand it. While the suggestion is attractive that payments for the war wounded began in the Periclean era, it is just as likely that these began earlier, in the aftermath of the victory over the Persians c. 454 BC. The blind Epizelus of Marathon fame should remind us that Athens had fought more than enough battles to provide him with company, sitting around the Agora, telling their stories to whomever would listen.

While the exact date at which the Athenians resolved to care for their disabled veterans may be unknown, it is clear that by the later fifth century, the Athenian *boule* or Council had responsibility for disbursing monies to invalid veterans. The Athenian Constitution reports that

> there is a law which orders that those holding property less than 3 *minae* and who are so disabled physically that they cannot work shall, after having been examined by the Council, receive 2 *obols* daily from the public funds. The Treasurer [for the invalids] is selected by lot.[45]

The property qualification and the amount of money distributed argues that the Athenians attempted to reach as many of the disabled as possible and provide them with just enough to survive each day. The low property qualification may also reflect the casualties suffered by poorer citizens, who provided the crews to Athenian warships. There can be little doubt that the ramming tactics used in ancient naval warfare would have left a number of men with arms and legs crippled by shattered oars and smashed hulls.

The Athenians may also have assumed support of the sons of men who fell in battle at about the same time.[46] These orphans were supported by the

---

43 See the discussion in Jacoby, *Die Fragmente der griechischen Historiker* 328 F 197 and Rhodes 1981: 570.

44 Sinclair 1988: 1 refers to various discussions.

45 Aristotle, *The Constitution of the Athenians* 49.4, with Rhodes 1981: 570 for discussion. The property qualification was substantially below that of the wealthy families who provided Athens with its religious festivals and fleet. The amount paid to invalids amounts to one-third of what a skilled craftsman could receive in a day's work. See Davies 1971: xviii–xxii.

46 Aristotle (?), *The Constitution of the Athenians* 24.3, with Rhodes 1981: 308–9.

state until they came of age (eighteen). Athens seems not to have been unique in its support of war orphans, as Aristotle reports that Hippodamus established such care in Miletus, and that other cities made similar arrangements for their orphans (*Politics* 1268a 8–12). During the great festival honoring Dionysus, the City Dionysia, Athenian orphans paraded into the theater, where they were presented to the assembled citizens, identified and then given a set of hoplite arms (Aeschines 3.154). Perhaps no other ceremony at the Dionysia, where the great dramas of the fifth century were staged, makes clearer the connection between theater and war, the *telos* or goal of the Athenian citizen.[47]

Over his long life, Sophocles witnessed many of these ceremonies. In view of his experiences as general and commander, it would surely be a bit odd if his dramas did not allude to the realities of war veiled in the language and story of myth. When Sophocles wrote *Philoctetes* c. 409 BC, invalid Athenians had been receiving state support for perhaps twenty to thirty years. In this drama Sophocles tells of a disabled soldier abandoned by his friends on account of his festering and foul-smelling wound. In this context Sophocles' *Philoctetes* acquires special significance: first, as a drama generally about the aftermath of war, but more particularly its effects on the survivors. When Sophocles wrote the drama, Athens had been at war with Sparta over two decades and Athenian soldiers and seamen had suffered accordingly. At the beginning of the play, Odysseus explains that he abandoned Philoctetes on Lemnos because "we had no peace with him ... he screamed and groaned ... all the camp was haunted by him."[48] This would seem to reflect life in Athens at the time, which would have resembled an armed camp. The streets of Athens were narrow to begin with and the houses were cramped together.[49] During the Peloponnesian War, space was even tighter, as many people from the country had fled to Athens seeking refuge from the annual Spartan invasions. In such close quarters people could hear the cries and moans of the wounded and, more disturbing, see their amputated limbs and smell the infections, as men slowly and painfully died from their wounds.

The less severely wounded, veterans like Epizelus and Nicomachides, could be heard on the streets and in the Agora, and what they had to say would have been unsettling. In the drama, when Philoctetes learns that Odysseus still lives, he reacts with bitter disappointment at his survival and the deaths of better men. Achilles' son, young Neoptolemus, responds that "war never takes a bad man but by chance, the good man always."[50] This

47 Observed by Goldhill 1986: 120.
48 Sophocles, *Philoctetes* 6–10.
49 See Wycherley 1978: 237–46. In some Greek villages today, such as Megalochori in Thira (Santorini), one can get the feel for this congestion and how you can literally hear what your neighbors are saying and doing in the house next door.
50 Sophocles, *Philoctetes* 437–8.

sparks a discussion on the idea of survival itself and prompts this soldier's philosophy from Philoctetes:

> [The Gods] find their pleasure in turning back from Death
> the rogues and tricksters, but the just and good
> they are always sending out of the world.
> How can I reckon the score, how can I praise,
> When praising Heaven I find the gods are bad?[51]

Philoctetes' reflections on the plight of the disabled and abandoned soldier could have been spoken as easily by Ron Kovic. Reared in the patriotic vistas that were 1950/60s America, Ron Kovic suffered a spinal injury that left him paralyzed from the chest down. As he describes himself, "I gave my dead dick for John Wayne."[52] Kovic's wound returned him home for "recovery" and treatment, first in the St. Albans Naval Hospital and then a Veterans Administration hospital in New York.[53] The resources of these facilities were severely stretched during 1968–70 as these years saw the greatest number of seriously injured returned to the US. Patient care was frequently sub-standard and worse:

> The wards are filthy. The men in my room throw their breadcrumbs under the radiator to keep the rats from chewing on our numb legs during the night ... There are never enough aides to go around on the wards, and constantly there is complaining by the men. The most severely injured are totally dependent on the aides to turn them ... The sheets are never changed enough and many of the men stink from not being properly bathed. It never makes any sense to us how the government can keep asking money for weapons and leave us lying in our own filth.[54]

Marginal care and occasional staff abuse account in part for Kovic's angry denunciation of the health care accorded wounded veterans. Many of these men, however, were angered by what they saw as a nation's rejection of them for having served in Vietnam in the first place. This "killing the messenger" attitude of many Americans at the time is conveyed by a story told by Frederick Downs upon his return home. After a booby-trap had taken off his left arm from the shoulder and left him with other assorted injuries, he returned to complete his education at the University of Denver, prosthetic arm and all. One day a stranger greeted him on the street and asked, "Get

---

51 Sophocles, *Philoctetes* 448–52.
52 Kovic 1976: 112.
53 Ibid.: 28, 32–9.
54 Ibid.: 38.

that in Vietnam?" When he replied yes, the man said, "Serves you right," and then walked away.[55]

While not all wounded or returning GIs from Vietnam suffered this kind of abuse, it remains clear that it occurred. In 1998, Jerry Lembcke, himself a Vietnam veteran, published *The Spitting Image* in which he rejected as apocryphal the notion that GIs returning from Vietnam were spat on, the equivalent of the urban myth that alligators live in New York city sewers.[56] Lembcke argues that the absence of newspaper stories or pictures taken by GIs or FBI agents proves that such incidents never happened. Entirely omitted, surely as anecdotal – a convenient way round an inconvenient piece of evidence – are the reports of veterans themselves. These range from David Bateman, a North Dakota delegate to Boys Nation with Bill Clinton in 1963, to my childhood friend Mark, who could both testify, place and date, to receiving a "spitting welcome" home.[57] Army nurse Lynda Van Devanter tells a similar story of spit along with curses including a believable, "Fuck you, Nazi bitch," upon returning home from Vietnam in 1970.[58] It would be specious to claim that every returning GI was ill-treated upon returning from Vietnam. In reality, most were simply ignored as American society went about its business, content to let the "under-classes" fight the war that touched them only if a relative was unlucky enough to get caught up in it.

Since the early 1990s, the Vietnam veteran has found his identity as well as his war-time trauma attacked by the conservative press and establishment. This assault has been underway since the publication of Wilbur Scott's *The Politics of Readjustment: Vietnam Veterans Since the War* (1993). In this work Scott argued that PTSD was a political-social construct of anti-war psychiatrists such as Robert J. Lipton and Chaim Shatan.[59] Eric Dean's *Shook Over Hell* advanced this conservative stance, taken up most recently by B.G. Burkett and G. Whitley in *Stolen Valor*.[60] Burkett and Whitley identified a number of fakes and fantasists who passed themselves off as Vietnam veterans and heroes when in fact they either never served in the military or, if they did, never saw Vietnam.[61] Such fraud and résumé-padding, however, have long been known. While there are many examples from the modern

---

55 Downs 1978: 11.
56 Lembcke 1998: 71–83. In D.L. Ulin's *Los Angeles Times* piece, "War Stories," July 3, 1998, the phrase "urban myth" is attributed to Lembcke.
57 Bateman recounted his incident on the ABC program "Nightline," July 20, 1998; Mark told me of what happened to him in 1968 and recently reconfirmed the incident.
58 Van Devanter 1983: 246–7, not cited by Lembcke, as also Downs 1978.
59 Discussed by B. Shephard, "Still in Shock," *Times Literary Supplement*, July 16, 1999, pp. 4–5.
60 See pp. 56–9.
61 Burkett and Whitley 1998, reported uncritically in the popular media, e.g. the *Los Angeles Times*, May 31, 1999, A1, 22.

era, the character is not unfamiliar from the ancient world.[62] When the Athenian politician Cleon rose in the assembly to tell the Athenians that he had a "plan" for defeating the Spartans trapped on Sphacteria, they burst out laughing (Thucydides 4.28.5). This is one of the few places in Thucydides' *History* where the historian notes laughter, and its occasion here must reflect Cleon's unfounded pretensions.[63] Burkett and Whitley also attack a number of prominent psychiatrists and trauma counselors who have spent decades investigating the nature of PTSD and those who have worked with veterans suffering from it.[64] In essence, their work is strongly anti-intellectual in that it fails to consider even remotely the advances made by the medical community since the World Wars in understanding the biology and psychology of trauma. Their position, as Shephard rightly notes, is a "medical version of the stab-in-the-back legend – that General Westmoreland could have won the war in Vietnam if the politicians and media had given him proper backing."[65]

Anti-intellectual in its understanding of modern medicine, the conservative attack also ignores the examples of Clearchus, Ajax, and Epizelus from the Greek world, who show that war-induced trauma was as much a reality then as after the World Wars and Vietnam. Such views are not simply academic concerns. Left unchallenged, the wider public will believe that PTSD and Gulf War Syndrome, for example, are imaginary constructs, and the danger here is that future generations will be left unprepared for the consequences of war and violence.

62 Severo and Milford 1989: 140–1, report three bank-robbers in 1860s New England, who explained to their victims that the Civil War had turned them into criminals. When they were finally caught, it was learned that they had spent the war as prisoners in New York's Sing Sing prison. Other examples of such fraud could easily be found.
63 See Lateiner 1977: 175. Cleon's plan worked, though the credit should be given to Demosthenes, the Athenian general already in command at Pylos/Sphacteria. Even at the time Athenians believed that Cleon had taken advantage of Demosthenes. See Aristophanes, *The Knights* 54–7.
64 Burkett and Whitley 1998: 152–3, 283–6.
65 Shephard in *Times Literary Supplement*, July 16, 1999 (see above n. 59).

11

AFTERWORD

For Lieutenants Bill Sullivan, Rod Ubermann, and Morgan Weed, killed in action,
1969–70, Republic of Vietnam

When Pericles addressed the Athenians on the eve of the Peloponnesian
War, Thucydides records (*History of the Peloponnesian War* 1.144.3) that he
told them:

> it must be known that war is inevitable, but that if we accept it
> more readily we will find our enemies less committed, and that out
> of the greatest dangers emerge the greatest honors for both city and
> individual.

Other sources confirm that the Greeks saw war as simply a bleak reality.
While it afforded young men, as Pericles implies, the opportunity to
emulate Achilles and win praise and undying fame, it was also recognized as
an unfortunate dimension to life, one grudgingly accepted as the necessary
complement to the happier events of domestic bliss. For present-day
American society, the inevitability of war is a view to which few would
subscribe. The United States has not fought a major war, one that involved
the massive mobilization of the country and its resources, since before the
fall of Saigon in 1975. Since then, excursions into Panama, Grenada, and
Somalia, the much greater effort of the Gulf War in 1990/91, followed by
the current undeclared war against Iraq and the war against Serbia have
brought to light the lingering aftermath of Vietnam and rekindled anxieties
over future conflicts.

In an essay titled "The Body Count is Back – Numbers Game," Ryan
Lizza of *The New Republic* described NATO's efforts to convince the court of
world opinion that Serb forces in Kosovo were being hammered daily by
NATO warplanes.[1] According to NATO spokesman Jamie Shea who, as
Lizza wryly observes, "seemed to relish the task," thousands of Serb soldiers

1   R. Lizza, *The New Republic*, July 19 and 26, 1999, pp. 16–18.

were listed as killed and hundreds of tanks, artillery pieces, etc. destroyed. When the Serbs finally withdrew from Kosovo, the absurd emptiness of these reports was made only too clear. NATO public relations attempts to quantify the unquantifiable evoked the memory of Vietnam and McNamara's criterion of victory – body count – and the bureaucratic mentality that sought to appease the media appetite for news. Lizza's essay rightly picks up on all of this as well as the strategic fog that plagued NATO's handling of Kosovo, a fog that has not lifted since the Serb military abandoned Kosovo and KFOR entered. NATO and Washington number-crunching, however, reveals not only the survival of the "Vietnam Syndrome," but the ease with which the public can be pacified with "Film at Eleven" photo-ops of [not] "Smart bombs" and deceptive reports of military success.

Kosovo also revealed both a government and a society reluctant to send ground troops into battle, particularly if the purpose and presumed threat were vague or distant. Whether or not future generations of Americans will go off to war to experience its horrors remains to be seen. A pessimist's view might be that the odds are good that future generations of Americans will indeed experience war, violence, and trauma, and then return home to face those who sent them off. Such is the view of General Josiah Bunting, super-intendent of the Virginia Military Institute, who believes this to be the case:

> [N]ot a few [will be] killed. It is the cost of doing business if you are a powerful democracy in the twentieth and twenty-first centuries. Surely in our national future crouch hundreds of wars, waiting silently for men, and now – barbarous to think – women to join them. For every Shiloh and Saratoga, there will be a dozen Khe Sanhs and Kuwaits. Our students should be ready for them.[2]

General Bunting's sobering remarks suggest that the questions posed at the beginning of this book are not merely matters of academic concern. Who should go off to fight these future conflicts that the general is so sure will occur? The volunteer-based armed forces favored by the US are currently below strength, and recruitment goals the last two years have fallen short.[3] With a booming economy there is little likelihood that this will change, and military forces will be further stretched. While there are efforts made to conceal the reality, it remains that those without education and opportunity, and access to it, are constrained to expose themselves to risks that the elites

---

2 Bunting 1998: 34.
3 See A.J. Bacevich, "Combat Unready," *The New Republic*, June 14, 1999, pp. 21–4, who notes *inter alia* that the Air Force pilot shortfall will reach 15 percent by the end of 1999, while there is a similar shortage of junior officers in the other branches.

avoid.[4] The contrast with ancient Greek society, in which the citizenry bore equally the burdens of military service, could not be plainer. There would seem to be another interesting point–counterpoint in the manner in which the ancient Greeks and modern Americans made their decisions to go to war. Such decisions are surely so important that they cannot be left in the hands of a few, but must be decided democratically.

It has been shown how a generation of Americans was deceived in almost criminal fashion and exposed to horrific situations of violence in which they were both its agents and objects. The questions that not only every American, but every citizen of a free state, should ask are: can this happen again? Can it be prevented?

4   This may be seen, for example, by investigation of those high schools in the US that are visited by armed forces recruiters. Invariably these concentrate their activities in those schools in which minority and working-class students are greatest in number; schools in affluent areas rarely receive pep-talks from recruiters. Similarly *The Independent* (UK) from July 11, 1999, carried an article in which the government advised young men without jobs and education to seek service in the armed forces.

BIBLIOGRAPHY

The bibliography cites only books and articles referenced in the text. Omitted are magazine and newspaper articles; citations of these are given in full in the notes.

Violence, culture, and society

Ambrose, S. (1994). *D-Day June 6, 1944: The Climactic Battle of World War II*. New York: Simon & Schuster.

——(1997). *Citizen Soldiers: The U.S. Army from the Normandy Beaches to the Bulge to the Surrender of Germany, June 7, 1944–May 7, 1945*. New York: Simon & Schuster.

Barthes, R. (1981). *Camera Lucida: Reflections on Photography*. Trans. by R. Howard. New York: Hill and Wang.

Bentley, M. (1999). *Modern Historiography: An Introduction*. London: Routledge.

Bodnar, J. (1992). *Remaking America: Public Memory, Commemoration, and Patriotism in the Twentieth Century*. Princeton: Princeton University Press.

Collingwood, R.G. (1946). *The Idea of History*. New York: Oxford University Press.

Curl, J.S. (1980). *A Celebration of Death: An Introduction to Some of the Buildings, Monuments, and Settings of Funerary Architecture in the Western European Tradition*. London: Constable.

Dean, E.T., Jr. (1997). *Shook Over Hell: Post-Traumatic Stress, Vietnam and the Civil War*. Cambridge, Mass.: Harvard University Press.

Friedman, M.J., Charney, D.S., and Deutch, A.Y. (eds.) (1995). *Neurobiological and Clinical Consequences of Stress: From Normal Adaptation to Post–Traumatic Stress Disorder*. Philadelphia: Lippincott-Raven Publishers.

Fussell, P. (1988). *Thank God for the Atom Bomb and Other Essays*. New York: Summit.

——(1989). *Wartime: Understanding and Behavior in the Second World War*. New York: Oxford University Press.

——(1996). *Doing Battle: The Making of a Skeptic*. Boston: Little, Brown & Company.

Ginsberg, A. (1996). *Selected Poems, 1947–1995*. New York: HarperCollins Publishers.

Graves, R. (1929/1957). *Good-Bye to All That*. Rev. 2nd ed., New York: Doubleday.

Hass, K.A. (1998). *Carried to the Wall: American Memory and the Vietnam Veterans' Memorial*. Berkeley: University of California Press.

Heer, H. and Otte, B. (eds.) (1996). *Vernichtungskrieg: Verbrechen der Wehrmacht 1941 bis 1944*. Hamburg: Hamburger Edition.

Herman, J. (1997). *Trauma and Recovery*. New York: Basic Books.

Holmes, R. (1985). *Acts of War: The Behavior of Men in Battle*. New York: The Free Press.

Huxley, A. (1937). *Ends and Means: An Inquiry into the Nature of Ideals and into Methods Employed for Their Realization*. 5th ed., London: Harper & Brothers.

Jennings, P. and Brewster, T. (1998). *The Century*. New York: Doubleday.

Jones, J. (1962/1998). *The Thin Red Line*. New York: Dell Publishing Group, Inc.

Keegan, J. (1976). *The Face of Battle*. Harmondsworth: Penguin Books.

Lawrence, T.E. (1926/1935). *Seven Pillars of Wisdom: A Triumph*. Garden City, NY: Doubleday, Doran and Company, Inc.

Linderman, G.F. (1997). *The World Within War: America's Combat Experiences in World War II*. New York: The Free Press.

Marwick, A. (1971). *The Nature of History*. New York: Alfred A. Knopf.

Mason, P.H.C. (1990). *Recovering From the War: A Woman's Guide to Helping Your Vietnam Vet, Your Family and Yourself*. New York: Viking Penguin.

Matsakis, A. (1996). *Vietnam Wives: Facing the Challenges of Life with Veterans Suffering Post-Traumatic Stress*. 2nd ed., Lutherville, MD: The Sidran Press.

McNeill, W. (1963/1991). *The Rise of the West: A History of the Human Community*. Chicago: University of Chicago Press.

——(1995). *Keeping Together in Time: Dance and Drill in Human History*. Cambridge, MA.: Harvard University Press.

Miller, S.C. (1982). *"Benevolent Assimilation": The American Conquest of the Philippines, 1899–1903*. New Haven: Yale University Press.

Mosse, G.L. (1990). *Fallen Soldiers. Reshaping the Memory of the World Wars*. New York: Oxford University Press.

Owen, W. (1973). *War Poems and Others*. Ed. with an Introduction and Notes by D. Hibberd. London: Chatto & Windus.

Popkin, J.D. (1999). "Historians on the Autobiographical Frontier". *American Historical Review* 104: 725–48.

Radcliffe-Brown, A.R. (1922). *The Andaman Islanders*. Cambridge: Cambridge University Press.

Remarque, E.M. (1929). *All Quiet on the Western Front*. Boston: Little, Brown & Company.

Romains, J. (1939). *Men of Good Will*. Vol. VIII: *Verdun*. Trans. by G. Hopkins. New York: Alfred A. Knopf.

Ruskin, J. (1903–12). *The Complete Works of John Ruskin*. Ed. by E.T. Cask and A. Wedderburn. 39 vols. New York: Longmans, Green & Company.

Saigh, P.A. and Bremner, J.D. (eds.) (1999). *Post Traumatic Stress Disorder: A Comprehensive Text*. Boston: Allyn & Bacon.

Sandoz, M. (1942/1992). *Crazy Horse: The Strange Man of the Oglalas*. Lincoln: University of Nebraska Press.

Sapolsky, R. (1997). *The Trouble with Testosterone and Other Essays on the Biology of the Human Predicament*. New York: Scribner.

Sassoon, S. (1968). *Selected Poems*. London: Faber and Faber.

——(1983). *The War Poems*. Arranged and Introduced by R. Hart-Davies. London: Faber and Faber.

Scarry, E. (1985) *The Body in Pain. The Making and Unmaking of the World*. New York: Oxford University Press.

Schmidbauer, W. (1998). *"Ich Wusste nie, was mit Vater ist": Das Trauma des Krieges*. Hamburg: Rowohlt.

Severo, R. and Milford, L. (1989). *The Wages of War: When America's Soldiers Came Home from Valley Forge to Vietnam*. New York: Simon & Schuster.

Shatan, C. (1973). "The Grief of Soldiers: Vietnam Combat Veterans' Self-Help Movement". *American Journal of Orthopsychiatry* 43: 640.

——(1982). "The Tattered Ego of Survivors". *Psychiatric Annals* 12/11: 1031–8.

——(1997). "Living in a Split Time Zone: Trauma and Therapy of Vietnam Combat Survivors". *Mind and Human Interaction* 8: 205–23.

Shay, J. (1994). *Achilles in Vietnam: Combat Trauma and the Undoing of Character*. New York: Athenaeum.

——(1995). "The Birth of Tragedy – Out of the Needs of Democracy". *Didaskalia: Ancient Theater Today* [An on-line journal]: 2, 2, April.

——(1999). "Mental Disorder After Two Wars: Sauce for the Goose, but None for the Gander" [review of E.T. Dean, Jr., *Shook Over Hell*). *Reviews in American History* 27: 149–55.

Shay, J. and Munroe, J. (1999). "Group and Milieu Therapy for Veterans with Complex Posttraumatic Stress Disorder". In Saigh and Bremner 1999: 391–413.

Silver, S.M. and Wilson, J.P. (1988). "Native American Healing and Purification Rituals for War Stress". In Wilson *et al.* 1988: 337–54.

Sledge, E.B. (1981). *With the Old Breed at Pelieu and Okinawa*. Novato, CA: Presidio.

Slobodin, R. (1997). *W.H.R. Rivers: Pioneer Anthropologist, Psychiatrist of the Ghost Road*. Rev. ed. Stroud, Gloucestershire: Sutton Publishing.

Solomon, Z. (1993). *Combat Stress Reaction*. New York: Plenum Press.

Sturken, M. (1997). *Tangled Memories: The Vietnam War, the AIDS Epidemic, and the Politics of Remembering*. Berkeley: University of California Press.

Thiele, H.-G. (ed.) (1997). *Die Wehrmachtsausstellung: Dokumentation einer Kontroverse*. Bonn: Bundeszentrale für politische Bildung.

Van der Kolk, B.A., Greenberg, M.S., Orr, S.P., and Pitman, R.K. (1989). "Endogenous Opioids and Stress Induced Analgesia in Post Traumatic Stress Disorder". *Psycho-pharmacology Bulletin* 25: 108–12.

Van der Kolk, B.A., McFarlane, A.C., and Weisaeth, L. (1996). *Traumatic Stress: The Effects of Overwhelming Experience on Mind, Body, and Society*. New York: The Guildford Press.

Watson, G.R. (1969). *The Roman Soldier*. Ithaca: Cornell University Press.

Weinstein, E.A, MD "Conversion Disorders". In Zajtchuk (1995): I, 4, 383–407.

Wills, G. (1992). *Lincoln at Gettysburg: The Words That Remade America*. New York: Simon & Schuster.

Wilson, J.P., Harel, Z., and Kahanal, B. (eds.) (1988). *Human Adaptation to Extreme Stress: From the Holocaust to Vietnam*. New York: Plenum Press.

Winter, J. (1995). *Sites of Memory, Sites of Mourning. The Great War in European Cultural History*. Cambridge: Cambridge University Press.

Zajtchuk, R. (ed.) (1994–5). *Textbook of Military Medicine*. 4 Parts. Falls Church, VA: TMM Publications Office of the Surgeon General.

Ancient Greece

Classical sources

All classical works cited in the text are listed here by author and title only. In general, the translations from which I have quoted are those most readily available to the general reader. They include the Chicago translations of the Greek tragedians under the editorship of David Grene and Richmond Lattimore; the Penguin editions of Herodotus, Thucydides, and Xenophon (translated by A. de Selincourt and R. Warner respectively); and R. Lattimore's translations of Homer's *Iliad* and *Odyssey*. I have also referred to *Carmina Archilochi: The Fragments of Archilochus*, translated by G. Davenport (Berkeley: University of California Press, 1964) and *Greek Lyrics*, translated by R. Lattimore (Chicago: University of Chicago Press, 1949). Note also the collection of Greek historians in F. Jacoby, *Die Fragmente der griechischen Historiker*, 3 vols in 17 parts (Berlin and Leiden: Weidmann and Brill, 1923–58).

Aeschylus, *Agamemnon*
——*The Persians*
——*Seven Against Thebes*
Archilochus
Aristophanes, *The Acharnians*
——*The Clouds*
——*The Frogs*
——*The Knights*
——*Lysistrata*
Aristotle, *Nicomachean Ethics*
——*Politics*
Aristotle (?), *The Constitution of the Athenians*
Cicero, *Oration to M. Brutus*
Demosthenes, *Funeral Oration*
Didymus, in Demosthenes
Diodorus
Diogenes Laertius, *Lives and Opinions of the Philosophers*
Euripides, *Andromache*
——*The Bacchae*
——*Cyclops*
——*Hecuba*
——*Helen*
——*Medea*
——*The Trojan Women*
Herodotus, *Histories*
Hippocrates, *Places in Man*
Homer, *Iliad*
——*Odyssey*

Pausanias, *Description of Greece*
Pindar, *Works*
Plato, *Laws*
——*Menexenus*
——*Republic*
Plutarch, *Lives* (including *Alcibiades, Pericles, Phocion, Solon*, etc.)
——*On the Cleverness of Animals*
——*On the Malice of Herodotus*
Sophocles, *Ajax*
——*Antigone*
——*Oedipus at Colonus*
——*Philoctetes*
Tyrtaeus
Xenophon, *Anabasis*
——*Hellenica*
——*Memorabilia*

History and criticism

Anderson, J.K. (1970). *Military Theory and Practice in the Age of Xenophon*. Berkeley: University of California Press.
——(1991). "Hoplite Weapons and Offensive Arms". In Hanson 1991: 15–37.
Berger, E. (ed.) (1984). *Parthenon-Kongress Basel: Referate und Berichte*. Mainz: von Zabern.
Bernal, M. (1987–91). *Black Athena: The Afro-Asiatic Roots of Classical Civilization*. 2 vols. London and New Brunswick: Free Association Books and Rutgers University Press.
Bétant, E.-A. (1843/1969). *Lexicon Thucydideum*. 2 vols. Hildesheim: Georg Olms Verlag.
Bloch, H. (ed.) (1956). *Abhandlungen zur griechischen Geschichtschreibung von Felix Jacoby*. Leiden: Brill.
Boardman, J. (1977). "The Parthenon Frieze – Another View". In Höckmann and Krug 1977: 39–49.
——(1984). "The Parthenon Frieze". In Berger 1984: 210–15.
Bosworth, A.B. (1988). *From Arrian to Alexander: Studies in Historical Interpretation*. Oxford: Clarendon Press.
——(1996). *Alexander and the East: The Tragedy of Triumph*. Oxford: Clarendon Press.
Bowen, A.J. (1992). *Plutarch: The Malice of Herodotus*. Ed. with Introduction, translation and commentary. Warminster: Aris & Phillips Ltd.
Burckhardt, J. (1998). *The Greeks and Greek Civilization*. Trans. by S. Stern, ed. with Introduction by O. Murray. New York: St. Martin's Press.
Burian, P. (1997). "Myth into Muthos: The Shaping of Tragic Plot". In Easterling 1997: 178–208.
Burkert, W. (1985). *Greek Religion*. Trans. by J. Raffan. Cambridge, MA.: Harvard University Press.
Camp, J. (1986). *The Athenian Agora*. London: Thames and Hudson.

Cartledge, P. (1987). *Agesilaos and the Crisis of Sparta*. Baltimore: Johns Hopkins University Press.

——(1997). " 'Deep Plays': Theatre as Process in Greek Civic Life". In Easterling 1997: 3–35.

Cawkwell, G. (1997). *Thucydides and the Peloponnesian War*. London: Routledge.

Craik, E.M. (1998). *Hippocrates: Places in Man*. Greek text and translation, with Introduction and Commentary. Oxford: Clarendon Press.

Croally, N.T. (1994). *Euripidean Polemic: The Trojan Woman and the Function of Tragedy*. Cambridge: Cambridge University Press.

Davies, J.K. (1971). *Athenian Propertied Families, 600–300 B.C.* Oxford: Clarendon Press.

de Romilly, J. (1992). *The Great Sophists in Periclean Athens*. Oxford: Clarendon Press.

Develin, R. (1989). *Athenian Officials 684–321 B.C.* Cambridge: Cambridge University Press.

Diels, H. and Kranz, W. (1961). *Die Fragmente der Vorsokratiker*. 10th ed., 2 vols. Berlin: Wiedmann.

Dodds, E.R. (1960). *Euripides Bacchae*. Edited with introduction and commentary by E.R. Dodds. Oxford: Clarendon Press.

Dover, K.J. (1974). *Greek Popular Morality in the Time of Plato and Aristotle*. Berkeley: University of California Press.

Easterling, P. (ed.) (1997). *The Cambridge Companion to Greek Tragedy*. Cambridge: Cambridge University Press.

Eder, W. (ed.) (1995). *Die athenische Demokratie im 4. Jahrhundert. v. Chr.* Stuttgart: Franz Steiner Verlag.

Fehling, D. (1971). *Die Quellenangaben bei Herodot*. Berlin: Walter de Gruyter.

Garland, R. (1985). *The Greek Way of Death*. Ithaca: Cornell University Press.

Ginouvès, R. (ed.) (1994). *Macedonia from Philip II to the Roman Conquest*. Princeton: Princeton University Press.

Goldhill, S. (1986). *Reading Greek Tragedy*. Cambridge: Cambridge University Press.

——(1988). "Battle Narrative and Politics in Aeschylus' *Persae*". *Journal of Hellenic Studies* 108: 189–93.

——(1997). "Modern Critical Approaches to Greek Tragedy". In Easterling 1997: 324–47.

Gomme, A.W., Andrewes, A., and Dover, K.J. (1945–81). *A Historical Commentary on Thucydides*. 5 vols. Oxford: Clarendon Press.

Griffin, J. (1980). *Homer*. New York: Hill and Wang.

——(1998). "The Social Function of Attic Tragedy". *Classical Quarterly* 48: 39–61.

Guthrie, W.K. (1967). *A History of Greek Philosophy*. Vol. I: *The Earlier Presocratics and the Pythagoreans*. Cambridge: Cambridge University Press.

——(1971a). *Socrates*. Cambridge: Cambridge University Press.

——(1971b). *The Sophists*. Cambridge: Cambridge University Press.

Hall, E. (1988). "When did the Trojans Turn into Phrygians? Alcaeus 42.15". *Zeitschrift für Papyrologie und Epigraphik* 73: 15–18.

——(1993). "Asia Unmanned: Images of Victory in Classical Athens". In Rich and Shipley (1993): 108–33.

——(1996). *Aeschylus' Persians*. Edited with an Introduction, translation and Commentary by E. Hall. Warminster: Aris & Phillips Ltd.

Hansen, M.H. (1991). *The Athenian Democracy in the Age of Demosthenes*. Trans. by J.A. Crook. Oxford: Blackwell.

Hanson, V.D. (1989). *The Western Way of War*. New York: Alfred A. Knopf.

——(ed.) (1991). *Hoplites: The Classical Greek Battle Experience*. London: Routledge.

Harris, E.M. (1995). *Aeschines and Athenian Politics*. New York and Oxford: Oxford University Press.

Harris, W.V. (1989). *Ancient Literacy*. Cambridge, MA: Harvard University Press.

Heckel, W. (1997). "Resistance to Alexander the Great". In Tritle 1997b: 189–227.

Henderson, B.L. (1927). *The Great War Between Athens and Sparta*. London: Macmillan & Company, Ltd.

Herman, G. (1994). "How Violent was Athenian Society?" In Osborne and Hornblower 1994: 109–17.

Heskel, J. (1997). "Macedonia and the North, 400–336 BC". In Tritle 1997b: 167–188.

Heubeck, A., West, W., and Hainsworth, J.B. (1988). *A Commentary on Homer's Odyssey*. Vol. 1: *Introduction and Books I–VIII*. Oxford: Clarendon Press.

Hirsch, S.W. (1985). *The Friendship of Enemies: Xenophon and the Persian Empire*. Hanover: Tufts University, by University Press of New England.

Höckmann, U. and Krug, A. (eds.) (1977). *Festschrift für Frank Brommer*. Mainz: von Zabern.

Hoffmann, H. (1997). *Sotades: Symbols of Immortality on Greek Vases*. Oxford: Clarendon Press.

Hornblower, S. (1987). *Thucydides*. Baltimore: Johns Hopkins University Press.

——(1992–96). *A Commentary on Thucydides*. 2 vols. Oxford: Clarendon Press.

How, W.W. and Wells, J. (1912). *A Commentary on Herodotus*. 2 vols. Oxford: Clarendon Press.

Hurwit, J.M. (1999). *The Athenian Acropolis: History, Mythology, and Archaeology from the Neolithic Era to the Present*. Cambridge: Cambridge University Press.

Jacoby, F. (1918). "Studien zu den alteren griechischen Elegikern". *Hermes* 53: 1–44.

——(1956). "Patrios Nomos: State Burial in Athens and the Public Cemetery in the Kerameikos". In Bloch 1956: 260–315.

Jeffery, L.H. (1976). *Archaic Greece: The City States c. 700–500 B.C.* London: Methuen & Company Ltd.

Jordan, B. (1972). *The Athenian Navy in the Classical Period: A Study of Athenian Naval Administration and Military Organization in the Fifth and Fourth Centuries B.C.* Berkeley: University of California Press.

Kagan, D. (1987). *The Fall of the Athenian Empire*. Ithaca: Cornell University Press.

Kallet-Marx, L. (1993). "Thucydides 2.45.2 and the Status of War Widows in Periclean Athens". In Rosen and Farrell 1993: 133–43.

King, K.C. (1987). *Achilles: Paradigms of the War Hero from Homer to the Middle Ages*. Berkeley: University of California Press.

Kirk, G.S., Raven, J.E., and Schofield, M. (1983). *The Presocratic Philosophers: A Critical History with a Selection of Texts*. 2nd edn. Cambridge: Cambridge University Press.

Kirkwood, G.M. (1958). *A Study of Sophoclean Drama*. Ithaca: Cornell University Press.

Knigge, U. (1991). *The Athenian Kerameikos: History, Monuments, Excavations*. Athens: Krene Edition.

Kyle, D. (1992). "The Panathenaic Games: Sacred and Civic Athletics". In Neils 1992: 77–102.

Larsen, J.A.O. (1955). *Representative Government in Greek and Roman History*. Berkeley: University of California Press.

——(1968). *Greek Federal States*. Oxford: Clarendon Press.

Lateiner, D. (1977). "No Laughing Matter: A Literary Tactic in Herodotus". *Transactions of the American Philological Association* 107: 173–82.

Lattimore, R. (1943). "Aeschylus on the Defeat of Xerxes". In *Classical Studies in Honor of William A. Oldfather*, Urbana, 88–93.

Lattimore, S. (1998). *Thucydides. The Peloponnesian War.* Translated with Introduction and Notes by S. Lattimore. Indianapolis/Cambridge: Hackett Publishing Company, Inc.

Lazenby, J. (1985). *The Spartan Army*. Warminster: Aris & Phillips Ltd.

——(1991). "The Killing Zone". In Hanson 1991: 87–109.

Lefkowitz, M. (1981). *The Lives of the Greek Poets*. Baltimore: Johns Hopkins University Press.

Lefkowitz, M. and Rogers, G.M. (eds.) (1996). *Black Athena Revisited*. Chapel Hill: University of North Carolina Press.

Lenschau, T. (1921). "Klearchos" (3). *Real-Encyclopädie der classischen Altertumswissenschaft*, A.F. Pauly, G. Wissowa, and W. Kroll (eds.) (1894–1972). 66 vols. Vol. 34, 11: 575–7.

Loreaux, N. (1986). *The Invention of Athens: The Funeral Oration in the Classical City*. Trans. by A. Sheridan. Cambridge, MA.: Harvard University Press.

——(1998). *Mothers in Mourning*. Trans. by C. Pache. Ithaca: Cornell University Press.

McCann, D. and Strauss, B. (eds.) (2000). *The Korean War and the Peloponnesian War. A Comparative Study of War and Democracy*. Armonk, NY: M.E. Sharpe.

Marincola, J. (1996). *Herodotus. The Histories*. Trans. by A. de Sélincourt. Rev. with Introductory matter and Notes by J. Marincola. Harmondsworth: Penguin Books.

Meiggs, R. (1972). *The Athenian Empire*. Oxford: Clarendon Press.

Mitchel, F.W. (1970). "Lykourgan Athens: 338–322". In *Lectures in Memory of Louise Taft Semple*, second series, 1966–70. Cincinnati: University of Oklahoma Press for the University of Cincinnati.

Mitchell, L.G. (1997). *Greeks Bearing Gifts. The Public Use of Private Relationships in the Greek World, 435–323 B.C.* Cambridge: Cambridge University Press.

Mitchell, L.G. and Rhodes, P.J. (eds.) (1997). *The Development of the Polis in Archaic Greece*. London: Routledge.

Momigliano, A. (1971). *The Development of Greek Biography*. Cambridge: Harvard University Press.

Mulroy, D. (1992). *Early Greek Lyric Poetry*. Ann Arbor: University of Michigan Press.

Neils, J. (ed.) (1992). *Goddess and Polis: The Panathenaia Festival in Ancient Athens*. Princeton: Hood Museum of Arts, Dartmouth College and Princeton University Press.

O'Brien, J.M. (1992). *Alexander the Great: The Invisible Enemy*. London: Routledge.

Ober, J. (1996). *The Athenian Revolution*. Princeton: Princeton University Press.

Orwin, C. (1994). *The Humanity of Thucydides*. Princeton: Princeton University Press.

Osborne, R. (1996). *Greece in the Making, 1200–479 B.C.* London: Routledge.

Osborne, R. and Hornblower, S. (eds.) (1994). *Ritual, Finance, Politics: Athenian Democratic Accounts Presented to D.M. Lewis*. Oxford: Clarendon Press.

Parke, H.W. (1977). *Festivals of the Athenians*. Ithaca: Cornell University Press.

Parker, R. (1996). *Athenian Religion: A History*. Oxford: Clarendon Press.

——(1998). Review of W. Burkert, *Homo Necans. Interpretationen altgriechischen Opferriten und Mythen* 2 (Berlin, 1997), *Classical Review* 48: 509–10.

Pelling, C. (ed.) (1997). *Greek Tragedy and the Historian*. Oxford: Clarendon Press.

Pritchett, W.K. (1971–91). *The Greek State at War*. 5 Parts. Berkeley: University of California Press.

Quinn, T.J. (1995). "Thucydides and the Massacre at Mycalessus". *Mnemosyne* 48: 571-4.

Raaflaub, K.A. (1997a). "Homeric Society". In I. Morris and B. Powell, *A New Companion to Homer, Mnemosyne*. Suppl. vol. 163: 624–48.

——(1997b). "Politics and Interstate Relations in the World of Early Greek Poleis: Homer and Beyond". *Antichthon* 31: 1–27.

——(1997c). "Soldiers, Citizens, and the Evolution of the Early Greek Polis". In Mitchell and Rhodes 1997: 49–59

——(1999). "Father of All – Destroyer of All – War in Late Fifth-Century Athenian Discourse". In McCann and Strauss 2000.

Rhodes, P. (1981). "A Commentary on the Aristotelian Athenaion Politeia". Oxford: Clarendon Press.

Rhodes, P.J. (1994). *Thucydides. Book III*. Ed. with translation and commentary by P.J. Rhodes. Warminster: Aris & Phillips, Ltd.

Rich, J. and Shipley, G. (1993). *War and Society in the Greek World*. London: Routledge.

Richardson, N. (1993). *The Iliad: A Commentary*. Vol. VI: *Books 21–24*. Cambridge: Cambridge University Press.

Roisman, J. (1989). "Klearchos in Xenophon's *Anabasis*". *Scripta Classica Israelica* 8/9: 30–52.

Rosen, R. and Farrell, J. (eds.) (1993). *Nomodeiktes: Greek Studies in Honor of Martin Ostwald*. Ann Arbor: University of Michigan Press.

Salmon, J.B. (1984). *Wealthy Corinth: A History of the City to 338 B.C.* Oxford: Clarendon Press.

Sealey, R. (1993). *Demosthenes and His Time: A Study in Defeat*. New York and Oxford: Oxford University Press.

Segal, C. (1995). *Sophocles' Tragic World: Divinity, Nature, Society*. Cambridge: Harvard University Press.

Shapiro, H.A. (1992). "Mousikoi Agones: Music and Poetry at the Panathenaia". In Neils 1992: 53–76.

Shipley, D.R. (1997). *A Commentary on Plutarch's Life of Agesilaos: Response to Sources in the Presentation of Character*. Oxford: Clarendon Press.

Sinclair, R.K. (1988). *Democracy and Participation in Athens*. Cambridge: Cambridge University Press.

Snowden, F.M., Jr. (1970). *Blacks in Antiquity*. Cambridge, MA: Harvard University Press.

Solmsen, F. (1975). *Intellectual Experiments of the Greek Enlightenment*. Princeton: Princeton University Press.

Sommerstein, A.H. (1996). *Aeschylean Tragedy*. Bari: Levante Editori.

——(1998). Review of E. Hall, *Aeschylus: The Persians*, *Journal of Hellenic Studies* 118: 211–12.

Stadter, P. (1989). *A Commentary on Plutarch's Pericles*. Chapel Hill: University of North Carolina Press.

Tritle, L.A. (1988). *Phocion the Good*. London: Croom Helm and Routledge, Chapman and Hall.

——(1989). "*Epilektoi* at Athens". *Ancient History Bulletin* 4: 54–9

——(1993). "Continuity and Change in the Athenian Strategia". *Ancient History Bulletin* 7: 125–29.

——(1996). "Black Athena: Vision or Dream of Greek Origins?" In Lefkowitz and Rogers 1996: 303–30.

——(1997a). "Hector's Body: Mutilation of the Dead in Ancient Greece and Vietnam". *Ancient History Bulletin* 11: 123–36.

——(ed.) (1997b). *The Greek World in the Fourth Century: From the Fall of the Athenian Empire to the Successors of Alexander*. London: Routledge.

——(1998). "Teaching the Vietnam War with the Greeks". *Perspectives: The Newsletter of the American Historical Association* 36, 8: 1, 36–40.

——(1999). "Leocrates: Athenian Businessman and Macedonian Agent?" In *Proceedings of the VI International Symposium on Ancient Macedonia*, Thessaloniki: 1227–33.

Voutiras, E. (1994). "Wortkarge Söldner? Ein Interpretationvorschlag zum neuen Poseidippos". *Zeitschrift für Papyrologie und Epigraphik* 104: 27–31.

Warner, R. (1946). *Xenophon. The Persian Expedition*. Translated with introduction by R. Warner. Harmondsworth: Penguin Books.

West, M.L. (1993). *Greek Lyric Poetry*. Oxford: Clarendon Press.

Wilson, J.B. (1979). *Pylos 425 B.C.: A Historical and Topographical Study of Thucydides' Account of the Campaign*. Warminster: Aris & Phillips Ltd.

Wilson, J. (1982). " 'The Customary Meanings of Words were Changed' – or Were They? A Note on Thucydides 3.82.4." *Classical Quarterly* 32: 18–20.

Winkler, J. (1985). "The Ephebes' Song". *Representation* 11: 26–62.

Winnington-Ingram, R.P. (1980). *Sophocles: An Interpretation*. Cambridge: Cambridge University Press.

Wycherley, R.E. (1978). *The Stones of Athens*. Princeton: Princeton University Press.

Vietnam

Anderson, D.L. (ed.) (1998). *Facing My Lai: Moving Beyond the Massacre*. Lawrence: University Press of Kansas.

Andrew, J.A., III. (1997). *The Other Side of the Sixties: Young Americans for Freedom and the Rise of Conservative Politics*. New Brunswick: Rutgers University Press.

Appy, C.G. (1993). *Working-Class War: American Combat Soldiers in Vietnam*. Chapel Hill: University of North Carolina Press.

Baker, M. (1981) *Nam: The Vietnam War in the Words of the Men and Women Who Fought There*. New York: William Morrow and Company, Inc.

Baskir, L.M. and Strauss, W.A. (1978). *Chance and Circumstance. The Draft, the War, and the Vietnam Generation*. New York: Random House.

Bill, J.A. (1997). *George Ball: Behind the Scenes in U.S. Foreign Policy*. New Haven: Yale University Press.

Bilton, M. and Sim, K. (1992). *Four Hours in My Lai*. New York: Penguin Books.

Broyles, W.J. (1990). "Why Men Love War". In Capps 1990: 68–81.

Bunting, J. (1998). *An Education for Our Time*. Lanham, MD: Regnery Publications.

Burkett, B.G. and Whitley, G. (1998). *Stolen Valor: How the Vietnam Generation Was Robbed of Its Heroes and Its History*. Dallas: Verity Press, Inc.

Cano, D. (1995). *Shifting Loyalties*. Houston: Arte Público Press.

Capps, W. (ed.) (1990). *The Vietnam Reader*. New York: Routledge.

Caputo, P. (1977). *A Rumor of War*. New York: Holt, Rinehart and Winston.

Dallek, R. (1998). *Flawed Giant: Lyndon Johnson and His Times, 1961–1973*. New York and Oxford: Oxford University Press.

DiLeo, D.L. (1991). *George Ball, Vietnam, and the Rethinking of Containment*. Chapel Hill: University of North Carolina Press.

Dittmar, L. and Michaud, G. (eds.) (1990). *From Hanoi to Hollywood: The Vietnam War in American Film*. New Brunswick: Rutgers University Press.

Downs, F. (1978). *The Killing Zone*. New York: W.W. Norton and Company.

Ehrhardt, W.D. (1986). *Passing Time: Memoir of a Vietnam Veteran Against the War*. Amherst: University of Massachusetts Press.

Hackworth, D. and Sherman, J. (1989). *About Face. The Odyssey of an American Warrior*. New York: Simon & Schuster.

Halberstam, D. (1988). *The Making of a Quagmire: America and Vietnam During the Kennedy Era*. Rev. ed. New York: Alfred A. Knopf.

Hasford, G. (1979). *The Short-Timers*. New York: Harper & Row, Publishers.

Hayslip, L.L., with Wurts, J. (1990). *When Heaven and Earth Changed Places*. New York: Plume.

Heinemann, L. (1977). *Close Quarters*. New York: Penguin Books.

——(1992). *Paco's Story*. New York: Penguin Books.

Hendrickson, P. (1996). *The Living and the Dead: Robert McNamara and Five Lives of a Lost War*. New York: Random House.

Herr, M. (1977). *Dispatches*. New York: Alfred A. Knopf.

Hersh, S. (1970). *My Lai: A Report on the Massacre and its Aftermath*. New York: Random House.

Holm, T. (1996). *Strong Hearts, Wounded Souls: Native American Veterans of the Vietnam War*. Austin: University of Texas Press.

Israel, F.L. and Schlesinger, A.M. (1966). *The State of the Union Messages of the Presidents, 1790–1966*. 3 vols. Vol. III: *1905–1966*. New York: Chelsea House.

Johnson, L.B. (1963-69). *Public Papers of the Presidents of the United States*. 8 vols. Washington, D.C.: United States Government Printing Office.

Kovic, R. (1976). *Born on the Fourth of July*. New York: Simon & Schuster.

Lanning, M.L. (1994). *Vietnam at the Movies*. New York: Fawcett Columbine.

Lembcke, J. (1998). *The Spitting Image: Myth, Memory, and the Legacy of Vietnam*. New York: New York University Press.

McMaster, H.R. (1997). *Dereliction of Duty: Lyndon Johnson, Robert McNamara, the Joint Chiefs of Staff, and the Lies that Led to Vietnam*. New York: Harper Collins Publishers.

McNamara, R.S., with Van de Mark, B. (1995). *In Retrospect: The Tragedy and Lessons of Vietnam*. New York: Times Books.

McNerney, B.C. (1994). "Responsibly Inventing History: An Interview with Tim O'Brien". *War, Literature, and the Arts* 6: 1–26.

Moïse, E. (1997). *Tonkin Gulf Resolution and the Escalation of the Vietnam War*. Chapel Hill: University of North Carolina Press.

Moore, H.G., and Galloway, J. (1992). *We Were Soldiers Once ... and Young*. New York: Random House.

Mulligan, J. (1997). *Shopping Cart Soldiers*. Willamantic, CT: Curbstone Press.

Murphy, E.F. (1993). *Dak To: America's Sky Soldiers in South Vietnam's Central Highlands*. New York: Simon & Schuster.

Ninh, Bao (1993). *The Sorrow of War: A Novel of North Vietnam*. Trans. by Phan Thanh Hao. Ed. by F. Palmos. New York: Riverhead Books.

Nolan, K.W. (1990). *Into Cambodia*. Novato, CA: Presidio.

Novak, M.L. (1991). *Lonely Girls with Burning Eyes: A Wife Recalls Her Husband's Journey Home from Vietnam*. Boston: Little, Brown & Company.

O'Brien, T. (1990). *The Things They Carried*. New York: Penguin Books.

——(1994). *In the Lake of the Woods*. New York: Penguin Books.

Olson, G.A. (1995). *Mansfield and Vietnam: A Study in Rhetorical Adaptation*. East Lansing: Michigan State University Press.

Olson, J.S. and Roberts, R. (1998). *My Lai: A Brief History with Documents*. Boston: Bedford Books.

Rawls, W. (1995). *Offerings at the Wall*. Atlanta: Turner Publishing, Inc.

Rottmann, L., Barry, J., and Paquet, B.T. (eds.) (1972). *Winning Hearts and Minds: War Poems by Vietnam Veterans*. Brooklyn: 1st Casualty Press.

Schroeder, E.J. (1992). *Vietnam, We've All Been There*. Interviews with American Writers. Westport, CT: Greenwood Press.

Schulzinger, R.D. (1997). *A Time for War: The United States and Vietnam, 1941–1975*. New York and Oxford: Oxford University Press.

Sheehan, N. (1988). *A Bright Shining Lie: John Paul Vann and America in Vietnam*. New York: Random House.

Sheehan, N., *et al.* (1971). *The Pentagon Papers*. New York: Bantam Books, Inc.

Siff, E.Y. (1999). *Why the Senate Slept: The Gulf of Tonkin Resolution and the Beginning of America's Vietnam War*. Westport, CT: Greenwood Press.

Smith, L. (1994). "The Things Men Do: Images of Women in Vietnam Novels by Combat Veterans". *Critique* 36: 16–39.

Stacewicz, R. (1997). *Winter Soldiers: An Oral History of the Vietnam Veterans Against the War*. New York: Twayne Publishers.

Studlar, G. and Desser, D. (1990). "Rewriting the Vietnam War". In Dittmar and Michaud 1990: 101–12.

Tatum, J. (1996). "Memorials of the American War in Vietnam". *Critical Inquiry* 22: 634–50 [with 38 figures].

Terry, W. (1984). *Bloods: An Oral History of the Vietnam War by Black Veterans*. New York: Ballantine Books.

Turner, F. (1996). *Echoes of Combat: The Vietnam War in American Memory*. New York: Doubleday.

Van de Mark, B. (1991). *Into the Quagmire: Lyndon Johnson and the Escalation of the Vietnam War*. New York and Oxford: Oxford University Press.

Van Devanter, L. (1983). *Home Before Morning*. New York: Warner Books.

Vietnam Veterans Against the War (1972). *The Winter-Soldier Investigation: An Inquiry into American War Crimes*. Boston: Beacon Press.

Warr, N. (1997). *Phase Line Green: The Battle for Hue, 1968*. Annapolis: Naval Institute Press.

Wilson, J.R. (1990). *Landing Zones: Combat Vets from America's Proud, Fighting South Remember Vietnam*. Durham: Duke University Press.

INDEX